Faye Huntington

From Different Standpoints

Faye Huntington

From Different Standpoints

ISBN/EAN: 9783337813284

Printed in Europe, USA, Canada, Australia, Japan

Cover: Foto ©Thomas Meinert / pixelio.de

More available books at **www.hansebooks.com**

"Perry leaned back in his chair and waited for Una's answer." — Page 124.

From Different Standpoints.

Alden, Isabella (Macdo[nald])

BY
PANSY & FAYE HUNTINGTON,
AUTHORS OF "MODERN PROPHETS," "DR. DEANE'S WAY," ETC.

BOSTON:
D. LOTHROP AND COMPANY,
FRANKLIN ST., CORNER OF HAWLEY.

COPYRIGHT BY
D. LOTHROP & CO.
1878.

From Different Standpoints.

1.

REDWOOD, January, ———

My Dear Sister Friend:

And are you lonely in the midst of the city's whirl? Do you miss your brother? I am free to confess that I miss my sister. If it seemed like banishment when the old doctor ordered me from the city, at such an unseasonable time of the year, the reality quite fulfills the seeming. I suppose you have as much of an idea of what this place is like as I had before I saw it, which was only something less definite than my idea of the palace and surroundings of the man in the moon. Shall I describe the quaint old farm-house? No, indeed! Quaint old farm-houses have been described by illustrious pens, until there is positively no opportunity for an original rendering of the subject. Please consult Irving, Holmes, Holland. Now I think of it, I fancy that this is not unlike the home where the family gathered at Thanksgiving, as pictured in "Bittersweet." Judging from what is brought out of the cellar, its stores would compare favorably with those of that underground apartment to which Danil and Ruth (was it Danil and Ruth?) paid a visit.

The family: Oh, yes! There's Uncle Nathan and Aunt Phebe, and Margaret, their daughter. And very kind they all are.

As to my health: I am improving slowly, but Dr. Mason assures me that I must not think of going back to my books before May or June. With the time I have already lost, it will be too much to make up. So farewell to ambitious schemes and dreams for this year. The class of '60 will have to find another name to hand down as their most illustrious representative. Seriously, I have small hope of being able to graduate with the class, though I manage to study a little. If it were not for this restless longing to get back to the University I could be quite contented here. Cousin Kate's husband is Mr. Fowler, pastor of the church in Redwood. I find him a very agreeable and intellectual gentleman, and I enjoy his society very much.

As for Cousin Margaret: What is she like? What should she be like, but a daisy? Are not all Margarets daisies? And is she not the purest and fairest of them all? But, like everything in this world, she is a puzzle and a contradiction.

With her mother she talks like a staid and experienced housekeeper; with her father she talks of business and accounts; while to me she discourses of books and authors, and thoroughly posted she is in modern literature, and also she is a fair Latin and Greek scholar. But in general society she is like half the young ladies one meets. Her talk is utter nonsense, and I am afraid she is a wicked little coquette. And yet she is the most saintlike Christian I ever came across. You see I don't know just what she is, or which of her moods is her real self. This morning she brought me my coffee. (I don't get up to breakfast with the family.) A very blue streak had come upon me. I said:

"Oh, Daisy, I am so impatient to be doing something! I really can not afford to lose so much time."

"Can you help it?" she asked.

"No," I snapped out the monosyllable like a cross dog. "If I could help it I shouldn't sit here fretting a great while."

"But since you can't help it, you'll do your best to make yourself miserable, and hinder recovery by getting up an indignation meeting all by yourself. Seems to me, Cousin Perry, I'd remember who it is that has this thing in charge, and not be quite so rebellious."

"But, Daisy, if you were a young fellow like

me, with your own way to make in the world, you'd feel as I do, that every hour is precious," I said, taking sips of the delicious coffee.

"To be sure," she answered, "hours are precious, whether we are making our own way or just making life pleasant for somebody else. But I can't help thinking that God knows what they are worth as well as we do, and if he puts us where we can't fill them with work of our own planning, it must be that he has some other for us, and we would better look around for it — or *within*."

In my ill-humor I was half vexed at what seemed to imply that a little inward searching, and casting out, would not be amiss; but she seemed so perfectly unconscious of having said anything impertinent that I had to pass it over silently. And after all, it is a fact that I need to ask what was the occasion for my being laid aside in this helpless fashion, just as my work was spread out for the years to come? Always supposing that there is an occasion for things, an overruling Providence as Daisy has it, what a comfort it would be to know whether that were truth or cant! I can fancy myself lying quiet, and at rest, even here on my bed, if only I could be sure that a great, wise, perfect Being saw the whole story of my life, finished, and knew just why the illness came in, and had his grand reasons for it. Una, it is splendid theory. The only trouble is I can't believe it; I wish with all my heart that I could; it would be such a comfort.

This is certainly a remarkable letter. You will give me credit for writing very few such. I wish you were here to help pass away the hours. I fancy you would like Daisy, though she is certainly unlike you as possible. By the way, that is a mark of wonderful genius, the ability to create so many people and have them so unlike each other.

There! I'm running off to theology again. It is time to close. In fact it is anyway. My pulse is about two hundred and eighty, I should judge, to guess by the way the blood races through me, and I am trembling like a leaf in the storm, all because I have attempted the writing of a letter. There's strength for you!

Una, write to me a long letter. Tell me everything. Do help to keep me alive through this dreary, weary winter.

As ever your brother,
PERRY HARRISON.

2

Dear Friend:

I wish I had something out of that cellar. Things in a city never seem to come out of cellars; never seem to have grown; they all feel as if they came from the South, or the West, in a freight-car, and were packed in sawdust, or ice, or something, for a week. Things to eat, I mean. Isn't it queer that every one has to stop work, or play, and eat? I do think that is one of the funniest things about us. Perhaps, however, your cousin Margaret doesn't eat! What an extraordinary lady she is! I should think you had sunshine enough, without any letters of mine, in which, by the way, you will find precious little sunshine; you forget that my attic is on the northwest side.

We have new boarders, a Dr. Ellenthorpe, (M. D.), who is as solemn as an owl, and full of business, and disapproves of the way in which you are pretending to get well. He volunteered his opinion; I didn't consult him. I was reading bits of your last letter but one, to Mrs. Ramsay, who, you know, has a motherly sort of interest in all creation, and among other things I read that Dr. Mason had ordered bourbon three times a day. Dr. Ellenthorpe was standing by the mantel, talking, as I suppose, with Laura Myers, or talking over her. I think anyone with brains may be excused from trying to talk with her. Just at that point he raised his voice and said:

"Your friend is unfortunate in his choice of physicians, if he has been encouraged to hope anything from the use of bourbon."

Somewhat amazed at his knowledge of matters of which he must necessarily be ignorant, I answered, curtly:

"Perhaps you are not acquainted with the disease for which it has been ordered."

He answered me with the utmost composure:

"It makes not the slightest difference what the disease is, except that in some cases it is more disastrous in its results than others. It is never beneficial. Tell your friend so, from me."

So, there you have the benefit of Dr. Ellenthorpe's advice, free of charge. He stands very high in high circles here. I didn't tell him so, but I believe it is good advice. I hate bourbon."

Another new boarder is Mr. Romaine. He is a carpenter. Think of Miss Alice Perkins having to dine every day with a carpenter!—or sup, rather. He takes his breakfast every morning before she is up, and the third meal he doesn't take at all. She says he is a master-builder; that sounds better than carpenter, you know. He is a good man, and some curious experiences grow out of his goodness. For instance, we have family worship in the large parlor every evening. I don't know how Aunt Ruth's consent was gained, except that people seem to have a way of consenting to what he wants done before they know it. Anyway, he announced, one evening, that after tea there would be prayers in the east parlor, and the boarders were all invited. There was a good deal of nudging of elbows, and some giggling, but a dozen or so strolled in, I among the number. Not being particularly interested in prayers, I had not the slightest idea of attending until I heard Ella Heath whisper to Charlie:

"What an idea! And he only a mechanic! It would be bad enough if he were a minister!"

"Aren't mechanics allowed to pray in Boston?" I said to her, with a very uppish sound to my voice. She is from Boston, you know. After that I had to go in, to look consistent. My tongue is always leading me into strange places; but it was real pleasant, after all. I never heard "Ortonville" sound so well. Mr. Romaine led the singing, and did it well. He reads well, too. It is a pity that Dr. Howe couldn't take lessons of him—*his* singing grows more intolerable to me every Sunday. This Mr. Romaine has a strange way of saying things. I sat near him, one evening, at prayers, and, after the singing, he turned suddenly to me, and said:

"Miss Eunice, do you mean to sing with the angels?"

His voice was as quiet and composed as if he had simply asked me whether I meant to sing in church next Sunday. I was a little bit startled, but I answered him promptly enough:

"I have never learned their tunes. I presume I should make discord."

"You must learn to sing by note," he said, smiling gravely. Then he went on with his reading.

Charlie Thorpe seemed to consider himself called upon to apologize. Did you know Charlie Thorpe? He is a student at the University. I'm sure I hope he'll learn something before he graduates; he is a perfect goose now.

"He really doesn't know any better," he said, referring to Mr. Romaine. "He is only a mechanic, you know."

"Better than what?" I asked, profoundly astonished.

"Why, than to address you in the manner he did a few minutes ago."

"But I thought he asked a perfectly civil question, in a perfectly respectful manner."

"I am glad you are pleased to judge him so

leniently," Charlie said. "But the fact is, that class of people obtrude their ideas in a very offensive manner, sometimes."

I am not given to wasting much talk on Charlie Thorpe, but on this particular occasion I seemed to be just in the mood to enjoy him. So I said:

"What class of people?"

He got out his hem-stitched, rose-perfumed handkerchief, and shook it. Then he said:

"Why, the working people; the lower classes, or whatever name you are pleased to call them."

Now, Perry, you know that, whatever may be my besetting sins, hypocrisy is not among them. So I said, very curtly:

"I don't know how to class people. If you are good at it, won't you give me my grade in society? My father is a shoemaker by trade, with a large family to support. My aunt, Ruth Brocton, keeps boarders for a living, and I, being her oldest niece, have the privilege of coming here and going to school, provided I will work enough out of school hours to pay for my board. Among other things that I do, I make your bed and put your room in order. To which class do I belong, Mr. Thorpe?"

I know he was astonished, and I think he was mortified, and that was all the good it did me, I suppose. Aunt Ruth says I was a goose; that I am not called on to reveal my poverty and housework to shallow-brained people, who will judge of my character and claim to respectability, even, by that rule. But I am not certain that I care how shallow-brained people look upon me, and I like to be myself, anyhow. What do you say, oh, most immaculate and orthodox Perry Harrison, with your sixty thousand a year, or something like it? Assuredly you do not belong to the working people (at least not now, when you lie in bed until noon waiting for a daisy to bring you coffee and theology), nor to the lower classes, allowing Charlie Thorpe to be the judge. In just what way shall we deal with addle-headed people who say words at us?

How does that Daisy of yours treat people whom she doesn't like, and can't like; who have not enough material in the region of their brains to suggest a liking? Or is she one of those gentle angels who like everybody? I wish I were.

Are you really getting better? Your hour for rising doesn't suggest very marked improvement, when one remembers you used to cheat even the sun himself into the belief that he had risen.

I am very sorry for your disappointment about the European tour. I quite looked forward to the pleasure of receiving foreign letters. I have as much expectation—rather more—of going up in a balloon as I have of going to Europe. All my knowledge of that fashionable locality must be secured by second-hand means, and I fancied you might be a good medium of communication. There is no telling, however. An unaccountable stupidity seems to come over European travelers the moment they get a pen into their hands—a sort of nightmare of dullness. Perhaps you would have been seized with it. I wish I could take a journey, if it were only to Brooklyn, just to see if I couldn't give a better description of it than people do. I shall always regret that Aunt Ruth insisted on economizing time in a sleeping-car, in our journey from Nassau to New York. I dare say I might have seen something to describe. I'm pretty well acquainted with the formula, for all travelers talk about alike.

Annie Ames is writing a book, or a sermon, or something; she scribbles half the night. What if I should write a book, since I can't take a journey! Could you give me a title? I wonder where Mrs. Stowe got her last one. Have you read the book? Ask your Daisy what she thinks of it.

I heard Mr. Parks preach, last Sunday. Perry, how did it happen that you never went to hear him? I wish I could go again; it was the best going to church I ever had. The singing! oh, the singing! I wish I could make you hear it. I told Mr. Romaine, in the evening, that I didn't particularly envy the angels, nor care about singing with them, as long as I could have such a good substitute as the two thousand voices in that church. What do you suppose his answer was? He excels in quotation. He said, in exactly the tone in which one would wish to hear those words quoted: "And the number of them was ten thousand times ten thousand, and thousands of thousands." I confess to you that the thought of that great company thrilled me wonderfully. I thought more about heaven for the next quarter of an hour than I ever did in my life before. The "art of putting things," says somebody (the "Country Parson," isn't it?) is a great art. I think Mr. Romaine has it.

I didn't mean to write you such a long letter. It is longer than yours; and you being a gentleman of leisure ought to do the most of the letter writing.

I don't believe they will get so very far ahead of you at the University; the students don't appear to me to be studying very hard. Think, for instance, of Charlie Thorpe getting ahead of you! I wouldn't make myself sick worrying about it. I think your Daisy gave excellent advice. I am interested in her. Tell me some more about her. Isn't your Aunt Phebe a character? or isn't she the one that your mother used to tell us about? If she is she would do to make a book of.

I met Dr. Mason the other day, and he inquired very particularly after your health.

"Let me see," said he, "Harrison is your brother, isn't he?"

"Yes, sir," I said, very meekly.

"So I thought. Well, how is your mother, now?"

"She is very well, sir."

He looked hard at me.

"Doesn't she have the rheumatism any more?"

"No, sir; she never had it." Then all in a giggle over his mystified looks, I said:

"You are thinking of Mr. Harrison's mother, I suppose. He is my adopted brother."

"Oh!" he said, and pushed his glasses up on his forehead and walked on, to consider it.

Where do you suppose I met him? At the door of the Fulton Street prayer-meeting! I stood at the corner, irresolute which way to turn, when Mr. Romaine came up, from the other side.

"On your way home?" he asked.

"On my way to a decision," I said. "I'm uncertain what to do with the next half hour. I've been delayed at school, and it is too far to go home, and stupid to stand here."

"I'm going to a very pleasant place to spend a half hour," he said, courteously, "quite near at hand. If you have the time, perhaps you would like me to show you the way."

The place proved to be the Fulton Street prayer-meeting. Remembering father's eager interest in the meeting, and his fondness for hearing about it, I decided at once to go, and give him an account of it. So there was where I met Dr. Mason. Did you know he attended prayer-meetings? I wrote father a very full account of the meeting, and in his answer was inclosed a slip of paper, which he said he wanted me to take, the next time I attended, and send it up to the table to be read. I'll copy the contents of the bit of paper for you; it was in father's handwriting?

"Prayers are requested for my dear daughter, who is away from home and in the midst of many temptations. I pray daily that she may give herself to Jesus. I ask you to join me in this petition. My daughter sometimes attends your meetings. Pray that God's spirit may find her there. (Signed,) AN ANXIOUS FATHER."

This is exactly like my father. He is as queer in his way as Mr. Romaine is in his. The *next time* I attend the Fulton Street prayer-meeting I shall send up that note! When do you imagine that will be? Perhaps I would better write a request for you. Do you feel the need of some help of that kind? If you would like any assistance from me, I shall be happy to give it.

Do you know whether your friend Eleanor has any acquaintance with Mr. Romaine? I think he knows her. I was speaking of her projected tour in Europe, and he asked me if she belonged to the Haddingtons, of Philadelphia. What can a mechanic know about the Philadelphia Haddingtons?

I wish you were here to give me a little help in my Latin. The house is full of University students, but I don't feel inclined to ask their assistance. I don't know any of them very well, except Charlie Thorpe, and I'm sure I know more about Latin than he does.

Don't wait as long as I did before answering; you have more leisure than I—no beds to make nor rooms to sweep. I must go this minute.

  Your sister,   EUNICE.

3

REDWOOD, Feb. 18.

My Dear Eunice:

Yesterday was the stormiest day of this season. All Saturday afternoon the snow fell softly and silently, yet very swiftly, so that, before dark, the fence-posts wore white caps rising like a Normandy bonnet; the fence-boards, and every branch and twig, had their line of white above, and the roofs of the houses and the chimney-tops all bore their burden of soft, white snow. Looking out, Aunt Phebe remarked: "It won't last long; snow always melts away quickly when it sticks to the trees."

But, even as she spoke, a fierce gust shook the tall lilac-tree before the window, swaying it back and forth, and leaving it bare and brown. And when Uncle Nathan came in to supper, he said, as he stamped and swept off the snow: "Shouldn't a bit wonder if we had a regular nor'wester after all."

Sure enough! before nine o'clock it blew a perfect tornado; shutters banged and doors creaked, and, all night long, the branches of a locust-tree rubbed against my window with a harsh, grating noise, that might have disturbed a person of weak nerves. Of course *I* didn't mind it! Yesterday morning, when I looked out, there was such a mass of snow in the air that the house across the way could not be seen, and the tempest kept up all day. Of course there was no church-going. Uncle, who is the soul of regularity and promptness, was kept at home from church—he says for the first time in five years. Margaretta says he is always there, and always early—so early and so regular that Mr. Pinckney, who lives half a mile below on the road to the village, says that he never looks at the clock Sunday mornings, but, when he sees Mr. Fuller coming, he knows it is time to begin to get ready for church!

But what was I to do, with a stormy Sunday on my hands, here in this out-of-the-way place? To be sure, I don't *always* go to church, under more favorable circumstances, as when I am in the city—or when it is pleasant out here—but then it is a satisfaction to know that you could go if you wanted to. Then, someway, it seemed yesterday as if the storm would last forever, shutting me off from my friends—except the few I have here. At first I thought what a good day to read! but books, like the weather, were never so dull. Even my beloved Emerson seemed strangely uninteresting, and I turned to Longfellow, feeling like a "forlorn and shipwrecked brother." But mercy! such a storm would wipe out, cover up, sweep away any *footprints* left for another's comfort or encouragement. No, books would not answer; I wanted real, living companionship. Daisy was reading a sermon (one of Beecher's, I presume) to her father and Aunt Phebe. But printed sermons are rather worse to listen to than spoken ones. Sermons need to travel a shorter road from the heart of the preacher to the souls of his hearers, to be effective. Then I essayed to write to you; and, will you believe it, I gave up that idea from conscientious scruples! Whose? They couldn't have been mine, you say? Well, I fancy such things are handed down through the generations. I think these belonged to Grandfather Fuller, and I have just found out, since I came here, that he bequeathed them to me. They wouldn't stand much of a chance for an existence in the atmosphere of the life I have been leading, but out here in their native air they grow and flourish. What a queer old place this is, to be sure! And you want to hear more about Daisy and the rest! I don't know whether you mean Aunt Phebe or Aunt Jane. They are both rather striking characters, in their way, and my mother is given to talking about both of them—in a very different key, however, Grandmother Fuller died years ago, leaving a large family, of whom Aunt Phebe was the eldest, and my mother the youngest. She (Aunt Phebe) brought them all up, helping to find matches for them, and saw them all married off. Besides the six or seven of her own brothers and sisters, she has had, at different times, the training of half a dozen nieces and nephews, and two other orphans. Just now she has *me* in hand, and she thinks her last undertaking the least promising. She has always lived here at the homestead, and, when Margaretta's mother died, uncle came back, and they have lived together ever since—that was when Daisy was a little girl. She says she remembers no other home, and no other mother. What a work that one woman has done! And, as Daisy said the other day, "Not one of them has turned out badly—unless," she added, laughing, "it is I." I remarked once to the old lady: "It is queer, Auntie, that you never married." "Lawful heart, child," she responded, "I never had time to think of such a thing! I was only just fifteen when mother died, and I have had my hands full ever since. And now don't you think Daisy here is trying to coax me into taking another child to bring up! *I* think it is about time I took a little *rest*." But she doesn't think any such thing. She will always be doing something for somebody, until her hand refuses to do her bidding. Aunt Jane, or, Mrs. Morris Fuller, as she wishes to be called, is Uncle Morris' wife, and she lives just across the way. She has never done anything for anybody that I can find out. I beg the lady's pardon, she sent me a mince-pie the other day—but I like lots of raisins in my mince-pies. She has taken to patronizing me. Wherefore? Because I am Wadsworth Harrison's son, and my Uncle Carlos left me fifty thousand dollars; and, furthermore, I am a university student. She honors me with the distinctive title, "My husband's nephew," and has invited me to tea—a great honor, I am told—and got out her silver service for the occasion. There is a story about that service, or connected with it, that I must tell you. (No matter how I heard of it.) Two years ago Aunt Jane said: "I am going to take the money I got for boarding those railroad hands and get a tea-set. I never can have any company until I do get one."

"Lawful heart!" said Aunt Phebe, "we have lots of company, and never had a silver tea-set;" and Aunt Jane returned:

"Yes, I know; common kind of company; but the people that I should invite are just the ones that I can't ask until I get new silver."

So she went to the city and bought the things, and that summer she had the Pendletons and the

Warrens to spend a fortnight. Then because old Mr. Warren took a fancy to Daisy, Aunt Jane took to patronizing her, but she manœuvred sharply to keep them from coming in contact with Aunt Phebe. I presume she feared that the honest soul would expose some of her weak points, and without doubt her fears were well-grounded.

Aunt Phebe is one of those persons who, having nothing to conceal for themselves, can not understand other people's necessities for subterfuges.

But it seems that demure little Daisy had her plans, and one morning she walked into Mrs. Morris Fuller's breakfast parlor while the party were lingering over their coffee, and invited them all over to the homestead to tea! Aunt Jane was thunder-struck, but recovering at once she said:

"I'm sorry, Margaretta, but we were going to drive to the lake, to-day. I was just going to send over to tell you to be ready at one."

"Never mind the lake," broke in old Mr. Warren, "we'll give up all the lakes in North America for the sake of taking a cup of tea from Daisy's hand at the Fuller homestead."

And Daisy ran home to get ready for "company." Presently Aunt Jane followed:

"How could you do such a thing?" she began.

"Why in the world didn't you consult me first? If I had suspected that you thought of such a thing I'd have told you better."

"No doubt, Aunt Jane," laughed Daisy, "so I didn't mention it until I was all ready."

"But you have only that old-fashioned china of your grandmother's; what will they think? I declare it is too bad! Your father is rich enough to have things like other people. If I were you, Margaretta, I'd make him get a set of silver."

I suspect that Daisy gave those eggs a good beating! She said:

"Won't you just tell me, Aunt Jane, who has things the most like other folks—we with our china and earthenware, like our neighbors, or you with the only silver tea-set within three miles?"

"Oh, well, Daisy, you know I don't mean country people."

"But *we* are country people."

"Well, there is no reason why *you* should spend your life digging away here, if you'd only let *me* manage it. What in the world possessed you to do this absurd thing?"

Daisy's cheeks got a bright color upon them just here, but she answered promptly to the last remark:

"Because I thought father and Aunt Phebe would enjoy a visit from Mr. Pendleton. You know they were school-mates, and he used to come here and frolic in this same old kitchen. He told me so; and I am going to give him a chance at some doughnuts, made after Grandmother Fuller's rule, even if we haven't a silver tea-pot."

So they all came to tea, and liked it so well that they accepted Uncle Nathan's invitation to "drop in any time," and there was always *somebody* "dropping in," and the next winter Daisy was invited to the city for a whole month of teas!

I said that old Mr. Warren took a fancy to her, but there is also a young Mr. Warren, of whom I hear but very little, *therefore*, I draw my own conclusions.

Your new boarder, Mr. Romaine, seems to have introduced a new quality into the character of the household. The religious element was rather wanting. I mean the real sort, that people *live* and *use*. I can think of half a dozen among those I know there who are members of churches, but you would never pick them out. I have a profound respect for such men as your mechanic. He evidently believes in his religion; it is a reality to him, whatever it may seem to me.

There is what they call a *special interest* in the churches in the village here. The evangelist, Rev. J. W. Briggs, is preaching every evening, and afternoons too. It seems very strange to hear of the people gathering from a circuit of several miles, evening after evening, coming to hear a person whom I take to be a very ordinary sort of a man. Yet, perhaps, it is not so very strange. People out here in the country have very little in the way of evening entertainments. I presume they are not critical as to the style and profundity of the preacher. They get their sleigh-ride, or their moonlight walk, all the same. Yet here is Daisy, with a clear, keen sense of the beautiful and the fitting capable of appreciating the loftiest sentiments and the finest eloquence, going steadily with her old father to spend hours in that dim, dingy, smoky old church; listening to an illiterate fanatic; for such I am sure he must be. I have not heard him. For once my invalidism does me good service.

I very seldom go out evenings, and ought not to do so at all during this severe weather. True, I have broken over the rule two or three times since I came here, but the circumstances were quite exceptional. Aunt Phebe generally stays at home, on account of her rheumatism, and we two have long talks. I have learned much of the history of our family (on the Fuller side), enough to make a book; but I shan't write one at present. Don't you do it either, Eunice. Words in books are such a time getting to the hearts of people. To be sure they reach a great many in the course of ages. But if one has really a burning message for the multitude it won't be so apt to go out if they get it direct from the heart through the lips. "But I'm a woman," you say. Well, there have been women with messages before now. But I wish your book was written. I want it to read *now*. I am tired of everything I ever heard of.

I wrote to Dr. Mason in regard to going to Philadelphia for a week, or, if that was not advisable, to New York. I thought that I might arrange to meet Tom and Eleanor there for a few days. But I received a speedy reply in the form of a telegram:

"On no account. Perfect rest is indispensable to complete recovery."

Indeed, I know very well that I ought not to undertake the journey. I am really gaining, but so slow that I get impatient. I shall appreciate strength of limb and vigor of mind if I ever get both back again. Eleanor feels hurt. Her last letter reads almost like a reproach. She has never realized how complete was my prostration, and this complete overturning of our plans is a great trial to her. I have written to her that she and her brother will be made very welcome here if they see fit to come for a few days before they sail. I confess I had almost hoped they might change their plans and postpone their tour for a few months.

I was going to remark, back there where

I branched off, that I think I can explain Mr. Romaine's knowledge of the Haddingtons—if it needs an explanation. I suppose you know that "a cat may look at a king;" and, for all I know, he may have had to do with the stately mansion she lives in.

Tell Miss Alice Perkins that she need not turn up her aristocratic nose at *any* man who does good honest work, and Charlie Thorpe—oh, well, arguments and advice are alike wasted upon such as he. But it might be a consolation to Miss Alice to know (seeing that *she* has to eat with him) that the *mechanic* has often entertained Tom Haddington and been entertained by him. Some day I will tell you the whole story. Now, it is enough to say that through this Romaine Tom Haddington, the aristocrat and the millionaire, saved what is worth more than money or ancestral name—his *manhood*. I have never met him, but I know him to be a noble fellow. I think there is no doubt of his identity with the *gentleman* you wrote about. I know considerable about him. His family wanted him to become a minister, but he seems to have thought that his religion would fit a mechanic as well as a minister.

The storm is over. I ought to have told you that long ago. I have been two days writing this letter, and the roads are now in fair condition; so Daisy tells me; and I have actually promised to go and hear that evangelist to-night. That is off of the piece with your going to Fulton Street prayer-meeting!

As ever your brother,   PERRY.

4.

NEW YORK, Feb. 18.

Dear Perry:

What do you suppose Aunt Ruth said to me this evening? I will give you a scene from our conversation. She sat at the round table, making up her account of the day's expenses. I sat biting the end of my wooden penholder. It was not that I couldn't think what to say first to you, but something in the book I had been reading came fresh to my mind just then, and I stopped to think it out.

"What are you doing?" Aunt Ruth asked, suddenly, stopping in the midst of her column.

"Writing," I said, dipping my pen in ink, and dating your letter.

"Who to!" You know Aunt Ruth isn't remarkably well posted as regards the arrangement of sentences.

"To Perry."

"What do you and him write to each other for?"

Did you ever happen to be asked that question? If you have been, I wonder what you said. I'm sure I didn't know what *to* say. I waited a little, but her keen, gray eyes were looking right at me; so I said:

"Why, for fun, I suppose; what does any one write letters to anybody for?"

"Humph!" she said. "You both pretend to be a world too busy to waste hours of time and quires of paper, just for fun. If you either of you had any earthly object, it would be different."

After Aunt Ruth went back to her adding, which by the way she does half audibly, so that I can distinctly catch the last half of every figure as it escapes her lips, I fell to thinking over her question: What *do* we write letters for? Do you suppose these long epistles can ever be utilized in any way, either for your good or mine; or even for our harm, if they can't be made to produce good fruit? Dear me! I believe I would rather do mischief than do just nothing. Of course, now, I enjoy your letters, and all that sort of thing; and I know you do mine. What a mercy it is that we don't have to waste time in being proper to each other. Well, never mind, we'll find out in the millennium, probably, why we enjoyed writing about every earthly thing to each other.

We have had a rich experience to-day. I may as well tell you that it was this over which I was biting my penholder. "To tell, or not to tell; that is the question." I decided to tell. I don't believe it will trouble you; in fact, I don't think it will surprise you; and it was so funny. To commence; your friend Eleanor is in town; dined with us to-day—that is she came to our dinner table as the guest of Laura Myers. Isn't that a strange friendship?. I wasn't introduced. The comical side of that struck me, too. "If Perry were here," I said to myself, "I wonder just how he would manage that?" After dinner we were in the parlor. Laura was discoursing with her usual sense.

"We have a very mixed table," I heard her say. "Not half so pleasant as it used to be; in fact, we are becoming decidedly democratic."

Your Eleanor's beautiful lip curled (and, by the way, you ought to tell her that the habit is very unbecoming to her style of face).

"I detest the word 'democratic!'" she said, scornfully.

"So do I," piped Laura. "But I think you would detest it more if you lived here. The house is even becoming the resort of day laborers."

"Indeed!"

"Yes. Did you ever know a man by the name of Romaine?"

"Not that I have any recollection of."

"Well, he is a character. You ought to be here one day, and see the air that he affects. He is a mechanic of some sort; goes to work at seven o'clock, and isn't released until six; but you would think he was king over us all. He really is rather fine looking; but he does such funny things. Don't you think he has prayers in this very room every evening."

"Insufferable," said Miss Eleanor. "Plebeianism of any kind is hard to endure; but when it comes to you with a religious whine, it is just unbearable."

"There he is!" was Miss Laura's next announcement. "Now, Eleanor, isn't he fine-looking?"

We all looked in Mr. Romaine's direction, and I really wish you could have seen what a contrast he presented to the foppish fellows about him.

"I suppose I shall have to introduce you," Laura said, with a sigh. "They all do here."

Miss Eleanor was queenly.

"Thank you," she said, "I have no desire to extend the circle of my acquaintance. You may spare yourself that trouble."

I'm sure you must be wondering where I was all this time, that I seemed to have the benefit of this conversation, and yet be ignored. That is it, precisely; I was ignored. I stood just at their back, looking over a list of paintings—a catalogue, you know—and waiting for the mail to be brought in, before I went up-stairs. On ordinary occasions Laura is friendly enough with me, but the presence of such an aristocrat as Miss Haddington was too much for her. She did not even glance in my direction. Presently I moved a little to one side, but it seemed that I was still within range of their tongues.

"Who is that pale-faced young girl with an unbecoming dress and a round collar? She stands at your left."

I have to inform you, oh most trusting Perry, that the hero of the unbecoming dress was your friend Eunice. The dress is unbecoming, I haven't a doubt. I have had it three winters, and am likely to have it three more; and round collars are out of fashion.

"That," said Laura, "is a niece of our landlady. She is a good sort of a girl; goes to school, and works for her board, or something of that kind. It is just some more of our democracy, you see."

"I see." You having heard the lady speak several times in the course of your life, doubtless know just how she said that "I see."

At that particular moment who should appear in our midst but Tom Haddington! I hadn't seen him in six months; didn't know he was in town. You know what a fresh, genial air he used to have. Well, he hasn't changed in the least. He went the rounds of the room, aided by Laura Myers, who had rushed forward to greet him, meeting old friends and being introduced to new ones, when, suddenly, he dropped Laura's hand, and his clear, ringing voice sounded through the room :

" Romaine ! as true as I am here," he said, and he held his hand out eagerly. " Why, man, where do you come from ? I as soon expected to see the President, and I would give more to see your little finger at any time than his whole body, much as I admire him."

All this time they were shaking hands in the most eager way, and Laura, for once in her life, losing sight of effect, stood looking on in open-eyed amazement.

" Why, Romaine," Tom commenced again, " have you seen my sister ? No ? She is here. Where is she, Miss Laura ? Oh, there she is, and you haven't met her ! That is an oversight; come right over here and let me introduce you. Eleanor, this is the best friend I ever had or ever expect to have, Mr. Romaine, of Philadelphia."

It must have been a transfer from the torrid zone to the frigid zone, in the region of Mr. Romaine's heart, to turn from Tom Haddington's greeting to receive his sister's bow. I don't care if she is your friend, Perry. I was provoked with her; she might have been more courteous to her brother than to ignore his friend in the way she did. I wonder what Tom would have said, if he hadn't suddenly been thrown into another surprise? He spied me, and rushed towards me, both hands extended.

"Why, Eunice," said he, "little Una, I thought you had gone home. How splendid it is to see you all here! Have you met my sister?"

Then, immediately, before I could answer his question, he asked another. You know Tom always used to ask at least two questions at once.

"Oh, Eunice!" he said, "seeing you makes me think of Perry. Have you heard from him lately?"

I stood near your lady, and I felt wicked, so I answered, promptly:

"I had a letter last evening; he is improving, though he seems to think rather slowly. He is impatient, as usual."

At that point I had the satisfaction of a full view of Miss Eleanor's face, and she gave me a prolonged and astonished stare. She had evidently heard of me before. I made another discovery, which is that Miss Haddington doesn't care to be absolutely rude to a friend of Perry Harrison. So, my friend, thank you for condescending to be known *as* my friend. It earned me a gracious reception, even though I *did* wear an unbecoming dress.

Now, why have I told you this long story? I hardly know myself, except because of the foolish habit of telling you all that happens in this house. I wish I were one of the good young ladies that one reads about in books, then I should have locked this story into the secret chamber of my own great heart, and borne my share of wrong in noble silence. Isn't that the way they do it?

This isn't answering your letter, is it? Well, there were two points in it that amused me. One was the idea of your being conscientious! I never suspected it! How does it make you feel? The other, the idea of your going to hear that country preacher! Truly, Perry, I thought you had more respect for your mother and your early education than to actually make light of preaching of any sort. It would have served you right to have caught another horrid cold; but I don't suppose you did; wicked people never get their deserts in this wicked world. However, since you will do wrong, give me the benefit of your experience.

What do you suppose I've done next? Gone into the Sunday-school and taken a class of little savages under my care! What on earth will I teach them! There are five of them—boys—with bare feet, or nearly so, even in this weather, and such hands! I don't think the idea of washing them can have entered their minds in a century. I presume you think they are not a century old; but in that you are mistaken; I'm sure they must have been created when the world was; they know all the evil in it, and there is so much that it must have taken some time to learn. Of course Mr. Romaine is the individual who had to do with my being so foolish. He was in great perplexity as to what he should do with them. Aunt Ruth came to his help.

"Why, here is Eunice; why don't you get her into it? She taught a day-school in Nassau, and managed first-rate, my brother said."

I laughed, of course.

"Why, Aunt Ruth!" I said. "I don't know what has become of your usual good sense. The idea of my being a Sabbath-school teacher!"

"Why not, child. It is a pity if you can't teach them to say their Bible verses. It can't be harder than staying in a little old schoolhouse with them all day, and you lived through that."

"But, Aunt Ruth," I said, "you know I had the amusement of whipping them to sustain my spirits, and I'm afraid that wouldn't look well in Sunday-school."

Meantime Mr. Romaine had evidently been considering. I'm not sure that he had heard a word that either of us had said, after Aunt Ruth's first sentence. He spoke at last, in a sort of doubtful tone:

"If you could manage them for me for one or two Sundays, until I could look around me, and—"

"Do better," I said, finishing the sentence, as he seemed to hesitate. And the truth is, Perry, I was piqued into taking it, because he evidently thought I couldn't do anything with them.

I wish I had time to tell you what a funny time I had with them last Sunday. That was my first attempt. I should have resigned all future care of them the minute I reached home, only Charlie Thorpe spoiled that by advising me to. I am resolved not to act on any idea that emanates from his brain.

This letter is to go by the next mail, and that closes in ten minutes. In my next I'll try to answer some of your remarks.

In haste,   EUNICE.

5.

Dear Una:

Your letter amused me considerably, the more as I had one from Eleanor by the same mail, in which she spoke of spending the day with Laura Myers, and of meeting my little friend Una, whom she pronounced "a very nice little girl." Now, I wish I could see your face as you read that! You would rather be called proud, haughty, disagreeable, almost anything else. Well, Miss Eleanor might not enjoy some things you said about her. But I venture the prediction that you will yet be fast friends, and I fancy that you might be very helpful to each other were you to be thrown much together. Wasn't it too bad that I wasn't there with you all! Yet I laughed when I thought what an incongruous set you were. Laura Myers and Alice Perkins, Eleanor and Eunice, Tom Haddington, Mr. Romaine and Charlie Thorpe! You didn't mention Charlie, but I suppose he was hovering about, as usual. Be careful, Una; the fellow has a heart.

I am looking forward with considerable certainty to a visit from Eleanor and Tom before they sail. I have not been quite so well for a week or two. The fact is, I have left off the bourbon which Dr. Mason ordered, and I find that my strength was, to a great extent, a fiction, gotten up from day to day by means of that same bourbon. It was a sentence or two in one of your letters awhile ago, with two or three more in one of Tom Haddington's, that led me to give it up. So you see you and Tom are in part responsible for my weakness and dullness.

It is fearfully dull out here. Dr. Mason knew what he was about when he sent me out here for quiet. Sometimes the stillness is so heavy that I can scarcely endure the burden. Yet I know that if I were in New York I should either break over the doctor's orders or die of a restless longing to get out. *Here* there is no special temptation to disobey. To be sure there is sleigh-riding, but the few times I have ventured out Aunt Phebe (in league with Dr. Mason, I suspect) insisted upon muffling me to the eyes, and so loading me with wraps that I could scarcely walk, and then burying me in cushions and buffalo-skins. Thus trammeled, with Uncle Nathan for driver, and sober old Billy jogging along, sleigh-riding became a tame affair—there is nothing exhilarating about it—and I sigh for the strength to hold and guide my own fiery Sir

Walter. Well, it is like anything else. Life bids fair to become a sober, jogging sort of an affair after all. I look at Uncle Nathan and at Uncle John, and wonder if I shall finally settle down to their sort of life; and then I look at Aunt Phebe and the rest of the sewing-society ladies, and think of you and Eleanor, wondering if these, too, had their ambitious dreams and plans away back in other days. There is just one word that expresses the life which these people live—*humdrum*. I hope my expected visitors will bring some life and energy from the outside world into this lonesome retreat. If somebody would only come in with a rush and a whir, and upset the quiet and order of this well-regulated community, what a relief it would be!

It is a fact, I am growing rebellious, I am sick of staying here. I want to be at work. I can not afford to waste so much time. I *must* get well. I told Daisy so this morning, and she laughed a little. "But if you *can't*," she said.

That's it—*fettered*. Now, think of it, Una. I mean't to graduate in July; go to Europe for a year or two; come back and—make a *mark*. Here I am, put back a whole year at the very best.

Do you remember (of course you do) the time I left Nassau for Williston, six years ago? And the talk we had about my future? How eager I was for the struggle—the struggle for an education with limited means? Do you remember how grandly I had chosen between "wealth and culture," in declining the fine position which was offered me in New York, and choosing to work my way up the ladder, standing then upon one of the lower rounds, a graduate of the country district school? How proud I was of sweeping the halls and ringing the bells that first half year at Williston! Don't laugh, please; but I used to imagine what I *would* say if anybody *should* snub me (which never happened) because of my poverty and my menial occupations. I would whisper to myself, "Now, Perry Harrison, don't you mind; some day you will stand head and shoulders above these fellows." Of course I was silly; but I think I really enjoyed being poor— the thought of being "a self-made man" was inspiring—and I think I was really a little bit sorry that Uncle Chester left me that sixty thousand dollars, because it spoiled my plans. But I confess to you that I have grown to think that "sixty thousand" dollars is a very handy thing to have. With the means to carry them out, my plans became broader, and my ambitious ardor increased. No need to tell you of my schemes— and some of them were so lofty that they might look ludicrous on paper.

Well, here I am! This room is exactly sixteen

feet square. I have strength to walk across it. I can look down the road and across the fields about a quarter of a mile. I can read, in limited quantities, a sort of light stuff called literature, and write gossipy letters. Whether or not this is the end I am unable to say. Daisy says—I'll tell you what *I* said first. My head ached. I threw down my book and looked over to the window where she sat, with a magazine, which she laid down as my book banged against the ottoman which obstructed its passage across the room. She smiled at my petulance, and I said, bitterly—no, I will not repeat the words I used, but I cursed the fate that keeps me here a prisoner, and she replied:

"Cousin Perry, it hurts me to hear you speak in that way of your best Friend. If you would only be willing to trust your future with Him—"

"Trust my future! If I am to judge of what your loving God will do in the future by the present, I might as well give up the ship first as last. Look at it now, and tell me if you call it love. I have worked hard, and I think fairly earned success. My prospects for carrying off University honors were at least fair, and then I should have been ready to use the advantages I had gained—gained, too, by hard, honest work —gained in spite of the hindrance of wealth— and here I am with, I must own, very little prospect of regaining my strength. Daisy, I feel that I have a right to life—a right to an opportunity to use my gifts. I have earned the right, and I do say that I can not feel that it is a just God that has set me aside at this point. It seems all wrong and cruel—so cruel."

"Don't Perry—*don't*."

Daisy's voice was full of sorrow, and I knew that I had pained her. I, conceited fellow that I was, fancied that it was sorrow for me—for my disappointment—and sympathy with my restless longing, and I was surprised at the vehemence with which she continued:

"Perry Harrison, I can not let you speak so of our Lord. I will not hear it. It is shocking! You can not know what you are saying. God cruel! I tell you it is not so. He is kind and loving, even when he sends things that hurts us. And as for your sickness, didn't you tell me the other day that it was your own fault—that you overworked? What's the use in blaming God for that? I wont hear it, I tell you; and don't you ever speak that way to me again."

I laughed a little—I could not help it. In her excitement she had crossed the room and stood by my chair, and she looked at me almost scornfully. I said:

"Well, little Margaretta, wait until your kind and loving Friend thwarts some of *your* plans, then tell me if you don't rebel."

"Perry," she said, while a sudden pallor came over her face, "you don't know what you are talking about."

Then she went away. I wonder what sorrow has shadowed her life so early, for there is a shadow. There was a whole book of revelation in that white face. Why does God make the gift a burden? A year ago I might have thanked him for life; but just now it does not seem much of a gift to be grateful for. I am almost sorry that Eleanor is coming. To see her radiant in health and beauty, and Tom overflowing with strength and energy, will scarcely improve my spirits and temper.

Later.—And now don't you think good old Aunt Phebe wants to take away one of my few remaining blessings! She came up to-night, after the rest had gone to prayer-meeting, as she usually does, to sit awhile with me. I was writing when she came, and as I laid down my pen, she said:

"Which one are you going to make read all that?"

"Oh, Eunice is the only person in the world to whom I should dare send such a long letter," I said, laughing. "Her patience is equal to anything in that line," I added.

"Well," said Aunt Phebe, with a long sigh, "I suppose you know what you are about; but it don't seem just right to be writing such long letters to one girl when you are going to marry another."

"Why, Auntie, Una and I have always been just like brother and sister. I write to her as I would to an own sister. Besides, there does not seem to be much prospect of my marrying anybody very soon."

"Well, well; I suppose you know what you are about," repeated the old lady. "But, my boy, I can tell you one thing—there'll be a heartache somewhere before you're done."

"Oh, no, Auntie. How can that be, when there is such a fair understanding all around?"

"Well, you'll find out; then you'll remember what an old woman told you." Then she added, with more energy: "I *know*—I've seen it."

Poor Auntie! She is giving herself unnecessary trouble about *us*, isn't she? I wonder what she meant; could it be Daisy? And is that some way the secret of the shadow which I fancy I have discerned?

I suspect that Daisy told of our talk this afternoon; for, as Aunt Phebe was rolling up her knitting-work, she said:

"Perry, when you look out in the morning, I want you to remember that over there, under that sheet of snow, there is a field of wheat, and remember that 'Bread grows in the winter night.'"

May 15.—Two months since I wrote the last line! And even now Dr. Mason's orders are imperative—not a line to be written or a sentence read! But what is the use of obeying? I may as well use up the little strength I have in this way, if I am never to have any for work that would amount to something. And that is just what they say—narrowed down, stripped of all qualifications, all consoling and mitigating (but unmeaning) words, the verdict reached is this: I may live! Oh, yes—live, breathe, exist for years! But as for ever getting strong enough to bear my part in the world's strife——

Una, do *you* call this justice!

PERRY.

6.

[AS WRITTEN IN EUNICE'S JOURNAL.]

We have had a busy week, and such a strange one! Surprising events followed each other so rapidly. In the first place, came that telegram. I believe I shall always shudder when I see a telegram after this. Mine was so short and so full: "Perry Harrison is dying. Come." How the room whirled, and how very strange it seemed to be up in the air and falling, with no solid place on which to fall. They say fainting is like that; if it is, I don't want to faint. I didn't faint quite, either, I felt that there was no time to lose in that useless way. I gathered my strength and went downstairs; went in search of Aunt Ruth, and said, speaking as calmly as I could:

"Aunt Ruth, I have got to go to Redwood."

She faced about on me, spectacles and all. She was looking over fruit, and she always wears spectacles during such work, and rarely at other times: so that makes her look more strange. I remember that even then I thought of the queer look it gave her eyes, and remembered that my eyes were said to be like hers, and wondered if mine would look like hers when I wore glasses. And all the time I knew, for I said it over to myself, that awful sentence: "Perry Harrison is dying!"

"To Redwood!" she said, drawing out the letters until each made a line. "Where on earth is that?"

"It is in Vermont, on the Vermont and Something Else Railroad. I don't remember just where it is, but I have got to go."

By this time Aunt Ruth seemed to have an idea that something was amiss. She took up her bowl from the chair before her, and pushed the chair toward me with her foot, as she said:

"Sit down, child; you look like a sheet. What on earth is the matter?"

I didn't sit down. I had a dim idea that if I should, the chair would go sinking down to that bottomless abyss that seemed whirling around me. But I answered, promptly:

"Perry is sick—Perry Harrison. You remember him? He is dying, the telegram says; and I want to start at once."

My Aunt Ruth froze into propriety in an instant.

"What an idea!" she said, in her most astonished tones. "As if you could go out there to see a young man who is no kind of kith or kin, even if he is sick."

How cold and horrible the words sounded.

"Why, Aunt Ruth," I said, speaking in a tremor of haste and pain, "he has been just like my brother all my life. He is just as dear to me as if he were my brother."

"Sho!" Aunt Ruth said, piling up the fruit carefully in the dish before her. "Of all the silly talk that girls get off, that is the silliest! Being like your brother don't give you and him the same name, and don't give you no kind of right, in the eyes of lookers-on, to go tearing around over the country after him. It ain't respectable, you see."

"I don't care anything about lookers-on," I said, hotly. "They may say and think exactly what they like. I never did care for gossip, and this is not the time to begin."

"I never saw one of them in my life that did." Aunt Ruth said it as composedly as though I was not at the very verge of endurance. "They none of 'em care for gossip. They are above it —in a higher sphere. It's a mercy that the most of them have old, wise heads, with a little common sense in them, to look after them, or they would all go to destruction together. I tell you what it is, child, even gossip ain't a thing to be run over with a sniff, as if it wasn't any account. As a rule, folks won't go at that work, unless they have a kind of foundation to start on."

For a moment I felt as though I must take up that great yellow bowl she was heaping with berries and hurl it at her head. How *could* she be so exasperatingly cool and argumentative when Perry was dying? But my very anger had a quieting effect upon my nerves. When they get to a white heat, they are stiller, outwardly, than while they are heating.

"Aunt Ruth," I said, and the sound of my own voice surprised me, "I am going to Redwood by this afternoon's train. If you will help me to get ready and go in a decent manner, I will be glad; and if you will not, I will run away. I am going on the five o'clock train if I live."

She suspended her horrible picking for two minutes, and looked me full in the face.

"Is the child gone clean mad?" she muttered. And despair took hold of me; for, really, I might talk of running away, and all that sort of thing, but I knew that I should have to get Aunt Ruth's permission, or stay at home. In the first place, I had not a cent of money in the world; and in the second—no, it is not so; I can honestly put that reason first—I was my father's daughter, I was placed by him in my aunt's care; and not even for you, Perry, could I go in direct opposition to her command.

"What in the world do you think you can do for him?" she demanded. "If he is so very sick, he may not live until you get there; and if he should, what is Perry Harrison to you?"

I sat down, then, on the chair. I felt myself falling. I did not say another word. Utter desolation got hold upon me. If I could have cried, I should have been glad; instead, I looked and felt like a stone.

Aunt Ruth worked away at the fruit. At last she said in a sharp, business tone, the one that belongs to her city life and her boarding house:

"What time is it?"

"I don't know."

"What time did you say that train went?"

"At five o'clock."

"And here are all these berries to can, besides the pies to see to for dinner. Well, what *has* to be will be, I suppose. Get on your apron and help me as fast as you can. If we've got to be ready by five o'clock, we shall have to fly, that's all."

Now, it had never once occurred to me that Aunt Ruth would think of such a thing as leaving her home and her work to go with me. And perhaps the perplexities that such a suggestion started were just the thing for my whirling brain;

From Different Standpoints. 59

at least it was drawn away for a moment from that awful sentence.

"Where can we go, Aunt Ruth?" I said, timidly. "Perry is not in a boarding-house, you know. He is with his aunt." Whereupon my aunt eyed me again, with bewildered eyes, over her spectacles.

"I believe the child thinks I am going to pounce right down upon him, as if I had come for no other earthly purpose!" she said; and added, reflectively: "Well, well, girls *are* fools." Then she deigned an explanation: "Why, we'll go to my Aunt Mercy's on your father's side; she lives a mile out. They didn't have any such high-sounding name as Redwood for it when I went there—it was Stony Hollow; and for a minute I forgot where that young fellow was. I haven't seen Aunt Mercy for a hundred years, more or less; but that ain't her fault. She'll be willing to see me, and if she ain't, there's no help for it: for you say you've got to go; and you always was headstrong. I s'pose you are attached to him. Poor fellow, he comes of a consumptive lot. But there's no use in making a goose of yourself, in my opinion. But we'll go, and no more words about it!"

After that sentence, I didn't know whether I wanted most to throw my arms around Aunt Ruth's neck and kiss her, or choke her. What I did, was to sit still and look over the berries. Well, Journal, she certainly managed that affair in a remarkable manner. I was too much excited to care then; but I can see now that I will be glad when I get home again. She remarked at noon, when the boarders who lunch at home had seated themselves, that they would have to be inconvenienced a little she was afraid, as she could not get Miss Hopper to superintend the house until to-morrow; and as she had made all her plans to go on a little vacation, and take the afternoon train, they would have to get along with what the cook and waiters could do for them for one day. They were all polite, and thought everything would be all right, and hoped she would have a pleasant time. Charlie Thorpe, of course, asked some questions. Was she going alone?

"No," Aunt Ruth said. She was going to take Eunice with her. She had been promising for ten years to visit Aunt Mercy; and for half that time she had been promising to bring me with her; but the right time had never seemed to come until just that minute. Then Charlie wanted to know if it was a long journey, and whereabouts in Vermont it was, and wasn't that the place where Perry Harrison had hidden himself.

"The very place," Aunt Ruth said, "and the poor fellow isn't so well as he was, I hear. I am glad, on that account, that we are going just now. Perhaps Eunice can cheer him up a little; they were children together, and have always been playmates."

Just then I could have hugged Aunt Ruth. How wise she was!

Well, we came. The awful line of miles between us was bridged at last, and we were landed at Aunt Mercy's door. This Aunt Mercy was a woman of whom I had heard indeed; but that was about all. I hadn't an idea as to what we were coming, and I didn't care. By that time I had begun to have great faith in Aunt Ruth's powers; so, as we clambered into Jonas Stiles' fruit-wagon, which was going right past Aunt Mercy's place, I clutched her sleeve.

"Aunt Ruth, I must see Perry to-night, some way; I don't care how, only I *must* do it. To-morrow may be too late."

Aunt Ruth's voice was sharp, even in undertone.

"You talk like a fool, child, if I must say so. How can we possibly manage it to-night? Pity's sakes! you ought at the very least to be going to marry him, by the way you act." Then aloud, she said: "Where is that young Harrison stopping, who came out here for his health?"

She seemed to know Vermont ways, and to realize that Jonas Stiles would know all about him.

"He lives in that farm-house yonder, just back of where you are going to stop; and I rather guess he come for what he won't find. He has been going on from bad to worse ever since he got here. I heard tell, this morning, that he was dying."

Oh, Journal, how *could* I bear this much longer? I felt like screaming. I wanted to say, Let me out! I *will* go to him this minute. I did open my mouth to speak; but Aunt Ruth put a firm hand on my arm, a hand that someway quieted me.

"I guess you may stop there with me, if he is so bad as that," she said, quietly. "I used to know his mother well, and I should like to see if there was a turn of any kind I could do for the poor boy."

The man agreed to it quietly enough. He was too good-hearted to think it strange.

"Will I take the young woman on?" he said, looking inquiringly at me.

"Oh, no," Aunt Ruth said; "she may as well wait for me. And"—no, he needn't wait; oh, not at all. If he would just set our trunk down at Mrs. Spencer's door, and say that we had stopped to inquire after a friend, we could easily walk the little distance. Then she said to me, as she watched him drive away:

"Now, I hope you are satisfied. For my part, I feel like a fool."

What did I feel like? I never can tell.

Our knock was answered by a young girl with a fair, pure face. I knew in an instant that it was Daisy. She took my hand and said, at once:

"Are you his friend Eunice?"

"Yes," I said, and my voice was perfectly quiet. "How is he?"

"He is living, and that is really all we can say. I am glad you have come. He seems to have been expecting you, for he asked twice if the train was in. But there is one thing: you must not go to him at all, if you can not be perfectly quiet and controlled. The doctor says that the slightest agitation might be fatal. And there is another thing: he will ask you at once whether you think he is going to die. The doctor will not have him told. I think it is all wrong, but I can not assume the responsibility; so I have to live a lie before him. And you must reconcile it with your conscience, as best you can, to do the same, or determine what to do. Only I ought to tell you this: that the doctor thinks that a knowledge of the hopelessness of his condition would be sure to prove fatal."

"And yet you think it is all wrong not to tell him. What a cousinly regard you must have for him!"

Yes, my Journal, I said just that hard and hateful thing to a lady whom I never saw before;

but she did not seem to hear it at all, or at least to heed it; for which I was very grateful. I mean I was afterward—I did not care then. After Aunt Ruth's admirable planning to have everything appear natural and reasonable— while she was talking earnestly with Daisy, as she threw off her duster, showing her what old and tried friends his mother and she used to be, and how sorry she was for the poor boy—one of those unaccountable whirling fits came over me, and for the first time in my life I fainted dead away. The next time I actually knew anything enough to remember it, I was lying in a sweet-smelling country bed. Aunt Ruth stood beside me.

"You are not to go near him to-night," she said; "and you needn't think it. You have had your way all along; it is time for me to have mine. I have been up, and the doctor is there; and he says he is not to see a new face to-night, nor be agitated in any way; and he says there is a mite of hope. And it's my opinion he isn't going to die yet awhile; he isn't, if *I* can help it. I am going to take care of him to-night myself. And you are to lie still and mind; or if you don't, that doctor says you will have a run of fever as sure as fate; and that will make a pretty mess." Saying which, she bustled away.

And there was I, who had traveled a day and

a night in feverish haste; who had neither eaten a mouthful nor slept a wink since I heard the news; and had finally reached over a space of three hundred miles, for the purpose of fainting away and being put to bed in the room under his, and having Daisy to nurse me! It was well such an experienced nurse as Aunt Ruth had come with me to take her place. When I did finally see Perry, it was a strange meeting. He was too weak to open his lips, and I was not allowed to open mine; so I could only hold his hand for an instant and smile at him like an idiot, and then rush away and cry like a boiling volcano—all of which was of great benefit to him! He is better. You may be sure of that, or I would not be going all over this to you.

We have been here two weeks. Aunt Ruth talks of going home and leaving me to Aunt Mercy's care. If I ever get to it, I am going to tell you about that woman. He is not by any means out of danger, but the smiling doctor grows more smiling, and begins to hint that a change of climate in the autumn may do wonders for him, if he should rally from this. But oh! that awful "if." And let me tell you, Journal, of something that I will tell to no one else. I will not let myself say it, only occasionally. But I don't believe it! This is a deceitful lull in a deceitful disease. And above all the other pain, there is one so strange and sharp, that I can not explain it. But he is afraid to die! Perry Harrison, with his splendid intellect and his splendid courage!—never afraid of anything earthly—is awfully afraid of this softly, shadowy thing, that looks so simple and quiet—this dying! I don't think I am afraid of it. I think I would like to try it. That horrible Daisy says people, even cowards, are not apt to be afraid of things that they fancy are far away from them.

"Are *you* afraid of it?" I asked her, and I spoke fiercely, as, someway, I can not help speaking to her. She answered, quietly enough:

"No, I am not. I know I should not be afraid to die to-night. But it is for no such reason as you give. It is because 'when I pass through the valley and the shadow of death, I will fear no evil, for he is with me, his rod and his staff will comfort me.'"

"Why don't you teach the secret of your fearlessness to him, if it is such a secret and such a wonderful thing?" I asked, and my tone was sneering.

She gave a weary sigh.

"There is just One that can teach that secret," she said; "and I have tried so hard to have Perry learn it of him; but he will not."

"If I knew what you are talking about—if there was anything in it all, and I had the secret

—I'd risk, but what I could get Perry to be interested in it," I said, bitterly.

She answered me in the same quiet, steady tone that she had all the time used.

"You know perfectly well there is everything in it. Why don't you get it for yourself, and try to impart it to him?"

Then she went away, and left me to think it over. It is very strange. I wonder if anybody ever felt so before? I want Perry to be a Christian. I do believe in it. I know there is truth in it. I want him to have the help that it can give, for I am almost certain that he is going to need it. But I don't want to be a Christian myself? I *can't* want to. I hate the whole subject. I would willingly try to be interested for Perry's sake. But I can't. My heart seems shut up. I am going down now to read to him. He will make some miserable selection—he always does —something that will throw him into a fever of thought, and do no good. What a stupendous failure living is!

7.

REDWOOD, August 10.

My Dear Eleanor:

What a strange fatality—Daisy would say "providence"—has separated us at this time!—led you across the Atlantic and fastened me here. There is absolutely no hope of my joining you this season. True, the doctor talks of a change of climate, but he wants to banish me to California. The fact is, I intend to go home just as soon as I am able to travel. If I can not find strength *there* I shall give up the quest—I have almost given up the hope. I know now that there was a time when the rest gave up they tried to cheat me into the belief that I would rally, while they had no idea that I would!

Poor Daisy! It must have been hard for her to act a lie; and it was only when the doctor said that the knowledge of my danger would be fatal—much he knew about it!—that she consented to go in and out with a falsehood on her face. What if they had let me die unwarned! I asked Daisy how she got along with it. Her answer puzzled me a little.

"Perry," she said, "they insisted that you must not be told, and I dared not take the responsibility; indeed, they declared that unless I promised to be calm and not hint of your danger I must be banished from your room entirely. There was one thing left for me to do: I prayed for your life as I never prayed before, that you might have another chance to make Christ your Friend."

Eleanor, someway I feel that I owe my life to Daisy's prayer. Skeptic that I have been regarding the power of prayer, I can not divest myself of this conviction. And, moreover, I feel that it may be well for me to look into this matter. My life hangs by a thread, and if, as these people say, I need a special preparation for whatever may be beyond, it is certainly time that I attended to it, and this is one reason why I rebel against this separation. You, Eleanor, know about this matter; at least, I suppose you do. You profess that religion which they say sustains in the dark hours, and makes it easy for men to die. I certainly need that, but it is all a mystery to me. You see how much I need you just now to throw light upon what I suppose is clear to you. Yet one thing puzzles me almost as much as the mysteries of this religion. You, Eleanor, have never seemed anxious about this matter. You have never asked me to embrace your faith;

never said that you prayed for me. And here is Daisy, with only a cousinly regard for me, overwhelmed with anxiety because of my unbelief. And Eunice too, though she is not a Christian herself, "wishes she knew something about it so she could help Perry." Are *they* over-anxious? Help me, if you can. Write often. I hope to be able to write longer letters soon. I find myself longing for Tom. I believe a sight of your faces would almost make me well again. Did I tell you that Eunice came to me when I was at the worst? She has remained here in Redwood ever since. Aunt Ruth came with her, and I am not sure that it was not her skillful nursing that brought me back from the brink of the grave. Everybody else was worn out, and just then she stepped in, with her strong, steady nerves and warm, motherly heart, and, as Daisy said, "put new life and hope into them all." Aunt Jane was entertaining the Warrens, from Albany, at the time, so she could only send over every day to inquire. She has since assured me that if I had not been so well supplied with nurses she would have asked her guests to defer their visit. What a nurse she would have made!

Here comes Eunice to read to me, and to remind me that I am disobeying orders.

As ever,   PERRY.

NASSAU, September 15.

My Dear Eleanor:

Since my last I have gained strength very rapidly. I have been to New York to consult Dr. Mason, who assures me that if I continue to improve at the same rate for the next six weeks, after that I may do whatever I like—go where I please—with one or two restrictions: I am not to re-enter the University, and I must not remain in this climate. Now, I propose to join you at Florence about the middle of November. I want you to consider seriously the proposition, that our marriage shall take place as soon as possible —say December first. We will spend the winter in Florence, and go to Germany in the spring. By that time I hope to be able to resume my studies, and may enter one of the German Universities. Dr. Mason would think me wild if I were to suggest that last idea in his presence. But I am not quite ready to renounce all literary work.

I went to the old place in New York. Saw Miss Myers and Charlie Thorpe, and the rest of them. I missed Tom's friend, Mr. Romaine; he was out of town. I had regretted this, for I had hoped to get some help from him. I am still turning over in my mind the matters of which I have written you concerning the reality of the religion of Christ. I am " almost persuaded;"

but, as I have said before, some things puzzle me and hold me back from any decisive action.

Oh, Eleanor!—my Eleanor! If you would only tell me—is there a reality in this thing? Do you know, *of your own experience*, that all the soul's needs are met in Christ? * * * *

Lovingly,　　　　　　　　　　　Perry.

[FROM PERRY'S JOURNAL.]

Nassau, September 20.

It is five years since I gave up journalizing. I do not propose to take up the practice again; but, being in a strangely unsettled mood to-day, and happening upon this old book, I have set out to write off my moodiness. Latterly I have had the habit of writing to Eunice whenever a fit of the blues came over me; but, to gratify a whim of Eleanor's, I have broken off the correspondence with Eunice. I am half vexed with Eleanor. If I did not know that a noble nature like hers is above such petty jealousy, I should feel that the request was an insult both to Eunice and myself. But of course I know that she has some reason for her unaccountable action in this matter. Her last letters have been exceedingly cold and unsatisfactory. But I hope that I shall not have to live upon letters much longer; and when we are together all will be explained. I have written to her urging that our marriage take place soon. I think it will be better so, and perhaps she will have more faith in her husband than she seems to have in her lover.

Dear little Eunice! I wonder if she cares much. I miss her letters. I wrote to her, telling her as gently as I could, that whatever time or strength I possessed for letter-writing ought to be given to my promised wife. She did not respond at all. She might have written once more. It looks as if she were vexed. To tell the truth, I believe that Aunt Phebe was right when she said that somebody would suffer or that somebody's heart would ache. *Mine* does. I want to see my little adopted sister just once, or to hear from her, to know that she is not angry with her brother Perry.

But this is not entirely the cause of my present unsettled mood. When I seemed to be near to death I felt that I needed something which I had not. I am convinced that a man needs a Saviour in the hour of death; and it seems to me that if I am going to depend on the Lord Jesus Christ for strength *then* that he expects something of me in this life—something more than a mere profession of his name.

Now, there is my Eleanor. She is a member of the Church. How does her life differ from mine? There is Daisy. But she is too nearly perfect—too near angelhood—thoughts of her don't help me. There is one person who is leading the kind of a life that I think a Christian ought to live. That is Mr. Romaine, and I have never seen him. I only know him through Tom and Eunice. I went to New York last week ostensibly to see Dr. Mason, though I cared very little about that. I went really to see Mr. Romaine. It was Tom Haddington's friend whom I wished to consult, religiously, instead of Dr. Mason, medically. But I was obliged to come away without seeing him, and I know not where to turn for help.

October 5.—I came to New York last evening, to make final preparations for my contemplated tour. To-day, about noon, I found myself in the vicinity of Fulton Street prayer-meeting, and, prompted by a sudden impulse, I went in. The meeting was in progress, and a gentleman, whom I failed to recognize, at the time, was speaking, and this is what he said: " Prayers are requested for a young man ill with a lung disease, and who is not a Christian." After reading the request from a slip of paper, the speaker added: " The young lady, whose hand I recognize in this paper, is herself not a Christian. I would add to the request this, that she be also remembered in the petitions." All at once it flashed over me that the gentleman speaking was Mr. Romaine, the young lady was Eunice, and the invalid young man was myself! Well, I staid to hear myself prayed for, and went out, saying, "Perry Harrison, you know that prayer will be answered, and you may as well yield the remainder of your skeptical theories. You have already come to believe in the power of prayer. You acknowledge that you believe that your life has been prolonged in answer to prayer. Why, then, do you not go farther, and begin to pray yourself?"

Well, why do I hesitate? The simple truth is, I am as ignorant as a child, of the very first principles of the Christian religion. I don't know what to do first. I wish——

October 6.—Just at that point there was a rap at my door, and Mr. Romaine entered.

"Mr. Harrison, I believe? Pardon my intrusion, but, hearing that you were in the house, as a friend of Tom Haddington's I felt like coming in to see you. My name is Romaine."

I was happy to see Mr. Romaine, and said so—gave him a chair, and we fell into a talk. Our mutual friendship for the Haddingtons furnished us with a topic to start off with, though I fancy that there is not much love wasted between him and my peerless Eleanor. The truth is, Eleanor is too aristocratic too live in our democratic country; and I suspect that she looks down a little upon Mr. Romaine. But he is a noble fellow, and I hope to be able to prove to her that he is worthy of our friendship and love, for I have already come to love him as a brother. Our talk drifted along, until, at length, I said:

"Mr. Romaine, I am glad you came in. I—, well, you prayed for me this morning?" He gave a little start, then said: "I've prayed for you a great many times during the last few weeks."

"Thank you. You are very kind to take an interest in my unworthy self." Then I thought we should never come at the point I wished to reach, by making polite responses to each other; and, while I was trying to begin again, he broke the silence by saying:

"As I have already said, I became interested in you through our mutual friends, and I will be frank and say that one object of my call here to-night is to ask you to give the subject of religion your serious attention."

"I have been doing that for several weeks," I replied; "but I tell you frankly that the lives of the most of the professing Christians whom I know have not impressed me favorably. Indeed, they have made me very skeptical concerning the faith which they profess."

"You believe in God and the Bible?"

"Yes. Though my interpretation of the Bible might differ somewhat from yours."

"And in Christ the Son of God?"

"Yes. That is, I am not sure about his being the Son of God, in the sense in which you mean it," I replied.

"In the Holy Spirit, and in his presence and power in the hearts of men?"

"There is just my trouble. People profess to be led by the Spirit. And look at them! Why, see *how* they are led! I can but think their own depraved hearts are leading them."

"Ah!" exclaimed my visitor, "you believe, then, that we have depraved hearts?"

"Yes, I do."

"And that we need a Saviour?—that *you* need a Saviour?" he asked, earnestly.

"I think I feel that," I said; "but I should not be satisfied with—well, to speak plainly, with the sort of religion that Laura Myers and Charley Thorpe have. I see very little difference in Charley since he became a Christian."

"Now, my friend," said Mr. Romaine, a half-amused look spreading over his face, and giving place to the look of earnestness which he usually wears, "will you tell me just how great would be the change in your life were you to decide for Christ?—I mean, of course, outwardly. You have no bad habits, no evil associations to drop off. The inner life would be all new, and the outer would be enlarged. You would be more of a man, and this is what Charley Thorpe has become—more of a man. You might exchange the theatre for the Young Men's Christian Rooms, and your voice would be heard in the sacred song and prayer. You might exchange law for theology. These are the changes *I* see in Charley, as you would, if you were with him long. And as for Laura Myers, if you will go down to our mission I'll show you something of what she is doing. I am not blind to the truth that there is a great deal of worldliness and inconsistency among Christians; but there is real, true devotion among them. The question is, Are you *willing* to be convinced of the reality of the Christian religion?"

"I certainly am," I said.

I was amazed at what he said of Charley Thorpe. I had only seen Charley Thorpe for a few moments, and had fancied that he had not changed at all. Now I remember that he seemed more manly, and never once spoke in the old flippant tone.

"I think you mistake me," I said. "I do not doubt the sincerity of all who profess to call themselves Christians. But I do not see much fruit. I want a religion that amounts to something."

Mr. Romaine did what seemed to me a very strange thing—he leaned back in his chair and laughed, to my vexation.

"Excuse me," he said. "But, my friend, will you tell me what has lifted the nations of earth out of the degradation into which they had fallen? What makes the difference between our own land and some others—Turkey, for instance—to-day? I think you will concede that the Christian faith does amount to something in its effect upon the masses. And how can that be unless it brings forth fruit in individuals? Now, my friend, if, as you say, you are willing to be convinced, will you make this your prayer, 'Teach me thy way, O Lord?' The Spirit is promised to guide into all truth. Will you not, instead of looking to the lives of others for proof, seek to know for yourself—by a personal experience—if there is such a thing as being renewed by the Holy Ghost, and united to Christ by a living faith? If you will put yourself in the right attitude before God—that of a penitent, seeking, believing sinner—you will find him ready to help, and you will be established in the faith."

But someway I did not like his phraseology; and I think I winced at being called a penitent sinner. Must I, then, class myself so low? I, Perry Harrison, boasting of my morality, secure in the consciousness of my integrity—must *I* come before God with the publican's prayer?

Perhaps Mr. Romaine divined my thoughts, for he quoted: "There is no difference, for all have sinned and come short of the glory of God."

Was there, then, no difference?

He rose to go. Holding out his hand, he said: "I wish you could reach a decision at once."

I don't know what came over me. I forgot my dignity, my morality, my pride, and only remembered that I had wanted to talk with this man—that I had hoped to get some help from him—and that, after all, I had not reached the point. The distress which I had now endured for weeks was growing quite unbearable, and I said, quickly:

"Don't go yet; tell me just what to do."

Just one moment he stood regarding me with a fixed look, then, with a low "let us pray," dropped upon his knees.

Reverently I say it, that prayer seemed to take me into the presence of the Saviour—the Saviour whom I had rejected. But how loving and tender he seemed! Surely my rejection of him was a sin for which I could never atone. I was ready to say, "I have sinned," and to cry for pardon, and when Mr. Romaine ended with, "Oh speak, now, dear Jesus, and bid him rest in thee, for in thee are the riches of grace, pardon, peace, love and joy," I added: "O Lord Jesus, I desire to be made a partaker of thy grace. Wilt thou pardon and accept me?"

Things certainly look differently to me to-day. It is as though I had changed my *standpoint*.

8.

FLORENCE, Sept. —, 18—.

My Dear Perry:

I hope you do not expect me to rave over the sights and sounds in this foreign land. If you do, you will be disappointed. I shall be much more likely to complain of the rain and the dampness. It is a very dismal evening; so horrid that mamma and Uncle Arthur have given up going out, much to my chagrin. The best opera of the season is to be given this evening. Uncle Arthur is a good deal of a bore, always having neuralgia or rheumatism, and imagining that there are draughts of wind in impossible places. Of all unendurable people a nervous invalid is the most trying. I shall pray to die outright rather than to live to be a burden to my friends, if ever I am reduced to the state of having aches and pains constantly.

I wish you were here to go out with me this evening; but then I comfort myself by reflecting that you, too, are an invalid, though not so trying a one as Uncle Arthur, I hope and trust.

Mamma tries to console me by reminding me that Uncle Arthur invited us to accompany him, because his health was so feeble he disliked to travel alone, and but for him we should not be here; but I am sure I would much rather have waited and gone abroad with you when you got well. I beg you not to try and take an ocean voyage until you are well and strong; it is the stupidest possible thing to drag through sight-seeing with one who feels more like being in bed.

Tom is going home by the next steamer. He has grown weary of idleness, he says; though I am sure Uncle Arthur has contrived to keep him busy. If it were not for appearances I would desert and go along; but mamma thinks it would be unpardonably rude to Uncle Arthur.

Perhaps you wonder why Tom could not be my escort to the opera; but you need not. He has a streak of propriety, or melancholy, or sanctimoniousness. Really, I hardly know what to call it, save that he has suddenly concluded that the whole world of operas are schools of Satan. I'm sure I don't know why, unless it is because his precious friend, Mr. Romaine, frowns upon them. What is there so extraordinary about that man? I failed to discover it when I saw him; but Tom raves about him as though he were not made of common clay at all. I wonder you don't attempt a bit of match-making now you are an invalid and at leisure, and try to unite the fortunes or the poverty of this remarkable man and your friend Una. It strikes me they would make a very romantic couple. To be sure he is alarmingly tall and she is painfully short, at least by his side; but then they are such superior mortals they would never think of being disturbed by any such commonplaces as that. It would be a positive trial to me. I am thankful that as you are so tall I grew to a reasonable height myself. I was reminded of it especially the last time I saw you and Una together. If you had had the remotest suspicion of how queerly you looked together you would have shrunk from the exhibition on Broadway. But all this would be no objection to the scheme which I suggest, as people of that class never have sensitive feelings. What a blessing it must be to be so constituted. Sometimes I could almost wish that I belonged to that class myself.

I have time but for a short letter this week. The weeks do pass so rapidly that it really seems as though I had hardly mailed one letter before the day arrived for another. The next time I go abroad, my dear Perry, I will not make such an absurd promise as that was, to write by every steamer; actually to be bound to a certain day for writing a letter, whether one feels like it or not, is altogether too commonplace for me. That will do for people like your little Una.

Perry, I know you are a remarkably good-hearted creature, but I fail to see how you can give so much of your time to such a morsel of humanity. If it were not too absurd I might almost be jealous! The idea of your actually missing her letters! That shows what a slave habit is.

Now, as to your suggestion about the ceremony, don't, I beg of you, think of such a thing as having it take place abroad. I detest that; one wants to be married at home, where one's friends can have the benefit. I advise that you do not try to come out this fall. Uncle Arthur may take a fancy to go home at any moment, and we are subject to his whims. It would be delightful to be gone when you arrived, wouldn't it? Of course I am eager to see you and all that; we have gotten beyond those formulas; but it would be much more sensible for you to stay at home. I can't, of course, tell you when we shall return, but I should not be surprised if it were to be soon. So at least do not make any plans for a month or two; and, in any event, don't expect me to listen to such an absurd proposition as a marriage in Florence. I am beyond the romantic age, and I want to be in my own home and get up a toilet worthy of the occasion, and have my friends admire it and all that sort of thing, and have a good time generally before I retire into private life. If I were at home I wouldn't, of course, object to a European tour for a wedding trip; but I always thought the other plan would be horrid; it would be almost like going to a minister's house, some night after tea, *a la* servant-maids.

But enough of that; I think I have convinced you what my taste is in the matter. There is one portion of your letter that I must not forget. It gave me much anxiety, because I thought you could not be so well as you suppose, or you would have certainly not been so "blue." I am sure it is not like you. I think it is very unwise in you to allow yourself to brood so much over such questions. Part of the letter I did not understand at all; it seemed almost like an implied reproach to me. If I did not know you were too gentlemanly I should fancy you thought I ought to have preached to you privately. Excuse me, my dear, preaching is not my *fôrte*. Of course I am interested in the subject, and of course it would be very pleasant for me to see you a Christian. In fact, I am not at all sure but you are one. At least I do not see the propriety of forcing such subjects on a person; in my opinion that does more harm than good. None but a certain class of fanatics are guilty of it. So that would be my answer to your query as to why I never obliged you to talk about your private feelings. I respect every one's private religious life. In my opinion religion should be unobtrusive. I half suspect that you have been coming in contact, either real or by proxy, with that fanatical Mr. Romaine. Such men should be silenced by law or in some other way. They do positive harm. Tom is not the boy he was before he knew him. He thinks nothing now of going directly contrary to mamma's approval and advice, and once he used to study to please her. I hope you see the beauty of a form of religion that leads one to disregard a mother's wishes! Believe me, my dear Perry, a person has not to take leave of his common sense in order to be a very respectable Christian. As to getting ready to die, that is all nonsense! You are not going to die. It would be much more sensible for you to get ready to live. I think people are not called upon to die, or to feel ready for it, until their time comes. Of course you would have felt very differently if you had been really going to die. Don't, dear, allow yourself to become a nervous hypochondriac, always talking about dying, and being prepared, and almost invariably speaking in a nasal tone, as if that were a part of the preparation. I want you to live and take care of me. It is as much a Christian duty to live as it is to die, especially when one has promised to take charge of some one else. So, for my sake as well as yours, I want you to give special attention to the duty of getting well. I should make a horrid nurse, and you may as well take that into consideration. Please give up the habit of writing about gloomy things; it retards your recovery, I am sure. If I were Dr. Mason I should prohibit you from talking with any but merry, genial people, who provoked you to laugh every two minutes.

There is Uncle Arthur's bell. I know what he wants as well as I shall when I receive his message: " Would it be agreeable for me to read the evening news?" No, it wouldn't! It is simply horrid, but it is one of the inflictions which come of being in Uncle Arthur's train. I shall not be so foolish again in a lifetime.

As ever,   ELEANOR.

[FROM EUNICE'S JOURNAL.]

NEW YORK, December 3.

Life is a queer tangle. Ever so many things have happened since I have taken the trouble to write about any of them. We are having a revival. Do you know what that is, my beloved Journal? No more do I; only it involves a great deal of going to meeting and makes some people act very queerly. I go to the meetings frequently—principally, let me own, for the pleasure of hearing Perry talk and pray. He is one of them. That seems so strange. I hardly know how it all came about, and I am not sure that I like it, after all. Perry seems so far away from me now. I'll tell you about his coming to New York. No one expected him. I hadn't heard from him in six weeks or more. My Lady Eleanor stopped that. I knew she would. At the same time I was provoked with Perry for being such an idiot as to let her manage him. So I meant to be awfully dignified when I saw him next, and I wasted my leisure hours in planning the way we should meet and wondering when it would be. I got up a good many stylish scenes over it, and they all collapsed in a most commonplace way. I was hurrying through the hall one morning when the bell rang. Maggie was down in the basement and I was right there, so I opened the door, and there- the dear boy stood. All I said was "Oh Perry!" and he held out both hands just as he used to do, and said:

"You dear little Una."

And I was so glad to see him looking so much better, and he was so thoroughly glad to see me again, that someway I forgot all about how I was going to act, and went back to the old ways. He made the shortest possible stay, and then rushed off to Nassau. He just begged of me to go along and see mother and the rest, but grim

Propriety, in the shape of my Aunt Ruth, wouldn't allow it. I told her Perry said it shouldn't cost father a cent, and she puckered her thin lips together so they were no wider than the edge of a case-knife, and said:

"Worse and worse!"

I wonder if I am a simpleton? It seems pleasant enough to take favors from Perry, even money favors. However, he made a short enough stay at Nassau, and then was back again, making preparations for his European tour. He told me he expected to be married out there. I didn't believe it any of the time. Someway I have never believed that he would marry that heartless, selfish girl. The very day after he told me he called me into the hall, and told me not to mention it, for he had changed his plans; did not know that he should go out at all this winter. I knew he had a letter by the morning steamer. No telling what was in it. Probably I shall never know. But that, or something else, made Perry awfully cross and disagreeable. He was just as moody as he could be. He snarled at his sickness, and at the weather, and at everything and every body. He never was as well satisfied with things that happened as he might be. This spell lasted for two days. During that time I did what I suppose was a queer thing. He looked sad and discouraged, and he is not by any means so well as he might be, and I felt worried about him all the time. One day Mr. Romaine was trying to talk sober to me. He is just as good as he can be, and I respect him more every day of my life. But I can't be sensible when I talk to him. I said:

"See here, you are wasting your powder. I have beds to make, and rooms to sweep, and lessons to learn. I haven't time to go to meetings or be good. Why don't you spend your strength on Mr. Harrison. He is rich and he is sick, and he is as dismal as an owl. He needs help, if you have any for him. If I were one of the praying people I would send his name up to be prayed for."

"Do you make that request?" he asked. And he sat down on the lower stair and took out his note-book.

"Yes, I do," I said. For what harm could it do? And I did want Perry to be more comfortable.

"Dictate it, please," he said, in a business-like way, "and I will present it at the meeting to-day."

So I did; and then I set my wits to work to get Perry to go to the meeting. I accomplished it, too, though he sneered and scoffed and said he believed less in religion than he ever did in his life before. But he went, and that I guess was the beginning of it, or the middle of it, or something.

The very next time I was beguiled into going to the meeting, which was less than a week afterward, Perry Harrison prayed! I was never so amazed in my life. Who supposed that a request for prayer ever amounted to anything only to make people feel a little more comfortable, as though they had tried to do something, and if they had failed it was not their fault. Since that time I have had my regrets—no, hardly that, either, but I feel left out. Perry is just as kind as he can be, but he seems different, and I can't explain even to myself how. He is preoccupied; thinks of nothing and talks of nothing but the meetings; he works day and night in them, and does more, so the others say, than any three of them. He gives a good deal of time and anxiety to me, but I feel farther away from the right way, if it is the right way, than ever I did. I am only half glad, now that Perry is so much better, that he has gone off on this road and left me. One thing is somewhat comforting. I don't believe my Lady Eleanor will ever be Mrs. Harrison. Something has entirely overturned Perry's plan of going out to her to be married. I hope and trust they have quarreled. If they have, and will only stay quarreled, it is all right. My worst fear is that Perry will get so good he will consider it his duty to make up.

NASSAU, February 16.

It is eleven o'clock. I have just come up to my room. Father is better to-night, and it is not my night to sit up, anyway. I have been over at the Harrison mansion all day, and you could never guess, you stupid Journal, what I have been about. Nothing less than helping to put Mr. and Mrs. Perry Harrison's rooms in bridal array. Mrs. Harrison, stupid old soul, sent for me this morning. They had received a telegram that the bride and groom would arrive by the midnight train, and she said Perry would so enjoy having my taste displayed. So I displayed it. Probably Madame Eleanor will re-arrange everything when she finds who had a hand in it.

Yes, Journal, our Perry is married, and the woman of his choice is a disagreeable purse-proud aristocrat! So much for his consistency in the religion which he has made such a show of. But I don't mean to blame Perry; he is probably deceived, like the rest of them.

What a silly world it is! Ever so many pretending to live on a higher plane than the rest of us mortals, and one needs a magnifying-glass to see any difference. I dare say Perry will be like the rest. He always was a dissatisfied being. If he doesn't grow worse instead of better I shall wonder at it. He will almost be excusable, too, under the circumstances; only it will be his own fault that he got into such a life. What am I talking about! Just as if he didn't consider his Eleanor all but perfect! Tastes differ, certainly.

Well, our pleasant days are over. It is all nonsense, our calling each other brother and sister. That will do to put on paper, but in real life it is evident that there is no such thing, outside of one's actual family.

It is five weeks since I came home. Father's sickness called me. School is over for me, for the present; I shouldn't be surprised if it were for always. Well, I don't know that I care. I have promised to go over and help Mrs. Harrison entertain the bride and groom. That old lady blindly refuses to see any difference between the Perry and Una of to-day and the Perry and Una of years ago. Well, why should she? Only I wonder how Perry and I shall behave. I don't feel as though I knew how to act. I believe I'm a dunce, and I mean to go directly to bed.

9.

[FROM PERRY'S JOURNAL.]

NASSAU, April 18.

It began that first morning after we came home.

And things have been a little unpleasant ever since—I mean some things—I must not speak of them to any one; and this is why I have come to this old book once more—it seems like a faithful friend, in whom I can confide my perplexities.

I meant to be a consistent Christian, and it seemed to be an easy thing to do—just to take up the work that came in my way—to live in all things according to the spirit of the gospel. I firmly believed that I—Perry Harrison—was equal to it. Why should I hesitate to take a bold stand for the Christian faith, having once been convinced of its reality? Why not be as ready and as strong to meet opposition here as I would be in any scientific or philosophical theories which I might have embraced? But I find a difference. I suspect that Satan does not trouble himself about scientific or philosophical theories, so long as religion does not get mixed in. Hence the votaries of science and philosophy do not find the wily enemy of souls interfering with their investigations, until they enter the broader field of thought which the Bible opens. Then he puts forth his strongest efforts, and he is sure to find out the weak points of the soul he means to conquer. And it seems to me that I am all weak points! *I*, who thought myself strong, cower and tremble before Eleanor's sarcasm! I shrink from mother's tender sympathy, and turn away from Una's thoughtful appreciation. It humbles me to find myself so weak, and it distresses me that I am proving myself such an unprofitable servant of the Lord Jesus Christ. The Christian way is so new to me; and, having all my life lived so far below my ideal of what a Christian life should be, it is not always easy to act consistently, in opposition to the wishes of another, and that other—my wife! I am still troubled about the same old puzzle—the conflicting views and practices of Christians in regard to conformity to the world. As we came from prayer-meeting, last evening—Eleanor never goes to prayer-meeting—Una said:

"Perry, I like your religion, it is so like my father's."

If that could only come true—if the living of

the one who, for so many years, was a father to me, might have so put its impress upon my life that it indeed should be like his, I must then approach nearer my ideal.

But Eleanor does not like Mr. Taylor, and she would scarcely be satisfied with a change in her husband that tended in that direction. Dear Eleanor, she has such perfect health, and such buoyant spirits, that I suppose I seem a little dull since I have been half an invalid, and she places it all to the charge of what she calls my " new notions."

Una had taken tea with us, and, stopping in on the way home from the meeting to get her fancy work, which seems to be a necessary accompaniment of going out to tea, she said :

" Mrs. Eleanor, you should have been at the meeting, Mr. Crampton was there, and his singing was heavenly ! "

"I thought that you and Perry looked as if you had just come down from the clouds," returned Eleanor. "I don't understand, Miss Taylor, how it is that *you* are so devoted to prayer-meetings ? Now, I am a church-member, but I never think of going to one ; and you, I believe, have not even that motive. I suppose, though, that in the country, people who are fond of going out have to take to prayer-meetings for recreation. I don't know but I may be obliged to go myself, yet, as a means of self-preservation."

Una laughed, and replied:

"I never thought of it in that light. I go because I was brought up to it, and my father would be shocked if I were to stay at home."

"Well," said Eleanor, "one goes because she was brought up to it, and the other because he has taken up the idea that praying is the one thing to be done in this life. Why, Miss Taylor, I have heard more praying since I was married than in all my life together—I mean, of course, except public prayers. I might as well have married a minister, and been done with it!"

"Perry *does* talk like a minister," said Una, wickedly.

"I know it! there is just my trouble!" Eleanor said. "I am going to set my wits to work to contrive a plan to get him out of this horrid way, so don't you oppose any plan I may *propose*."

"Of course I shall be ready for anything, even a fancy ball!" returned Una, laughingly, gathering up her things to go.

But to get back to that first morning. Eleanor sat at the head of the table—the place which my mother insisted upon yielding to my wife at the outset. Now, ever since my father died, I have sat in his place at the table, and, year by year, been growing more and more to act in his stead as the head of the house. But the family altar, broken down at his death, had never been re-established. I had been slow to take up this duty, even after I became a Christian, and my mother and I sat at our table and went about our work without even a word of prayer. But I had decided that it could be so no longer, and, as we sat down to the breakfast-table, I said, though my voice trembled:

"Mother, Eleanor, this is a good time to begin it; let us ask God's blessing."

When I had ended, Eleanor said, in her smoothest tones (and how sharp they are, sometimes):

"Well, Perry, that was well done. You certainly have a very easy way of putting things. What next, by way of surprises?"

"Family prayer, I suppose, will be next in order. But that ought not to be a surprise in a Christian household, and I should not think it would require any very great skill in the putting of the question in an easy way."

"Putting the question may be easier than carrying out the idea," she answered. "It may do very well in the country, but it could never be done in the city."

"Do you mean to say that there is no such thing as this in city homes?"

"No, of course I don't mean that. You ought not to take me up so. I mean in a home like ours, for instance. Mamma never comes down to breakfast before ten o'clock, and sometimes uncle does not come at all. Tom and I take breakfast together, unless I happen to have been out late. You could never get the two or three together in our house"—and Eleanor's silvery laugh had just the least bit of sarcasm in it.

"But here it is very different," I said.

"Oh, yes. But then you must not expect me to be as good as I am this morning, as a rule. I am not used to such abominably early breakfasts, and I suspect that you will have your family prayers all to yourself."

All this good-humoredly, and I could not decide how much of it she meant. It all struck me as trifling, and I knew my mother thought so. And I made reply, perhaps a little wickedly:

"You forget that I have a mother; and I think that, with the presence of the servants, the service can be kept up."

"Oh, now, Perry, don't be disagreeable! Of course I think it is the orthodox way to have family prayers when practicable, and where it is to one's taste, but I never could endure the thought of being obliged to be prompt. And then it would be so embarrassing when we have company—I mean people who don't believe in such things, like uncle, or mamma. Now you think I am awfully wicked, I know, but it would seem queer to have a young fellow like you conducting family worship like Deacon Taylor! Will you have us read a verse around, as they probably do over there?"

"Eleanor!"

"Well, my dear, I thought that I would like to have everything explained, so that I might have a clear perception of what was expected of me. Seriously, Perry, your religion is making you gloomy and old-fashioned. You are not a bit as you used to be, and I believe I liked you better before."

"That is a complimentary thing for a wife of a week to say of her husband," I said, laughing.

"I can't help it; it is true. You have grown solemn as an owl, and I expect every day to hear an announcement of your determination to renounce the pomps and vanities of the world."

"I have done that already," I said. "And have you not done the same?"

Just here mother spoke for the first time during this conversation:

"Eleanor, remember that Perry has been an invalid so long, and is still so far from being strong, that it is not surprising he should have lost some of his old vivacity of manner. For my part, I think the change is not altogether for the worse. A man in his position, as the head of a household, and the manager of an estate, ought to be a man of some gravity. There is, to me, great gratification in the thought that the loss to this community, in the death of the father, may yet be made good in the son."

These were pleasant words to hear from the lips of a mother who is not given to flattering or petting her boy. My mother was never demonstrative in that way. Indeed, my childhood's petting was all under the roof of that little brown house down the road—by Una's mother. And yet no son ever loved and trusted a mother more than I love and trust mine.

Eleanor is not given to pouting, but she came near it then. Perhaps she felt my mother's words as a rebuke, though I do not think they were intended as such. Anyway, the conversation dropped just there!

My Eleanor has not been accustomed to a religious atmosphere—I mean of the spiritual sort, such as Una and my Cousin Daisy have breathed all their lives. True, her brother Tom is developing a grand Christian manhood, but he meets with much opposition from his mother and uncle —the one a Christian in name, the other an avowed unbeliever. He told me he longed to introduce a new order of things into their home, but his mother said it could not be mentioned as long as the uncle was a member of the family.

My poor attempt succeeded better, though Eleanor's disrelish of the proceeding troubles me greatly. She frequently does not come down to breakfast, and so is not present at worship. I wish she felt differently, and I can but hope that she will grow to be more in sympathy with my views and feelings. Sometimes I fancy that she feels she has been wronged—that the old, unbelieving Perry Harrison was more to her taste than the grave man whom she married. Two years ago, before my long illness, I held life very lightly; it was something to be enjoyed—money, talents, education, love—all its good gifts were only valued as they were so many more aids to the grand good time I meant to make of life. Ah, my estimate of life was a very low one! I thought my standard was high—but how low and mean it seems to me *now*, viewed by the light of the revelations of the last few months! With more exalted ideas of the importance of life, with an ever-present remembrance of opportunities thrown away, wasted time, strength and money, is it any wonder that I am consumed with an eager longing to be about the work which so much needs to be done, and for which there are so few laborers? And is it strange that this desire has changed levity into seriousness, trifling into earnestness?

March 28.—I received a little note from Daisy, the other day; it was written in response to a letter in which I told her that I had adopted her theory, and could now thank the Lord that I had been laid aside for so long as a useless member of society. This was her reply:

REDWOOD, ———.

My Dear Cousin:

"O sing unto the Lord a new song: for he hath done marvelous things. His right hand, and his holy arm, hath gotten him the victory."

"I love the Lord because he hath heard my voice and my supplications."

DAISY.

"Dear me!" Eleanor said, when she read the note. "What a sentimental lot of friends you managed to draw around you! Do you know I don't like the idea which that implies. If you had been a real outcast—a miserable, low sort of a fellow—and somebody had picked you out of the slums and filth of the city and made a man of you, why then there would seem to be some sense in quoting that verse about marvelous things and a 'great victory.' You were always respectable and honorable, and I can't see what there is to make such a fuss about."

"But, Eleanor, if 'there is joy in heaven over one sinner that repenteth,' may not we on earth rejoice when the prodigal comes home?"

"I don't, in the least, know what you mean by comparing yourself with the prodigal," she returned, pettishly.

And how could I explain to her—how make her understand what seems clear to me, that there is no difference—" All have sinned, and come short of the glory of God."

We are going to New York for a few days. Eleanor is bored with our country ways, and needs a change. I have been urging Una to go with us, but no one seconded my efforts, and the little lady herself only laughed and asked me if I had lost my senses. She has been here all the evening helping Eleanor with her packing. Someway the two get on together better than I expected. I had fancied that Eleanor did not like Una, but there seems to be a wonderfully good understanding growing up between them; and, as Una knows how to make herself useful, she is often here doing little bits of things for Eleanor. I have no doubt about my enjoyment of the projected trip, but for one drawback—I dread to leave mother alone. The weather is still very cold and cheerless. I think it was a mistake our letting our faithful Jenny leave us. She understood mother's needs so well, and could do for her what no one else can. But mother feared that the new daughter of the house would not understand Jenny's position, and might not like the familiarity into which she had grown from being so long my mother's companion. So, thinking that Eleanor's society would compensate for her loss, she decided to let Jenny go; and a new home just then opening to the girl, it was an easy thing to do. But I think now it was a mistake. We did not look forward to just such an emergency as the present. However, Una will spend much of the time with mother; so I shall feel easier.

Eleanor is full of anticipations, and happy talk of city gayeties. And I can not deny that it will be pleasant, for I like the whir and whiz of the city. I have written to Tom to meet us there, and it will be a pleasure to meet Mr. Romaine again. But Eleanor quite positively refuses to stop at Mrs. Brocton's, her reason being that "the very sight of that Mr. Romaine gives her the nightmare!" So we go to a hotel.

Well, I hear Eleanor bidding Una good-night, so I conclude that the last trunk is packed. I heard the carriage driving up some minutes ago; Jackson must be taking her home, as it is raining. Eleanor is too thoughtful to let the child walk home in the rain. I am glad they are fond of each other.

10.

[FROM EUNICE'S JOURNAL.]

NASSAU, April 18—.

It is April Fool's Day. A most appropriate name. I wonder what genius originated it? The only mistake is not to have it fitted to all the days. The world is just made up of different classes of fools. Of course, in that case, I am one of them; but I can't help that.

I have just come home from the Harrisons, where I have been helping Mrs. Perry get ready for a trip to New York. I have been there all the afternoon and evening. It is wonderful the number of little things she contrives to find for my plebeian hands to do. Perry took himself off to his study early in the evening. I was glad of it, for his grave, somewhat troubled face, makes me feel wicked. Still, if he had staid down stairs, I would not have had to plod home in the rain and the darkness. They pressed me to stay until the coachman returned, but as he had gone on a five-miles' errand for Mrs. Perry, and it was after nine o'clock, I did not care to do so. The elder Mrs. Harrison was distressed; feebly hinted that Perry would not like it at all, and that he ought to be called, which neither Mrs. Perry nor I would allow; she, for the reason that she did not mean him to walk home with me, and I, because I meant that he should not go out in the rain. Mrs. Eleanor made light of the walk; said she presumed I was used to going alone, and that I wouldn't mind it any more than a robin would. For reasons known to myself I pretended to agree with her, and made my escape, running home across lots, frightened half out of my wits, the truth being that I am not accustomed to being out alone in the evening. I got my feet wet, and, what was worse, splashed my new brown calico dress with ugly mud. I am sorry about the dress, for Perry likes it, and Mrs. Perry doesn't; two reasons for *my* liking to wear it.

It is as good as going to the theatre to watch the life being lived at the Harrison homestead nowadays; nothing more incongruous can be imagined than the different elements which compose that family. If one had not such a sore feeling for one of the actors, it would be funny to see them try to assimilate. Perry spends his days, and I dare say his nights, in an effort to reconcile his elegant bride to the simplicity of her surroundings. One can not help wondering why on earth she married him. She is not rich, to be sure—that is, not remarkably so—but neither is he, and she must certainly have been able to secure wealthier prizes in the matrimonial market than that. How I hate such expressions, sounding like a third-rate sensation novel! And yet I can't help thinking that they fit her life. What can possibly make the difference between that woman and her husband? Why couldn't they have had one or two ideas in common? Being both of them educated, refined people, why *don't* they think alike? Since both of them are professing Christians, one would suppose that there, at least, their interests might touch, but they do not. If anything, I think they are more at variance in regard to that than anything else.

Well, what is the use of my writing about them? They have their own battles to fight. I have promised Mrs. Harrison, senior, that I will go over in the morning and see them off. That means that I promised Perry to come and see to it that his mother did not miss them very much at first.

"She will miss Eleanor," the absurd boy said, with a solemn face. "Being so constantly with her for several weeks, of course it will make a different house to have her out of it."

Undoubtedly it will! For the sake of his

peace of mind I am really glad that he does not know what a delightful "miss" it will be! For Mother Harrison and I, although neither of us would own it to the other for the world, are of the same mind concerning this element in the household.

Now I am going to bed.

Friday Evening.—The woman seems actually to be angry at him for having caught a cold! They did not get to New York, after all. I went over yesterday morning, according to promise. I waited until it was almost time for the carriage to take them to the cars, but I found them sitting at the breakfast-table.

"You will be late," I said. "The train is in, and they don't stop but twenty minutes."

Then Perry attempted to explain to me how their plans had to be changed by reason of the severe cold he had taken. But he was so hoarse it was almost impossible for him to talk.

"How *did* you get such a distressing cold?" I asked him, and his wife answered:

"Foolishly, of course, just as all such colds are contracted. He would persist in going out to the prayer-meeting, yesterday noon, though it was raining at the time. Generally he is very particular about the rain; but he seemed to think that for a prayer-meeting the laws of health would be suspended."

Mother Harrison looked disturbed, not to say vexed, over this, and answered with spirit:

"Indeed, Eleanor, I don't think it was the prayer-meeting. It rained very little at noon yesterday. If he hadn't gone in search of that worsted last evening, and got his feet wet, it would all have been well."

"Of course the poor worsted must be blamed," Mrs. Eleanor said, with a laugh that jarred on one to hear. "The prayer-meeting couldn't be at fault; it was very absurd of me to hint such a thing; I shouldn't wonder if two or three of them indulged in to-day would cure him. Meantime, I was very wicked to want a skein of worsted. I hope I will never be guilty of such a sin again."

Poor Perry looked excessively annoyed.

"There is no blame to be attached anywhere," he said, hoarsely. "I take cold easily, I know, and should have been more careful of myself. It is nothing serious, I trust. I am chiefly sorry for your disappointment. Perhaps I may be well enough to go by to-morrow."

But he isn't; he is hoarser than ever to-night, and his mother says it is because he exerted himself to talk with Eleanor, so that she would not have too dull a time last evening.

I went over to-day to take the magazine. Mrs. Eleanor met me at the door of their room, and informed me that she didn't see but I would have to do my patient up in pink cotton and lay him away on a shelf till spring; he is absolutely good for nothing in the winter.

I could have choked her. The poor fellow looked so pale, and coughed in that horrid, hollow way that seems to almost cut me in two; and yet he sat so erect and tried to make light of the matter.

"Why don't you soak your feet and go to bed?" I asked him, the minute I caught sight of his pale face.

"Yes, and drink catnip tea, or ginger, or whatever other horrid dose it is they fix; and pile on the blankets, or old-fashioned comfortables, it ought to be. Isn't that the way they do things in the country?"

"They take care of people when they are sick," I said crossly, "if that is what you mean. Perry, I'm afraid you will have another attack of congestion if you don't let yourself be cared for in time."

His mother gave me a gratified glance.

"I have been coaxing him all the morning to lie down and let me try to sweat him," she said, anxiously.

"So have I, I am sure," added his wife. "I think the process must be a very interesting one, from all I have heard of it. I should suppose it might add greatly to his appearance. Miss Taylor, if you understand the affair, perhaps you wouldn't mind superintending it."

It was evident even to Perry's blinded eyes that she was trying to insult me. He looked so utterly distressed, and yet so appealingly at her, that I shut back the indignant words that were crowding to my lips, and left him with his mother.

This is what marriage means, is it? What a sympathizing, tender friend she is! How much one, sick and suffering, would like to have her around! Oh, I am sure I hope with all my soul that she will never be so utterly unendurable to Perry Harrison as she is to me. I hope he will never, *never* discover his mistake, for it is surely a mistake. They haven't an idea in common. I will hold my peace; I will help to blind him if I can; for to realize what she is, and what he has done in marrying her, would be too dreadful for a man like Perry Harrison.

Closing her journal with a sense of disgust over that, and, indeed, almost everything else, Miss Eunice Taylor made herself ready for rest, revolving in her mind the resolve so lately written down, and wondering much whether that would involve the remaining away from the Harrison mansion. In view of the feeling, amounting sometimes to absolute disgust, which she had for his wife, could she hope to appear so friendly before Perry as to satisfy him, and help him to hug the delusion that he had chosen wisely and well? On the other hand, if she remained away from there, how long would it take the idle eyes of their little village to see, and the idle tongues to concoct possible reasons? Besides, what would Perry say? Thinking about it did not help her out of the bewilderments; and, with a petulant wish that they would go off to New York and stay there, she tried to dismiss the subject from her mind, without coming to any decision further than that she would stay away for awhile, and see how it would seem.

This resolution lasted until about three o'clock the next afternoon, when the little maid who ran errands for the Harrisons came with a message that she would come over for awhile. The message was from the mother, and Eunice at once obeyed it. The elder lady met her in the hall, and sunk her voice into a whisper, as though she already felt the divided lives that had begun in that household.

"She has gone to lie down; says she has a headache; and poor Perry hasn't eaten a mouthful to-day. The doctor says he musn't go on so; he must keep up his strength. I thought maybe if I should go down myself, and make him some real nice beef tea, he would eat a few spoonfuls, only I didn't like to leave him alone, and I would as soon disturb Queen Victoria as *her* out of one of her naps. So I just thought I would send for you to come over and amuse him a little while."

"What an idea!" murmured Eunice. But she went forward to the sitting-room without further comment, and found Perry sitting in the great arm-chair before the fire, his head thrown wearily back on the pillow, and his whole air one of dejection and disheartenment. He brightened visibly as she entered.

"This is kind," he said, trying to sit upright. "Eleanor is lying down. She is not very well to-day; but she has been gone a long time; I dare say she will be down soon."

"I hope not," muttered Eunice; but she said it under her breath, and then aloud:

"Does your head ache? Put it back again on the pillow. Why do you try to put on ceremony with me? I'm your nurse, and you are to do as I tell you; your mother said so."

He laughed and obeyed her, but in a moment the troubled look came back.

"I am so sorry about this illness, Una," he said. "It is such a disappointment to Eleanor. Of course she is anxious to see her mother; and having made all her plans, and written when she was to be there, it is a real trial. Several engagements that she looked forward to will have to be broken. I feel so sorry that her life with me should begin in disappointment, and one way or another she has a good many of them."

"Of course it is a trial," Una said. "But I dare say she will have grace to bear it, especially when she remembers that there *are* heavier ones even than this, which come to some people."

How could she help a touch of sarcasm in her voice. Perry did not smile; he looked grave, almost displeased.

"She is not used to disappointment," he said. "Her life has been a very sunny one, and she is intense in her nature. Her plans mean a great deal to her."

Some people have a way of calling that a selfish nature, Una thought; but this thought she kept to herself. Perry was silent for a minute, then he broke forth again:

"Sometimes I think it is a providence placed in my way that I may not carry out the programme we formed," he said. "I have been in trouble about that, Una. It is a wonderfully hard thing to know what to do."

And the young man rolled his head restlessly on his pillow, as if the whole business of life were an enigma to him.

"What is the matter with New York?" Eunice asked, in her intense sympathy for him, and her desire not to show it, making her voice almost rough.

"Well," he said, hesitating and flushing painfully—it was a delicate subject to touch—"you know, Una, the sort of life to which Eleanor has been accustomed in New York, and you know that it can not be in accordance with my present ideas of life and duty. To what extent should I be justified in doing violence to my own feelings in order to give her pleasure? That is one bewilderment, and there are a dozen others."

It was almost impossible for Eunice not to be ugly in her answer.

"But, Perry, how do you expect me to understand what you mean? I know you claim to have been converted, whatever that involves; but so does your wife, and I can not see why your tastes should not accord. How am I expected to understand you when she does not?"

My lady had the benefit of a pair of very stern, very rebuking eyes just then, from a head that sat erect without the aid of a pillow, as he said:

"You need to remember that my wife's father was very different from yours; and my wife's mother *is* very different from yours—an almost infinite difference there is between them. There is a good deal of power in education, Una."

Clearly, if she wanted to cast a shadow over the fair name of his wife, she had not attained her object; but she really had no such object, and was thoroughly ashamed of herself. She hastened to speak soothingly, realizing that his color was coming and going in a way that would speak ill for her success as a nurse.

"Of course there is," she said, quietly. "There are not many fathers and mothers in the world like mine, and I know it. Perry, if I were you I wouldn't worry about New York till I reached there. Your business just now is to get well. Besides, I wouldn't go to being pokey about my religion. You are just the sort of person that they make fanatics of. I dare say there are ever so many harmless things that your wife would enjoy which you will set yourself to believing are wrong. I wouldn't do it."

This she said honestly, with a desire to help him—to soften a little the discussions which she knew were sure to come between himself and wife. But he had a way of silencing her.

"Is your father a fanatic?" he asked.

"Never mind my father," she said, brusquely. "Let me lift up that pillow and make you more comfortable."

A few minutes of silence, then he broke forth again:

"Do you know what Romaine is doing. Splendid fellow! He has gone to preaching. He doesn't call it that, either—'Talks,' he says it is;

gathering in those who will not go to church, and singing to them, and telling them the story of Christ. I can imagine what it is, and how he does it. I would rather hear him than any minister I know. I tell you what, Una, I wish *I* were a mechanic, a day laborer, or any sort, with the opportunities they have for working among their fellow men. Someway I can't get close enough to anybody to do any good."

"I don't believe it is being a mechanic that makes the difference," Una said, briskly. "And you musn't talk nonsense, if you are sick. I shan't allow it. The idea of you, with your leisure, and your money, and your chances, wishing yourself somebody else! It is absurd. If I had your opportunity and your notions I'd risk but that I would find work to do."

"What would you do, Una?"

"Do! Everything. I can think of a dozen things that want doing awfully. The trouble would be to decide where to begin."

"But, Una, that is generalizing. I can do that splendidly. Come down to actual, practical work, and tell me what you would do if you were situated exactly as I am at this present time."

"I would keep my head still, and not rumple up that tucked pillow-slip in the way that you are doing. As for work, when you are well enough, why, to begin with, look at the factory boys and girls in this town, beginning work at half-past five in the morning and working till six at night, year in and year out. What chance have they for becoming men and women? How are they going to know how to read their Bibles, or write their names, or form an intelligent opinion about anything that is going on in the world? Nice citizens they will make by and by! You'll be called on to spend your money in building penitentiaries and prisons for them. I'd have schools—evening schools—in pleasant rooms, and I'd have maps, and charts, and globes, and all sorts of things to help them, and nice, pleasant, well-dressed people to teach them and to shew them how to act. And I'd have little lunch-rooms, where they could get a cup of coffee and a dish of ice-cream for barely what it costs to make them, or hardly that; where a boy could invite the girl he thought the nicest in the world to come and take some refreshments, and pay for it himself, and feel that he was manly. There are ten thousand things I would do. I could help at some of them myself, if I had a chance, though I don't know anything about being a Christian."

Perry's eyes had grown bright while she spoke, now they glowed with pleasure.

"That sentence is full of thought, Una," he said, "and I see, as you say, a hundred avenues opening. As soon as I am well enough we will plan it all. I am sure Eleanor would be interested in some work of that kind."

At this point his pillows fell on either side, and Una went to arrange them.

"You must sit still," she said. "This position is not conducive to eloquence. What will your mother say to such a rumpled state of affairs?"

At that moment the door opened and there entered, not his mother, but his wife, immaculate in rich winter toilet, and elegantly gotten up as though she were about to sit down to a New York dinner-table with honored guests. She paused in the doorway and surveyed the two: Una with her hand still patting the pillows into place, and her husband, with his flushed, eager face settling back among them.

"Really," she said, "is that a tableau?"

"No," answered Una, with utmost coolness. "Only a headache, and a perverse patient, who tumbles his mother's drapery around and drops the pillows. I have been taking your place of nurse while you rested. Now that you have come I suppose I may be relieved. I think his head ought to be bathed in cologne, or something cooling; he is feverish."

Then she went home, and that night she wrote in her journal this:

He thinks he can interest her in night-schools,

and ill-smelling, ill-dressed factory girls and boys, and homely lunches! What idiots men are! Oh, Perry Harrison! what is to be the end of it all? Was I helpful or a hindrance in starting this new train of thought for his feverish brain to work on? Yet I honestly fear, if he doesn't have something to work on that will interest and draw him away from himself, he will die.

11.

The entries in Perry Harrison's journal were too few, and at such long intervals, that the connecting links in the history of these people must be supplied by the chroniclers of their lives and fortunes.

The thought which Eunice Taylor put into the restless brain of the invalid stuck fast, and so grew upon him—so amplified itself that he could not wait until he was well again to let some of its outgrowths develop into action.

The next time Eunice came over to the Harrison mansion, this time summoned by Mrs. Eleanor, who found the work on political economy which Perry wanted read aloud quite too dry reading for her, the subject came up again; indeed, Perry very soon interrupted the reader to say:

"Now, Una, about that idea you advanced the other day. I have been revolving it over and over, and while I see the work to be done plainly enough, the question is just where to take hold. Can you suggest?"

Eunice closed the book.

"Why," she began, "with so many wrongs to be righted, so many evils to put down, so many wretched homes to be brightened, so many miserable lives to be led up out of the darkness, it does not seem as though there need be any questions as to what to do."

"It isn't a question of *what* to do, but where to begin; it bewilders me to think of all there is to do."

"I see," said Eunice. "You remind me of myself, when my room gets topsy-turvy. I have sometimes stood in the midst of the confusion with a feeling of utter despair. It would seem that I could never get things to rights. Articles that belonged on the bureau would be partly on the bed and partly on the table, and things out of the closet partly on the chairs, and maybe some of them strewed over the floor, and the books all awry and things stirred up generally. No matter how they got into that condition, they have got to be cleared up, and the puzzle is where to begin. I feel like sweeping everything off tables and bureau into one promiscuous heap and hoisting them out of the window. But the thing I *do* is to reach out and take up the article nearest me and put it into its place, and then turn round and take up the next, and so on. Moving one thing makes way for another to take its place, and before I know it the room actually gets into some sort of order, and then if I am called away before it is all done I have still accomplished something."

"So you would not advise me to sweep out existing habits and customs all at once, but just take up the matter nearest and right that, and the rest will follow."

"Well, yes, something like that. Things won't right themselves while we stand looking at the evils. We have got to take hold."

"Yes. And now, Una, tell me just *where*."

Perry leaned back in his chair and waited for Una's answer, while she looked away, down the hill into the valley below, where the tall chimneys loomed up, and the low tenement-houses were visible through the leafless trees.

"Well," he said, after awhile, smiling, "will it be cottage prayer-meetings or a temperance society?"

"Neither," returned Eunice, emphatically. "You might about as well set a music-box playing in the center of that room of mine, and expect the hats and shawls and all the rest to marshal themselves into their places. My friend, these people have not been educated up to temperance societies nor cottage prayer-meetings. How many would come, do you suppose, if you were to give notice of such an entertainment?"

"Not many, I presume," answered Perry, wearily.

"Besides," resumed Eunice, "it is the boys and girls that I am thinking of. I shouldn't expect to do much for the others. I think," she resumed after a few minutes, "that there is a nice room over Mr. Clark's store that might be fitted up comfortably. I am sure that you could get it, because I heard Mrs. Patten talking about it. She has opened a shop in the village, and would have liked that room, but it was rather beyond her means and larger than she needed. Shouldn't wonder if it would be just the thing."

"For what?" asked Perry, laughing.

"Wait till I get through, can't you, you impatient mortal! Don't you know that I always get it out, all that I want to say, even if I do sometimes begin at the wrong end? Now I would respectfully suggest that you secure this room, and fit it up with carpet, seats and platform, and put up curtains, kalsomine the walls and hang up some pictures, and then get some views or maps or something to illustrate the subject you decide to have presented, and then, by way of opening, give a little entertainment—something that will be instructive and pleasant, too—and then present the matter of an evening school. I don't believe I would make it a charitable institution, either. These people like to be independent; but you can study that out while the work of fitting up the room is under way."

"Does Mr. Clarke own the building, do you know?"

"I think so. Father would know about that."

"Well," said Perry, "as soon as Thomas comes home I will send for Mr. Clarke, and perhaps he will enter into this work. Any way, he will know whether or not the room is suited to our purpose."

"My dears," said Mrs. Harrison, who had been sitting listening quietly to the talk, "are you sure that you have counted the cost? You know that this thing, once started, must be carried on, or it will be worse than not to begin at all. Perry, remember your own frail health, and remember, too, that your wife's tastes and wishes have now to be consulted in your movements."

"I hardly think," said Perry, with a touch of pride in his tone, "that Eleanor will set her tastes or wishes in the way of any plans for the good of the class of people whom we propose to benefit. Indeed, I am depending largely upon her help—hers and Una's. They, with their strong, willing hands and hearts will, I expect, carry out the plans which I may lie here and make."

This with a faint laugh, as if he were trying to make light of his weakness. And in his feverish anxiety to begin he could scarcely await the return of the servant to arrange for an interview with the village merchant.

In the midst of this talk Eleanor returned from a drive, which she had taken in solitary grandeur in the family carriage. She had been to the loan library in a neighboring village, and came back with a package of books more to her taste than any she found in the Harrison library.

"There," she said, as she entered, looking so handsome in her magnificent attire that even Eunice was forced to admire her, "I hope that you have finished that stupid book; I was bored to death with it, and I don't believe that Perry found it as interesting as he pretended. I have brought home the newest novels, and now, my dear, I shall be your most devoted reader. I declare," she continued, picking up from the table the book which Eunice had left open at the last page read, "I don't believe you have been reading at all. This is only two pages beyond the place where I left off. I know that much about it, if I did not find it interesting."

"It is true," said Perry, "that we have talked more than we have read, the reason being that I wanted the benefit of this young lady's idea upon a subject that just now interests me. Let me tell you about it."

"Oh, don't trouble yourself," said Eleanor,

haughtily. "I assure you that it can be of no sort of interest to me. Miss Taylor and myself are not likely to have many ideas in common."

A look of pain swept over Perry's face, but Eunice seeing it, forced herself to laugh, while a flush rose to her cheeks.

"Probably not," she said, "unless it be on the subject of fancy-work. Cross-stitch is cross-stitch the world over. But I must go now. Good-by, Perry; good-by, Mrs. Eleanor. I'll bring over the invalid's dinner to-morrow. So get up an appetite."

In the course of the talk with Mr. Clarke, when that gentleman called in response to Perry's message, he asked, innocently:

"Will your wife be one of the teachers."

I believe that even Perry Harrison, with all his loyalty toward his wife, had a vision of her face as it would have looked had the question been asked in her presence, and thought of how she would have scorned the connecting of her name with the enterprise brought that pained expression to his face as he replied:

"I think not. It seems to me that it would be better to have paid teachers. I want to remove the enterprise as far as possible from the appearance of a charitable institution, and put it somewhat on a business footing."

"It will be a failure," predicted Mr. Clarke.

"The people do not care for education, and you will not get pupils enough to pay a teacher. I am sure it must fail."

"As a profitable business venture it may in a sense, though I am not sure that we shall not all reap the benefit in the future. Anyway, I take that part of the burden and responsibility."

The talk and planning went on, and soon afterward the work of fitting up the room began. That room! Even Eunice Taylor's hopeful heart almost failed her that morning when at Perry's request she went to look at the capabilities of the place. A dark stairway leading up to a damp, cheerless lumber-room—that was what she found. But a few days later, the carpenter having opened and repaired the shutters, letting in the blessed sweeteners—the pure air and the sunshine—the kalsominer having done his work, the glazier and the painter having departed, leaving pleasant reminders of their visit, she again paid a visit to the place, which had now a "hall." How different it was! Perry was with her. Eleanor had rather ungraciously declined to accompany them. The stairway had in some mysterious way been made a sharer in the benefit of air and light, and the clean, sunny apartment into which they stepped out of the little ante-room was a surprise and a delight to both of them.

"Well, Una," said Perry, "do you think we can make anything of it?"

"If you had seen it as it was the other day you would think it made already," she replied. "But of course it needs some furniture."

"What is the first thing?" he asked.

"I should say a carpet," she replied.

"Aren't you rather extravagant in your ideas?" asked Mr. Clarke, who had come up with them.

"Perhaps so. But did you ever know a woman to acknowledge that?" she responded, laughing.

"You know the class of people that you will get in here are not accustomed to carpets," said Mr. Clarke.

"That may be; but if they were used to all the refinements of life I suppose that this room would not have been needed at all," returned Una.

"Mr. Clarke thinks the boys and girls are not educated up to carpets," said Perry, with a meaning glance at Una. "But, really, Eunice, is that necessary?"

"Perhaps not; but I like carpets; it is a weakness of mine."

"Well, then, we will certainly have the room carpeted, out of consideration for your weakness."

Carpeted, and furnished with a sort of combination of seats and desks, the "hall" was like a little bit of paradise let down among the dingy homes of the boys and girls, to many of whom home was only a place where they ate and slept, home loves and associations being ignored.

One gloomy, drizzly day, at the very last of April, Eunice plodded her way homeward, having driven the last carpet-tack, and hung the last picture at exactly the right angle, and having taken a last look to see that the "welcome" was hung in the most conspicuous place. She was alone, as she locked the door and pocketed the key, as Perry had suggested when he drove off with Eleanor. An hour later she said to herself:

"Well, this is rather early in the history of this enterprise to have the whole thing shifted to my shoulders. I have a mind to throw the key into the pond. It will be just like my lady to insist upon going to the moon and dragging Perry with her, on the very day of the opening. Who knows but I may have to make the speech myself! I wonder if that Mr. Romaine *will* come."

Of course the refitting of the unused room had not gone forward without causing much talk and wonderment. How at least two people of our acquaintance looked at it will be seen from letters written at this time.

This from Eleanor to her mother:

NASSAU, April —, 18—.

Dear Mamma :

Was ever anything so provoking! Since my hurried note, telling you of our detention, I have waited with trunks packed, hoping that he would be able to start. But Perry's mother and confidential friend have been too much for me. If we had held to our original plan and got off that first morning it would have been better, to my way of thinking. Then Perry could have had the benefit or Dr. Mason's advice, instead of being sweated and toasted and soaked by this country doctor, who knows about as much as a school-boy. To tell the truth, mamma, this husband of mine has to be petted and dosed, and dosed and petted, and as I am a poor hand at such work they have to call in the neighbors. He is almost as nervous as Uncle Arthur, and a great sight more fortunate in having some earnest sympathizers. You see, mamma, if Perry were real sick (I mean alarmingly) I could never run on at this rate; but they do make such a fuss over a little cold. I have a cold myself; I caught it by going into the east wing to sleep. Perry coughed so incessantly that I did not sleep any the night before. The room was horribly cold, and the miserable wood fire went out, so that I got a chill. But nobody minds it.

I haven't the slightest idea when we shall go to

New York. I unpacked to-day; for, though Perry is now able to be out, he is so busy with a new scheme that it would be impossible to get him away; and, besides, it is now so late that I don't care to go until just before we go to Newport, to get my outfit; for I mean to go to Newport, though I expect to go under difficulties.

Mother Harrison informed me yesterday that the sea air was bad for lung complaints, and that Perry ought to live on the mountains, the air was so invigorating. All that woman lives for is to see that Perry does not do some of the innumerable things which are not good for him. They—I mean *we*—live in a horribly plain way. You would never dream that the Harrisons, mother and son, were worth a hundred thousand, more or less. The house is as old-fashioned as a country meeting-house, and the furniture—well, I always did hate claw-footed tables and old, musty-smelling wardrobes and sideboards and old-fashioned silver. It is nothing but a miserable little factory village, anyway, with not more than two or three families whom one would care to visit. Several have called, some of them formally, but some of those horrid factory people, with no style. Don't you think I will be likely to return the calls of that sort of people! And yet Perry and his mother seem to take it for granted that I will go poking around on factory lanes and into common tenement-houses, making myself agreeable to everybody!

And now what do you think is the latest? The chief talk at breakfast, dinner and supper for the last fortnight has been a quixotic undertaking which Perry and his adopted sister have planned and begun to carry out. They tried to get me into it, and I believe that Perry was actually half vexed that I did not fall in love with his scheme on the spot, and spend all my energies during the day and lie awake nights contriving plans for the furtherance of his enterprise, which, as nearly as I can find out, has no name, but if I were called upon to give it one I should call it a gigantic humbug, though whether or not they will succeed in humbugging anybody but themselves remains to be proven. I don't believe in pulling down all social defenses and taking the rabble into intimate companionship. For my part I don't believe in making such a fuss over that class; they can look out for themselves. I hate this talk about elevating the masses and educating them up to things. I told Perry that the first he knew he would have them elevated above us, and I preferred to keep on the upper layer myself. He thinks I'm wicked, and Miss Taylor looks at me with those great brown eyes of hers in a way that makes me want to shake some of the conceit out of her. That girl is here half the time. You see it is this way: A long time ago, when Perry was a little fellow, his mother was absent several years, traveling in Europe for her health, and Perry was left with these Taylors, and they are just the sort of people to presume upon that fact for the rest of their lives. But Perry and his mother can not see that, and they think the girl the pink of perfection; and as for Father Taylor, Perry quotes him and patterns after him until I am growing to detest the whole family.

Perry tells me that he has written to Tom to come up here with Romaine next week. I want to see Tom, but I believe I would about as soon forego that pleasure if I must take a dose of Romaine with him. But, if Tom comes, I wish you would enclose me a package of trimmings, etc. I will enclose a list. There isn't a decent milliner or dressmaker here, and I should have been wearing my winter hat still, only Miss Taylor made up that drab velvet for me. With the aid of the fashion-plate she managed to get up quite a respectable affair. She is really quite handy and has exquisite taste. I wonder that she does not take up a trade.

Good-by for a little,   ELEANOR.

This from Perry to Mr. Romaine:

NASSAU, April —.

Dear Friend and Brother:

I hoped to have been with you ere this, speaking face to face of the things of which, knowing so little, I am desirous of knowing more; but, as it seems, I have been held to this place by a Providence whose planning hand I am learning to acknowledge. There is a work going on here, and some special services have been held, and a few have come into the light. I was confined to the house for the most part by illness, to my great sorrow, and yet I ought to acknowledge that I was about to run away for a little when the Lord saw fit to lay me aside. And here in my seclusion a new light dawned upon me, and I am learning ways in which to work of which I had not before dreamed. The work has been commenced, and now I want, if possible, you will come up here for a day or two, and help and advise with me. Can you come? We are going to open an evening school, and I have about as much idea of how the thing should be done as I have of the mysteries of a fashionable milliner's shop. Now, come up, and bring some ideas; and if you cannot come *possibly*, then write me just how you do these things. But if you can make it plain to be your duty to come out here and help a feeble worker in the cause of the dear Master, why then come at once. The evening school is not the whole of the plan, but the rest will be unfolded in time. I am so filled with joy when I think of the means which God has put into my hands to use for his glory that I only regret that I have so long held the trust as a talent wrapped in a napkin.

Yours in Christ,   PERRY HARRISON.

12.

[FROM EUNICE'S JOURNAL.]

We are living at high pressure during these days. The number of things which have been accomplished since I last wrote here, if any one were obliged to give them in detail, would fill a volume.

In the first place—no, that is the second place. Well, let me begin at the beginning, and give the whole story. This journal of mine is a wonderful comfort to me, after all; it takes the place of the innumerable letters I used to write to Perry. I wonder what he has done with my letters? Journals are more endurable than people; they can't exasperate one with hateful words or sneers or tosses, as Mrs. Eleanor constantly does, and they can't distract one with trying to run a dozen ideas at once, as Perry does. The beginning was that Perry worked and worked over that one idea until it really seemed to take such possession of him that he could think of nothing else. He has hired and furnished a room, and had an opening gathering in it, and commenced an evening school. Now I'll go back and give it more slowly.

From the very beginning I had a great deal to do with the enterprise. Perry seemed to think as a matter of course that I was enlisted, and the way he worked me showed his genius for commanding people, at least. Meantime Mrs. Eleanor worked him, in a ceaseless fever, to get him off to New York. It was the very last place where he should have gone. But she almost tormented the life out of him; at least it seemed to me that she would.

Mother Harrison was in a perfect tremor of anxiety, and at last she resolved on a bold move, in which she took counsel of nobody, though I know I get half the credit of it from Mrs. Eleanor. The very day that we had done the last things to the new hall (it isn't a storeroom or lumber-room anymore) preparatory to our opening—I mean when *I* had done the last things, for I was finally left to work alone, Perry explaining with a very flushed face that Eleanor, not understanding matters, had made an engagement which it was imperatively necessary to keep. I was very good-humored; said, "Of course," and that I could get along nicely. Didn't I understand that he, poor victim, couldn't help it? I also understand that Mrs. Eleanor is very anxious that we two should quarrel, therefore I will *not* quarrel with Perry. No, not if he does all the absurd things that there are left for him to do. And he is in a fair way for it. "Blessed are the peacemakers." Let Mrs. Perry have the comfort of feeling that she is keeping the peace between us.

When I got ready I locked the hall and went over to Mother Harrison's. She entreated me to stop to tea; she didn't expect Perry and his wife home until after tea, and she was worried about his being out in the night air riding, and needed my company, so she said. I wasn't hard to be entreated; in fact I said to myself as I locked the door, that if she wanted me I would stay and have tea. We were sitting cosily over our cream-toast, when Perry and his wife arrived, he looking blue and cold, she looking disgusted. The mother and I flew around to make them comfortable.

"I didn't expect you," the mother said. "Eleanor seemed to think that you would take tea with the Wilburs."

"I didn't dare, mother," Perry answered, and his voice sounded hollow. "The night is setting in so damp and foggy I felt that I ought to be at home."

Then his wife gave that disagreeable little laugh of hers, and said to his mother:

"You ought to pat him on the back, and say 'Good boy.' He is improving so rapidly under your tuition! I dare say he will be ready for a glass case soon!"

What any of us would have answered to that heartless speech is more than I know, had not a diversion occurred. But in the meantime the door-bell had rung; there was a bustle in the hall, and presently there walked in, unannounced, two gentlemen. Perry and his mother looked, and exclaimed, and sprang forward in greeting, Perry exclaiming:

"Oh, Romaine, this is *so* good of you!" While at the same time, his mother said:

"Dr. Mason! This is more than I had dared to hope."

It transpired that the mother, in her great anxiety over her son's condition, had written to Dr. Mason asking his advice about New York air, which letter he had answered in person.

"I am on my way to a medical convocation of importance," he explained, "and I stopped over one train."

"Young man, I'd like to see you alone for about fifteen minutes, and have a talk with you." This to Perry.

It resulted in their almost immediate adjournment to his room. Mrs. Eleanor was asked to accompany them, but declined, on the plea that she was cold, so she waited their return in haughty silence, while the elder Mrs. Harrison ordered fresh tea and toast, and I tried to entertain Mr. Romaine.

When the gentlemen returned Dr. Mason addressed himself at once to Perry's wife:

"Madam, it is my misfortune to be obliged to step in, very often, and upset the happiness of families, or their plans, which in some instances amounts to their happiness. Now I have to tell you that you must keep your husband away from New York this spring. The city is at its nastiest. Just at present not a desirable place for any one, mud and rain alternating, or rather mingling, in delightful stickiness and mistiness. He is not in a condition to travel, nor in a condition to breathe city air with benefit, if he could travel. Moreover, he needs to avoid the salt air entirely—mind, I say *entirely*—during this spring and summer. It goes against me to forbid his coming in my vicinity; I should like a dab at him and a chance for a fee; but in justice to my conscience I shall be obliged to forego those pleasures. If my advice were asked further, I should say a quiet sojourn in a delightful country home like this, with a chance to breathe pure air, and with a day now and then of unmitigated sunshine, and a green landscape about him, was the place for him, through the spring, and at least the early summer. Now, dear madam, give me a cup of your tea, and then I must be off again."

This last sentence addressed to the mother. And so absorbed was he in that cup of tea that apparently he lost entirely the smoothly-rounded sentences of the wife.

"I am sure, Dr. Mason, we ought to be very much obliged to you for flying down here and assisting at the burial of ourselves in this out-of-the-way place. Not only for the spring, but the summer! It was very thoughtful in Mr. Harrison's mother to plan such a delightful surprise; she really deserves a vote of thanks. The place is quiet enough, certainly; neither is there any lack of green things, if that is important."

I haven't patience to tell you about the rest of that evening; and, besides, I feel such a queer sense of mortification for Perry, when I think of it, that I find I don't want to dwell on it. But the question of New York is certainly settled, and, for the mother's sake, I am glad. No one ventures to dispute Dr. Mason's orders. We walked home in the fog, Mr. Romaine and I; he talking about the new enterprise, and apparently taking it for granted that I was enlisted in it, body and soul.

"It is a splendid thing," he said, "not only for the physical and intellectual. Mr. Harrison will never be contented to stop with those. It is grand to see such talents and such wealth as his consecrated, isn't it?"

What was I to say?

"It is nice to see him occupied with something that interests and amuses him," I said. "He has been wretchedly sick again, and, unless he has some hobby to ride, his soul will eat up his body; therefore I am helping. But it is a wild idea, all the same. When it began it was reasonable enough; it was to be a pleasant room to sit in, and there was to be a place for refreshments on a cheap scale. But this night-school business, and classes, and all sorts of things, I don't know about; or, rather, I *do* know—I think it is folly. They are well enough off, as regards their learning. What is the use of their being educated? What will they do with their education?"

Don't be stupid enough, journal, to suppose that I meant a word of this; it savors too much of Mrs. Eleanor's style for me to say it, even if I thought it. I don't mean to say it on all occasions, but I felt just like getting up an argument with this man, to hear him talk. I might as well have tried to argue with the gate-post.

"A place of refreshments!" he said, "what do you mean?"

And he actually made me enter into details of that idea of mine, and explain how this could be, and that, and finally declared that the idea was a good one, and should be carried out at once in a certain place that he knew of, whether we did it here or not. Perhaps he did not even hear what I had said about not believing in the other ideas; at least he ignored it.

The first evening at the hall was funny—some of it. They came out wonderfully well, the boys and girls and their fathers and mothers. But Perry had previously made the blunder of inviting the minister, and the doctor, and Judge Colman, and Esquire Fenton, in, to make some *remarks*. He says he will be chary of "remarks" in the future. They said the most idiotic things! You wouldn't have supposed that one of them had a grain of sense. Mr. Watson, in the pulpit, is a sensible enough man, but he knew no more how to talk to these people than if he had lived in a dictionary all his life, and just stepped out that evening to look around. I don't think there were ten words, leaving out the conjunctions and prepositions, that were understood by those to whom his speech was addressed. He tried to pat them all on the head, metaphorically, and succeeded; at least they felt about as flat as though he had. Esquire Fenton was pompous and patronizing to the last degree; said "My dear friends" every two seconds, and wanted them to try to realize what these self-sacrificing people had been doing for them, and how the "dear young brother" had spent money as freely as water in their behalf, and was willing to "spend and be spent" for them.

Poor Perry gnawed his moustache and wiped the perspiration from his forehead, and looked despairingly at Mr. Romaine, who stood with folded arms, leaning against a post, for there really was not a vacant seat in the room, though it is quite a large one. As for me, I laughed; it was all so absurd! Gathering those men and women up there and talking to them as if they were third-rate pieces of putty, because they worked in a factory!

Esquire Fenton got through at last, which is a wonder, for he is one of those who possess the "gift of continuance" to an alarming degree. Then Mr. Romaine sprang up the steps of the little platform, as though he was very eager to speak; and I think he was.

Dear me! Why can't men be more alike, or more unlike, or something? Why should this mechanic be superior to those cultured men of society? Superior, not in words, but in that rare and subtle and indescribable thing which we name *tact?* His words were few, and simple, but spoken with such quiet earnestness, and common-senseness, that he won the attention and the heart at once. In the very midst of his talk, or, rather, while one was fearing that he was going to finish the *talk* and begin a set speech, he said: "Now let us have a song together," and instantly his rich, full voice seemed to fill the room. He sang a familiar hymn, with a chorus that those to whom it was not familiar could catch at the second hearing; and certainly they joined as if they were glad to do so. Then he prayed. He has a way of praying as though he were sure that the Lord heard every sentence, and he succeeded in making me feel so, too.

"Grand man!" Perry said of him the next morning, when we were talking the matter over, and actually there were tears in his eyes! He does get up such an enthusiasm for people.

"What a wonderful way he has of winning hearts," Perry continued, and then he propounded the same thought over which I have been whining: "I wonder what made such a difference between his talk and the talk of those others?"

His wife explained it to her entire satisfaction:

"He is one of them, Perry; he comes from the scum himself, and therefore can easily accommodate himself to their comprehensions. I think that is simple enough."

Now, Perry is rarely dignified to his wife; he can answer me haughtily enough when he thinks I have said something very foolish; in fact it reaches the realm of actual snubbing sometimes (I rejoice in that word, it is so expressive), and he can, in a gentle, entirely dutiful, but wonderfully effective way, put down his mother, when occasion requires; but Queen Eleanor is allowed, as a rule, to think that every word of hers is well chosen; at least, so far as I can see, and for aught I know, he thinks so. But that day she jarred. His voice was calm enough, but the tone was cold.

"I was wondering rather, Eleanor, how it was that his words suited *me* exactly; the very inmost depths of my heart were stirred, and the words of those other men did not move me."

"There is no accounting for tastes," Mrs. Eleanor said in her most supercilious tone. And Perry answered in his very coldest ones:

"I find that to be true."

As for me, I had the strangest mixture of feeling during this little conjugal aside. A wicked sense of satisfaction in seeing that Perry had brains enough left to know when a friend, to whom he was extending hospitality, was insulted, and a real pang at the thought that his idol was soiled before him. Poor Perry!

Well, we have our school fairly under way; not with a salaried teacher, according to Perry's first notion. Mr. Romaine scoffed at that.

"Where will you find him, or her?" he asked.

"Teachers who are willing to accept payment are of course easily found. But what you want, in this enterprise, is *soul*—a heart bursting with a desire to do good in just this new and difficult line that is open. Such teachers there are, doubtless, who ought to be paid, and who would do good work for pay, but they have to be hunted for, and sometimes the hunt takes long. Meantime here is the field white to harvest. Where are the laborers?"

"What shall we do, then?" Perry asked, nervously.

He has thrown his whole soul into this enterprise, and if it fails I am afraid it will break his heart.

"I should advise classes," Mr. Romaine said, "somewhat after the industrial-school style. Let Miss Taylor, here, take a class of boys, and Mrs. Harrison perhaps would take the older girls." This with an inquiring glance at Eleanor, who answered in her haughtiest tones:

"I prefer none. I haven't been educated for a school-teacher, and my talents do not lie in that direction. I have nothing whatever to do with this enterprise. You may count me out."

"I will take a class of girls," Perry said, quietly. And Mrs. Eleanor, I think, realized that she had overreached herself. I am sure it had not once before occurred to her husband that he could actually give personal attention to classes. However, he held to it, and was obstinate when his mother ventured an argument on the plea of health, and put me down sharply when I tried to second her. His wife said absolutely nothing.

So we have our classes. Mine amazes me—appalls me! There are nine boys in it; great, rough, uncouth fellows. They don't know what to do with their hands or their feet; and so they shuffle the one and make all sorts of uncouth disposals of the others.

"What shall I teach them first? The Twenty-third Psalm?" I asked Mr. Romaine one evening when we were first organized, and I shall have to own that I asked it with a supercilious air, worthy of Mrs. Eleanor herself, and a wicked desire to make fun of the whole thing, or appear to. His answer was prompt and quiet:

"By all means, if you can do it through your life. They are not quite ready for the verbal teaching yet. I should first attempt a lesson on the art of keeping finger-nails in order, or something of that sort, with those who need that kind of help."

"I thought cleanliness was *next* to godliness," I said, conscious that I was being very silly, and yet not seeing my way out into sense.

"It is—the *very* next," he said. "And you

have doubtless discovered that the 'next things' sometimes have to be brought forward as though they were 'first things.'"

I think I shall make a queer teacher. This is the way I began:

"Boys," I said, sitting down before them, and every one of them was grinning (that is just the word that expresses it) and nudging each other's elbows and shuffling each other's feet, "if you had each five dollars to put in the savings-bank, and it would draw five per cent. interest, how much money would you have if you left it there fifty years?"

They stared at me. I think they had an idea that I was going to ask them if they could spell "baker," and knew the Lord's Prayer, and would each like a card to keep, with "thou shalt not steal" printed on it. They looked as though they were in expectation of something of that sort. Then one of them, Dan Baker by name, answered me, and if I am not mistaken in him the answer is an index of the boy:

"What difference does it make how much it would be?"

"If you were to have the money after it had lain there multiplying itself for fifty years, wouldn't it make a difference?"

"No danger of that," he said, shrugging his shoulders.

"I don't see how you can be sure of any such thing. You are not so old but that you may live for fifty years, and you certainly may be able to earn five dollars to put on interest."

"What *is* interest, anyhow?" Joe Stoner asked. "I mean, how can people afford to pay interest on money?"

They all regarded me curiously, evidently interested in the question. And I then and there explained to them, to the best of my ability, the laws of borrowing and lending in money matters. My ability, in that line at least, is not remarkable, and I floundered once, and called on Perry to help. He explained briefly, but very clearly, and with an air of surprise over the turn that affairs had taken in my class, and then went back to his work, setting me down, I dare say, as a very strange teacher.

But the boys acted as though they might have begun to have a dawning feeling of respect for me; I fancy they thought I considered myself very wise, and were rather gratified to see that I was not above an appeal to Perry. I set every one of them to work calculating the sum that five dollars would earn in fifty years, at five per cent. compound interest. Of course they knew nothing about the laws of computation, but I waited to see what the law of common-sense would do. Not one of them reached the right solution save Dan Baker, and his somewhat sullen face flushed rosy red over the information that he was correct. The amount of the sum seemed to amaze them all. And whatever is or is not developed by our evening school, in my opinion savings bank accounts will be startlingly on the increase.

Although my class and I had a good time, we were as unsystematic and rambling as possible. But next time we are going to do better; we are to select and read any article of interest that we find in the papers. I am anxious to see the selections.

I am curious over Perry's class; he was eager and absorbed, and they were very attentive, but he volunteered no information concerning them, and went home alone with a grave, preoccupied face.

13.

Perry writes, May 15:

We are fairly under way. It is too soon to look for result, but we have started out better than I could have hoped.

Romaine—what a prince among men he is! He came up in response to my letter and spent several days, helping us in organizing, etc., and now we are quite in working order. The workers are few in number, but perhaps others may come to the front in time. Eleanor does not fall in with our ideas as yet, but I am certain to interest her after a while. As the work goes on, she must see it in another light. The atmosphere of fashionable life, which she has breathed all her days, is not conducive to the development and growth of human sympathies.

Una is an efficient helper, though I have thought that her interest grew out of a desire to gratify me, rather than from a longing to help others. At least so it seemed at first; but I think that she is becoming quite eager in her wish to help those boys of hers. They already begin to look up to her, and to quote her as authority. Only this morning one of them assured me that a certain thing was so and so—for Miss Taylor said so. My little lady will have need to be cautious as to the opinions she advances, if the boys are going to rest so implicitly on her word. The other evening I was coming out from the city by train. As we reached our station, Joe Stone boarded the train, and bought two or three papers of the newsboy on the platform. I wondered a little, especially as he did not invest in the trashy papers that a boy of his class might very naturally be supposed to be interested in, but took one of the best of the New York dailies, and a first-class weekly of our own city.

Someway Thomas had misunderstood me, and failed to meet the train; so I walked home. Starting out, I said:

"Well, Joe, I am going your road a little way. Shall I have your company?"

For answer Joe stared at me; but we walked along together, and I remarked:

"I think you are one of Miss Taylor's boys?"

"*Yes, sir!*" he replied, with more emphasis than politeness.

"Do you have pretty good times in that class?"

"I *tell* you *we do!*"

"What are you doing with so many papers? Have you turned newsboy?"

"Oh, no—some of these are for the boys. I only keeps one. You see Miss Taylor she asked us would we pick out *suthin'* we liked, and bring it to the class, and then she said we'd talk about it, and she'd tell us all she could. So you see we have to have city papers, 'cause you know there ain't nothing in the Nassau paper worth taking in."

I could not help laughing at this youngster's disparaging criticism upon our enterprising weekly.

"Well, what do you find that is worth talking over?" I asked, curious to know what this novel method of teaching brought forth.

"Well, you see, sir, we can't any of us make head nor tail out of a good deal that's in the papers; but some things we can get hold of enough to talk about. You know, sir, that a fellow has to know something afore he can take in what is told to him. I think it is like you have to have a standing place when you are going to tackle any kind of a job. So you see we don't get into the big pieces yet, but pick out some of the bits that we find in the corners. Last time I found this."

And Joe fumbled in his pockets, shifting his papers from one arm to the other, until he brought out a rumpled bit of paper, which he handed to me. It was a scrap entitled "Something for

Boys to Remember," being one of those bits of advice to boys which fill up the odd spaces in the paper, and which seldom find readers; and perhaps it was only because Joe Stone *must* find something that he clipped it from his paper.

"Well," I said, "that is good. But what did Miss Taylor say about it?"

"Why, she said there was never anything truer than them words. She says it is the man or boy that drives right along that succeeds, and that laziness makes half the villains in the world; that it is because so many people want to live without honestly working for a living that makes them cheats and liars and thieves. And I guess she's right."

"And so you mean to make a man of yourself?" I said, at the corner, where his path led one way and mine another; and Joe answered, with a beaming look:

"Well, maybe."

"And how about the rest of your class?"

"Oh, they all brought something. Some of them were real cute. Dan Baker—he's the sort of a fellow as always says, 'What's the use?'—but he brought in something. I didn't 'spose he would, but he likes Miss Taylor first-rate. I expect he will keep on coming."

I noticed that the boy hesitated, as if he had something more to say; and at last it came out.

"Miss Taylor told us about savings banks, and I've got sixty cents saved up toward my dollar!"

"Have you? Well, that's good. I'm glad you've made a beginning."

Then we said good-night, and he ran off with a springy step, born, I'm sure, of that sixty cents and the prospect of a bank account.

Well, I don't know but Eunice has started out right. Once get them upon the upward grade, with a hope before them, and there's little fear of their falling back to old ways. The glow of an ambition is already lighting up that boy's face. And he will never have a dollar which will be worth half so much to him as the first savings bank investment. It is a first step toward the development of that boy's capacities. If Una can get a hold upon their hearts, and kindle in their brains a flame of ambition, and light up their future with hopes, it will be a great work. Even this is worth all the money and care expended. Now, if only she could lead them higher—if she could inspire them with the very highest of all aspirations—if she would come herself to the fountain! Strange that the daughter of such a father should stop short of the crowning glory of a woman's life. The love of Christ shining out, softening the sharp angles of her character, is all she needs to make her a very queen among women—fit to rank beside my own peerless Eleanor. Poor Eleanor! I am sorry for her. Dr. Mason, with his insuperable decrees, has laid a shadow across her path, which I have not been able to lift. I am so dull and uncompanionable nowadays that I have no doubt she finds me a stupid fellow to have around; and I do not wonder that she sighs for the delights of New York. Una runs over almost every day, and lights up the old house. She is becoming almost a necessity to Eleanor. I presume that the two are even now puzzling over the last new stitch, as described in the *Bazar*. Well, I am glad that the two are good friends. Eleanor is sometimes a little sarcastic, but Una seems not to mind it half as much as she does my frowns.

There, I forgot. I meant to ask Eleanor to go down to the hall with me to-morrow morning, and put some of her work upon the blackboard. I want to illustrate my lessons by means of some diagrams, and neither Una nor myself have the skill to sketch a three-legged stool. But my wife is something of an artist, and, if I can persuade her to work in cheap crayons, I shall have made an advance in the direction in which I am anxious to move.

As to my own evening class, they puzzle me. I didn't begin, like Una, by plunging into business calculations, but we were about as informal and rambling, that first evening, as we could well be. I said:

"Now, if we are going to meet together regularly, let's get acquainted as soon as we can. I shall have a great many things to tell you, and I expect that you will have a great many to tell me. I shall want to know what you do with what I teach you, and you will have to be looking out for chances to use the knowledge you gain for the good of others. So you see while I teach you, you will be teaching me, and we shall all, in turn, be able to help somebody else. Do you see?"

They hung their heads, and looked as shy and awkward as it is possible for uncultured girls, of twelve years, to look; but one of them ventured to raise her eyes to mine, and I said:

"What is it?"

"Nothing; only I don't think we could teach *you* much."

"Don't you? Well, we shall see."

A vase of spring flowers stood on the table near us, and, as we talked, I had taken the vase in my hand, and, turning it around to admire the dainty blossoms, I said:

"I wonder where these came from?"

"Oh, I can tell you!" said the girl who had already spoken, and whose name is Emma Cole. "I found them over on the hills, and gave them to Miss Taylor, and she fixed 'em up. I think they are real pretty."

"So they are. Can you tell me the names of them?"

Now I am fond of flowers, but I can never remember the names of even the commonest ones. Emma's face was a study. The idea that any one should be so deplorably ignorant as not to know the names of the simple flowers which were as familiar as Greek roots to a college professor.

"Why, don't you know? That is the Mayflower! We always get them in the spring. They grow over on the hill. I think that is the only place around here where you can find them. The way I *learnt* about them was, a lady, an artist, they call her—one that paints pictures, you know—came out from the city one spring, and she came to get these flowers. She said somebody told her as how they *growed* out on the hills, and she wanted some to make pictures of. And I went with her to show her, and she telled me lots about flowers. I wish I could remember it all. But I never forgot the name, 'cause the lady herself looked like a Mayflower."

All at once Emma became conscious that she was talking considerably, and drew back, blushing.

"Well," I said, "I am very much obliged to you for telling me about these flowers. You see you *have* taught me something before I have even begun my lesson. And now I will tell you about these Mayflowers—why they are named so—and then we will study these cards which I have brought."

Thereupon I gave them a lesson in history, telling them the story of the Pilgrims and the Mayflower, making it as much of a story, and as little of a history, as I could. We all grew eager and absorbed in it, and one of my little girls, drawing a long breath, exclaimed:

"Oh, wasn't it awful to lose all one's friends and cross the ocean! I couldn't do it, ever, no way!"

Could I resist the impulse to tell them another story—the story of Him who left home, and the host of shining angels, to enter upon a life of sorrow, and meet a death that was beyond the starvation and the savage butchery of the Indians in suffering and ignominy? So, beginning with the grand old chorus of the angels, and ending with that resurrection morning, I rehearsed the old story, and, at the close, one of the class, Hattie Stone, said:

"I like that last story the best. Don't you, girls?"

"Now," I said, "I have told you this story because it concerns you and me. It is to help you to grow into the likeness of this Friend that we have begun these classes. It should be the end of all our living to get ready to live with Him, and the more we learn the better we shall be fitted for it. Let us always have first in mind and heart this thought, that we belong to Christ, and are to do all our work, and all our study, for his honor."

I knew, or thought I knew, that I was getting beyond their depth, but I did not know how to do any better.

But that some idea had entered their heads was evident from the question of Hattie Stone:

"Do you mean that the Christ you say we should work for is the same Christ they preach about on Sundays? I never heard them much of a Sunday, but I have heard 'em talk at funerals."

"I mean the same one."

"And do you mean that, if we get the lessons you give us, and do our work all honest at the factory, that it will make a difference to Him?"

"Yes, I mean that."

"Well," said Hattie, "I like *that*. It is nice to think that somebody cares."

Hattie settled back in her seat, and betook herself to the study of some cards which I had brought. Having ascertained that all my class could read a little, we made arrangements for the next evening's lessons, and then it was time to close.

I am not sure that I am not making a failure. Someway I can not make an altogether secular thing of it. I can not rid myself of the impression that their souls need my first care. And, while I know Una is wise in leading her boys, by natural and easy steps, up so a higher plane, I can not help longing to lift my girls at once out of the darkness, and set them upon the sure foundation. I do know, of my own experience, that all knowledge seems clearer when viewed in the light of Christian faith, and this is why I want to begin with giving them some knowledge of the truth.

My mind is full of schemes. I have already made arrangements to open lunch-rooms. We shall, for the present, have coffee and sandwiches, with perhaps pie and doughnut, and, later, as the warm weather comes on, we shall have ice-cream, and, very likely, fruits. I have written to Romaine to find some person who understands the cream business, who will come out for a time; but I have in mind a suitable person to take charge of the whole concern, after a little training. It is a widow, who is not strong enough for factory work, and who seems a nice sort of a person, and would, I think, be glad to get a chance to do something toward supporting herself. Not that I imagine that the business will be very profitable, at first, but it may work into something.

Then, to go farther, there is the project of keeping the hall open as a reading-room, but perhaps it will be best to wait until fall for that. It may not do to run too many new ideas at once.

All this time mother looks on curiously, while Eleanor prophesies that we shall come to naught. Perhaps so; but we shall have tried to do something, and I can not think that our efforts will fall to the ground utterly worthless.

14.

[FROM EUNICE'S JOURNAL.]

That Joe Stone is going to be a nuisance. I shall have to choke him if he makes trouble between Perry and me. I might have known that I couldn't work in company with such a sensitive conscience as Perry has lately developed. There is a sort of third-rate theatre in town—no, I am not sure that it is third-rate. People who are posted in regard to such things say it is a very decent affair; not at all behind most of the colloquies that are performed in our public schools. Now, I have been brought up not to go to theatres, either first or third-class, and I fancy that this one, at least, would hardly be to my taste, but Joe Stone has not been so brought up; indeed, he has not been brought up at all. He has come up, in the most helter-skelter fashion. Theatres are not beneath him, even though they were much lower in stamp than this one. He talked with me about going. He wanted to go "like blazes!" he said. He is not remarkably refined in his language. But, then, he was "savin of" his money for that bank account, and he didn't know as I would think it just the thing to spend it in any such way. What did I think about it?

Well, I am of an economical disposition, and it seemed important to me that Joe should learn to save his money, so I counseled wisely and prudently; and Joe, with a long-drawn sigh that showed how much self-denial he had, and how much influence I am getting over him, relinquished the idea of the play, and settled himself to the sum in addition that I had given him. All would have gone well had not accident and folly put me in a position to play Lady Bountiful. It happened on the very next evening that Lou Parsons dropped in to spend a social hour. He was gayly complimenting our little town on the number and variety of entertainments which it could boast, and drew from his pocket a shower of blue and yellow tickets, in order to count the number of ways in which he had been favored during the last two or three weeks. I, looking on, made this silly remark:

"It must be fun to be employed in a business that, according to etiquette, demands free tickets to everything under the sun. I wonder if there isn't a vacancy in the printing office? I could learn to set type, I am sure. Would that entitle me to free tickets? I should really like some."

Whereupon he immediately produced from

another pocket two crisp tickets for the said theatre, and with a very low bow presented them to me, with his compliments, saying, with a solemn air, that he thought perhaps I would like to choose a companion to accompany me, therefore allow him to present two. Of course he knows that I never attend such places any more than he does himself. He is a good, prosy young man, and, so far as his conscience on these subjects is concerned, is quite equal to Perry himself, though what is reasonable enough in Perry is perhaps foolish in him. The traveling theatre is, of course, miles beneath Perry's mental calibre, but I should think might afford an evening of innocent enough amusement to Lou Parsons. However, I was very glad to get the tickets, for there suddenly flashed before me Joe Stone's wistful face and his expressive, if not elegant sentence, that he wanted to go "like blazes!" Here was a chance for him; a chance, also, to teach him a lesson in brotherly courtesies, for I had no doubt that his little sister Hattie wanted to go also, if not "like blazes," then with all the force of her pretty, pink-cheeked strength. That child is wonderfully pretty, and has a sort of native grace that is very fascinating. She is in Perry's class, and I like to watch her. There is a girlish friendship between her and my rough Dan. I mean to watch *it*. Perry calls all his class "little girls," and, from some of his expressions, I think he considers them all about twelve years old. That is as much as a man knows! Because they don't do their hair in frightful knots on the top of their heads, and wear dresses that he steps on every time he moves, he thinks they are little girls. There isn't one of them younger than fourteen, and this little Hattie is nearly, if not quite, sixteen; though she is so small and slight that it is not strange he should take her for much younger.

Well, I gave my tickets to Joe, with the hint that now he had a chance to show his brotherly consideration and make Hattie happy. The intense delight in his eyes, as he said: "Miss Taylor, you are just a brick; that's what *you* are!" was so genuine a compliment that I hardly had the heart to remind him that "brick" was not an elegant term to apply to a lady. I took the tickets to him in the factory, and went home from there in a most satisfied frame of mind. I had excused Joe from evening class, and assured him that no doubt Mr. Harrison would excuse Hattie; but he would better go and see him, for that gentleman wants the classes to be very particular to get excused when they need to be absent. He wants to keep everything in business-like shape.

Imagine my surprise when, at the usual hour for school, he shuffled in, cheeks burning red and downcast eyes. My first thought was that he had lost the tickets. I turned to him eagerly, but he hung his head, and muttered his explanation in such a way that I had to lean toward him to make any sense of it.

"Oh, Miss Taylor, you won't think I didn't like them, 'cause I did, very much; and I think it is all bosh, just as you do; but then he is real good to Hattie, and he has helped father keep his place, and so I don't like to, you know. But it's awful silly, and mean, too."

"Joe, what on earth are you talking about?" I asked him. With his face growing redder every minute he muttered:

"Why, the tickets, you know. I went to him just as you said, and he didn't like it at all; talked a long time about them low theatres, not wanting me to take Hattie there, and being disappointed, and all that. And I couldn't, you know, could I, after all he has done?"

"Oh!" I said, enlightened suddenly. "You mean Mr. Harrison didn't want you to go to the theatre. Of course you were not to go unless you chose. I dare say you did right to please Mr. Harrison. He has done a great deal for you; he is worthy of being pleased."

At the same time I was boiling with rage. What right had Perry Harrison to interfere with my scholars and my plans for their development? If he is going to manage things in that way he may teach his own classes. I shall desert him, and I shall tell him so the first opportunity.

Eunice Taylor's next opportunity to speak her mind to Perry Harrison was on the next afternoon. She went over to the Harrison mansion by appointment with Perry's wife, and found him alone in the library, his wife not having completed her afternoon toilet. He did not wait for her to speak her mind; evidently his heart was full of the subject.

"Oh, Eunice," he said, "what *could* have become of your good sense? Is it possible you thought it was wise to teach Joe Stone to waste his time and money on third-class theatrical amusements? Such teaching would hardly do credit to our new enterprise."

Now, if Mr. Harrison had known it, there were wiser ways of broaching such a subject than he had chosen; it made Eunice's eyes glow.

"Indeed, Perry," she said, "I'm glad you mentioned that. Do you know I think you are interfering with my class in an unpardonable manner? If I'm to teach them I must have liberty to teach what *I* think and not what *you* think. If you want the class yourself, why take them by all means. But if you want me to keep them you must let them alone."

"Why, Una!" amazed by her words, and

still more by her tones. "I don't know you to-day; I thought you desired my advice and help in your work? You have told me so, I am sure."

"Advice is very different from interference. *I* don't think it would have been an unpardonable sin for Joe Stone to have taken his sister and gone to the hall the other evening. I am not a saint, like you, and therefore I have no such wholesale condemnation for play actors, as you good Christian people seem to think it is your duty to feel. I dare say they are as respectable as the rest of us. Anyway, I should risk poor Joe being harmed by an evening's entertainment of the sort, especially when he wasted no money on it; I took care of that."

"I know," said Perry, stopping in his walk up and down the room. "You were kind enough to give him tickets, and I have no doubt with the best intentions; but, my dear child, why do you profess that you have no scruples against theatre-going when your father thinks and you have been brought up to think so differently? Surely you are not sincere in this!"

"I am, perfectly sincere," Una said, her eyes still flashing. "It may not be to my taste to spend an evening at the theatre, and I may consider it to come within the range of Joe Stone's taste to do so. Anyway, I furnished him the means, and would do so again without a scruple."

"Una," said Perry, in a low quiet voice, contrasting strangely with her excited one, "the theatre is no place for a *Christian*."

"That may be, but I'm not a Christian, neither is Joe Stone nor his sister. I don't want you to go nor your wife, though she tells me there is no place of amusement that she enjoys more in the world. I am entirely willing that you should keep her from going, if you can; but Joe Stone and I have a right to go if we want to, and can get a chance."

"I thought we were friends and that we thought alike, and that our tastes and our work were in sympathy," he said, speaking low, and pausing in his walk long enough to look into her angry eyes. "If I am mistaken, Una, I regret it more than I am able to tell you. But I still think that, in a great measure, I am responsible for this attempt at an evening school, and I have promised the Lord Jesus Christ that, so far as my influence reaches, it shall tend toward leading these boys and girls into his kingdom. To that end I work; all other motives and aims are secondary, and must bend to that one. I want your help in this, but if you can not give it I must do without it. Still, it is right that you should know I will throw all my influence toward that end, and shall have to come in contact with your ideas as often as they come in contact with my sense of right."

He might have put it more gently. But Una was already ashamed of her outburst and touched by the evident distress in his face and voice. So all might have been well had not Mrs. Perry Harrison at that moment glided in through the half-open door.

"Quarreling, I really believe!" she said, in her silvery voice. "You and Una! Who would have suspected such a thing possible! My dear child, you see none of them are to be trusted. Though certainly I thought Perry would keep his temper before *you!* What can be said in the most meaningless sport by some women takes tone and force said by others."

And there was that in Mrs. Harrison's tones which made the angry blood rush into Una's cheeks. As for Perry, he went out from the library without speaking another word to either lady, and a few minutes thereafter passed down the walk leading to the front gate. Mrs. Harrison seated herself among the cushions on the sofa, and got out her bright-colored wools.

"They are a sad set, these gentlemen," she said, carelessly, "especially the Harrisons. This one has inherited all the family temper. My dear Una, you may be thankful that you escaped his hands."

What was there in her tone that made this sentence so insulting? Under any circumstances it might, perhaps, have been pronounced coarse; but it jarred on Una's nerves like the cut of a knife on clear flesh. She lifted her head haughtily, and said, while her cheeks burned:

"Mrs. Harrison, may I ask what you mean?"

An air of well-bred surprise was Mrs. Harrison's answer.

"Mean?" she said, innocently. "Why my dear child, you can not have supposed me to have remained ignorant of what is village gossip! I should have expected *you* to be better versed in village life than that. You know, of course, that it is said my husband was so ungracious as to desert you and ignore your claims after devoting himself to you since your babyhood. Of course *I* understand just how much truth there is in all this; I am only trying to amuse you with an account of what is being talked; you are reaping laurels, I assure you; the good people of the village can not say enough to show their admiration of your forgiving spirit, in that you have taken him to your heart as before, and are even willing to make yourself a tool to carry out his quixotic schemes. Seriously, my child, I wish you would not be so patient with his whims; he is capable of going to all sorts of extremes. Sometimes I am really afraid that he will determine that the Mormon theory is correct, and conclude that he must have two wives at least in order to carry on his grand plans successfully—one to afford intellectual stimulus, you know, and one to do the work. Don't you let him make such a drudge of you. It is a real shame! I *told* him that I should interfere if he persisted in spoiling your prospects for life in this way."

What was Una to answer to this strange, coarse, insulting, cold-blooded address, conveyed in the most insinuating tones? Give her credit for self-control and a degree of forbearance that was almost Christian, in that she said not a single word, but gathered up her work, that had fallen to the floor, and rising glided out of the room—out of the door—stopping only to seize her straw hat from the rack in the hall, then away across the meadow to her home.

She wrote a note that evening—brief, and yet containing much. This was it:

PERRY:—Your wife has insulted me; and not only me, but you. From this time we must be as strangers.

EUNICE TAYLOR.

In her journal she wrote that night, as late as midnight:

I have been stabbed to the very heart, and Perry Harrison's wife has done the work. I wonder if all mortal wounds open people's eyes to their own follies and mistakes? Mine did. I see most plainly why those cold, cruel words stung so. I *have* been left by Perry Harrison! Deserted! Not that he ever meant it—not that I ever knew he did it until this day. I know now, by the pain and the bitterness, that he ought never to have been to me what he was—what he *is*. I know that he treated me as no man should treat a woman, save that one whom he loves best on earth; by which I only mean that he was patient with my mistakes, gentle with my faults, considerate for my comfort, giving me to understand by constant, endless, nameless attentions, that I was always in his thoughts, an object of special interest. This he had no right to do; this I had no right to accept; for I knew then, as well as I know it now, that he was engaged to Eleanor Haddington. I was not true to her nor to myself, and he was not true to her nor to me, and it is these truths that cut. Aunt Ruth was right—there is a sting. Oh, Perry! Oh, Eunice Taylor! You are not strong, nor self-reliant. You have no friend to help you; you do not know what kind of help you want, nor which way to turn, nor what to do. God help you! No, God can not help you, for you have not asked his help. No, and I will not! Is not Eleanor Harrison a Christian? Doesn't she go to church every communion Sabbath, and sit in her elegant robes in the corner of the Harrison pew, and nibble a crumb of the sacred bread, and touch her lips to the gold-lined goblet? Shall I touch it, after that? *I hate her!*

15.

Perry Harrison had been more annoyed by the disagreement between himself and Eunice than any one guessed. He could hardly believe that they had actually quarreled, and yet that was what his wife had named it; and now that he recalled the scene and the words spoken he confessed that it looked and sounded like a fierce dispute. He had been so hurt and disappointed, first that Una had been so untrue to what he had believed to be her ideas of right, derived from her own father's teachings, and, secondly, that she had so passionately resented his interference, as she was pleased to call his attempt at remonstrance. And then he questioned within himself whether he had been altogether without passion; whether his words had been well chosen and spoken without anger; whether he had not been more anxious to make people think as he did than zealous for the truth.

There is a class who talk largely about allowing people to think for themselves, but I have noticed that these are the very ones who want everybody to think exactly as they do, and they are apt to look upon those who do not arrive at the same conclusions as beneath themselves in intellectual capacity.

Perry Harrison was not one of this class. Still he had very strong convictions, and it hurt him to find that Una had less firm ideas upon a matter which seemed to him of great importance. Someway a prop upon which he had leaned had suddenly given way, and he felt more alone in his work, and even in his Christian life, than ever before; and, strange as it may seem, he felt not the slightest prompting to turn to his wife for sympathy and help. He had already learned that with all her years of experience Eleanor Harrison stood yet upon a low spiritual plane; not that he put the thought into form, even in his most secret heart. Not at all. He had not yet been disenchanted. Disappointed he often was in his wife; grieved that she could not enter into his plans and sympathize with him in his aims; but he had a thousand excuses which were no shams to him. He really thought her the most lovely of women—"a queen among women" —he was wont to call her; and so she would have been but for one grand defect. Supremely selfish, and without sympathy and thought for others, she seemed what we rarely find, an utterly heartless woman; and yet she could be the most fascinating of mortals. She always had a host of admirers. Even Eunice Taylor sometimes yielded to the charm of her manner when she chose to be gracious, and then that young lady made up for it by writing in her diary spiteful things about her neighbor.

"And now to make matters worse these two had to quarrel!"

That was what Perry said when, the next morning, he received Una's note. Strangely enough that explosive little billet did not quite overwhelm the gentleman. He was inexpressibly grieved, but not hopelessly so. You must remember that he was ignorant of the real state of affairs. No breath of the village gossip had reached him, and even had he heard every ill-natured remark which had been made he was so sure of his own and Una's good faith and trust in each other, in a brotherly and sisterly way, that he would scarcely have thought to connect it with Una's outburst, as revealed by the slip of paper which he twisted and twirled in his fingers, while he bit his lips and wrinkled his forehead between his exclamations of vexation and dismay.

"At last Una has taken offense at some of Eleanor's unguarded and sarcastic remarks."

That was the way he explained it. He did not wonder much, for he had been often surprised at the cool manner with which Una received remarks which even to him sounded harsh and unkind. But he always said, "That's Eleanor's way," and secretly rejoiced over Una's good sense. But now she had actually taken up a feeling of resentment, and he was so sorry! It had followed so closely upon his own little misunderstanding—that made it less easy to bridge over. What a silly child she was, to be sure! What could it have been to call out such a spiteful little note as that? Of course Una was sorry before this, and would give worlds to recall her note. On the whole he would just ignore it, and let it be as if it had not been; not a word would he breathe of it even to Eleanor, and when he saw Una he would act just as usual. It was only one of the child's little outbursts. How well he remembered them in the old, childish days.

How far away those days were now! There was the same friendly greeting when he met Una's father and mother; but the old freedom was gone. He no longer ran in every day as he used to, whenever he was at home. He had not thought of it before, but things were changed, certainly. He would never cease to love those dear friends of his boyhood, and he recalled the grasp of the hand and the words of cheer with which he was welcomed when, a few months before, he came back to them with a new hope in his heart, a new aim in his thoughts and life; and with these memories, and the sad, hard sentence of that note mingling in his thoughts, Perry Harrison bowed his head in heaviness of heart. Not that he believed for a single moment that the friendship was really broken—it was too firm for that; but there was something disheartening about it all. Bearing as it did upon the success of the work he had undertaken, what was to become of that? And with a sense of his weakness, and a desolation for which he felt he had no adequate cause, he betook himself to his usual occupations.

Matters stood in this way for a day or two, then Eleanor took occasion to say, at dinner:

"I wonder what has become of your ally, or confederate, or whatever you choose to call her? She has not been here since the day you quarreled. Was it so serious?"

An amazed look spread itself over Mother Harrison's face.

"Perry and Una quarreled!" Then directly to her son: "Not seriously, I hope?"

"I think the little difference *we* had could scarcely be called a quarrel," replied Perry, with a slight emphasis on the *we*, which Eleanor noticed, and it caused her color to rise; but Perry did not look at her, and she could not determine whether or not he knew of the finishing up of that last visit of Una's. She had an instinctive feeling that she might do well to move cautiously, lest she should call down upon her own head something that would not take the form of blessings.

Pursuing his policy of ignoring Una's note, and its threat or declaration, Perry said, as he rose from the table:

"Mother, Eleanor and I are going to ride into town this afternoon, and if you will go with us we may as well carry out our intention of visiting the artists' studios. Let Katy run over and tell Una, and tell her to be ready at three."

Eleanor's eyes flashed; and she laughed a little, scornful laugh.

"The Sultan has spoken! Let all the Sultanas obey!"

"As they please," returned her husband.

Katy brought back a note from Una. It was this:

Dear Mrs. Harrison:—I am sorry to disappoint you, but I can not go this afternoon. Will you please say to Perry that I will try to meet my class to-night.
   Yours,   Una.

To this Eleanor said, with another scornful laugh:

"You see, Perry, one of your subjects has rebelled. Will she lose her head? I believe that is the usual method of dealing with the refractory ones. I suppose it serves as a salutary lesson for those who remain."

Mr. Harrison did not even smile at what might have been an attempt at pleasantry. He only said, in a low tone, which could not have been meant to reach other ears:

"I did not think she meant it."

His mother said:

"Well, never mind; another day will do as well. I don't feel very well myself, and we must remember that Una is not a young lady of leisure. She has many home duties from which your wife is free. I sometimes think that we are growing exacting in our demands upon her time."

"I am sure," said Eleanor, petulantly, "that I am willing to pay Miss Taylor for all she has done for me. Only Perry made such a buzz about my ears when I spoke of it that one would think, to hear him, that he had received a personal insult. However, I presume I shall make no more demands upon her valuable time. But Perry can keep her busy running after his boys and girls whole half days, and every day in the week, and nobody seems to think that *his* demands are unreasonable. I told him that I should interfere, and I always keep my word."

This with a significant glance toward her husband, which he appeared not to notice. He was determined to carry out his policy of ignoring the fact that there had been trouble anywhere among them.

"Then, Perry, if only you and I go, you will drive in the phaeton, won't you?" asked Eleanor.

"Yes, if you prefer," replied Perry, in a listless tone, as if the whole affair had grown to be a matter of the utmost indifference to him—as, indeed, it had. He had been planning this way out of the trouble, and, man like, he fancied that, if they could only be brought together in some such way, all would be harmony again. You see it had not entered his head that there could be any serious cause for Una's pique. He felt vexed at Eleanor, and more vexed with himself, and had decided that they ought to make the advances. And now his plan had failed. To be sure it might be, as his mother had suggested, that she was hindered by home duties; yet it was like Una to *say so*. Then, on the other hand, her sending word that she would be at the hall was a good omen. He would wait and see how it would all come out.

But, in spite of his resolve not to worry, he was silent and moody, and Eleanor voted him cross as a bear! and, when he exerted himself to entertain her, she grew sullen, and would not be entertained. Altogether they had a most uncomfortable afternoon. Driving home, in the early twilight, Perry said, as Eleanor continued to reject his efforts to entertain her:

"Eleanor, what is the matter? I don't understand you at all, to-day."

"You are not more unfortunate than I am," she replied, coldly.

"Then I am to infer that you do not understand yourself?" he asked, smiling.

"You are to infer no such thing! I understand myself perfectly," she said, with spirit. "You know very well that I mean that I do not understand you!"

His reply was gentle, and full of concern:

"I do not know what you have difficulty with; I am not conscious of dealing in ambiguities; I believe in straightforwardness. It may cause a little pain, sometimes, but I believe it is always better in the end to be straightforward."

"It is a pity that you had not adopted that theory earlier in life."

Eleanor's tone was sharp and bitter. And Perry knew by that, more than by the words which, in themselves, were ungracious enough, that, behind all, there was something which, as yet, he could not guess. And, straightforward as he was, he dared not ask either his wife, or his friend. You need not suppose that he knew that he feared anything. Had he not quite convinced himself that Una had only taken offense at some of his wife's cutting remarks, which, following close upon his own dignified, and, perhaps, somewhat sharp, remonstrance, had cut deeper than usual? What a nuisance it was, anyway! They were all getting on so beautiful together, and now everything was spoiled? Again and again he bemoaned the state of affairs.

They drove to the door in absolute silence. There was an unusual stir about the house, and, on the steps, they were met by Dr. Webb, who, with a grave face, held out his hand to Perry.

"It is your mother," he said, in response to Perry's anxious "What is it?"

"I was called in two hours since. Did you not meet the messenger we sent for you?"

"We met no one," was the reply. "We came home by the river road."

"That explains it. We feared you would be delayed, and Miss Taylor and I took the liberty of sending a dispatch to Dr. Mason. I dared not wait, as every hour is important."

"Then my mother is living?" almost gasped Perry.

"Yes, and I can bid you hope. But I felt that I needed the counsel of an older physician, and Miss Taylor thought that Dr. Mason would be your choice."

"That was right. But what is it? Is it—"

"That which we have feared—paralysis."

Perry bowed and passed on, joining Eleanor in the dining-room, followed by the doctor, who insisted upon their taking some refreshment, while he explained further.

It transpired that Eunice, seeing Perry and his wife pass, and concluding that Mother Harrison was alone, ran over to make a call in their absence, thinking, doubtless, that the good mother need not be distressed by any suspicions of trouble. On entering the little sitting-room, she found Mrs. Harrison lying partly on the floor and partly on the lounge, and insensible. Here was work for her strong nerves and ready wit. Calling the servants, she gave her orders quickly and quietly. The doctor was sent for, and a messenger despatched for Perry, while with the aid of the frightened women, she got the stricken woman to bed.

All this Perry learned from the doctor, who was emphatic in his praises of Una's efficiency.

"She is with your mother; she said she should stay until you came. I presume you and your wife will stay up to-night? I will be in again in an hour, and we will make arrangements for the night. Meantime I will go down to the office, and see if I can hear anything from the doctor. I suppose we can not hope for his arrival before ten o'clock to-morrow?"

"What is the man thinking of?" exclaimed Eleanor, as he went out. "Are there no professional nurses here? I never sat up with a sick person in my life! It makes me sick to lose my sleep, and I could never endure sick-room odors. I think it is constitutional—the mortal dread I have at the sight of suffering."

At this moment Eunice Taylor's white face appeared in the doorway.

"Perry," she said, and her voice was like a sound from the grave, "I think your mother made en effort to speak your name just now. Will you go to her?" Then, as he passed her, she whispered—and her voice was an inspiration, so intense was it in its anxiety—"Perry, be strong—oh, be strong."

16.

Life at the Harrison mansion was strange and exciting and bewildering during the next few weeks. The coming of the uninvited guest, who had established himself in the household during the absence of the son and daughter, changed all plans and regulations, and made strange havoc with the petty quarrels that had been going on.

Eunice Taylor, in her pity and sympathy for Perry, forgot that she was angry with him, that they were to be as strangers, and went forward with her quick, kind words of strength, almost as soon as he arrived.

Settling down upon the early terror and bustle, followed a night of anxious watching, that weariest kind of watching, in which the anxious hearts can do nothing *but* watch and wait. Eunice had not had any plans for the night, but they were promptly made for her by Dr. Webb.

"Stay with her to-night, won't you, Miss Eunice? I shall send Mrs. Bacon here, and she is a good enough nurse, and the family will be here, of course, but yet I think it would be better for you not to leave her."

Of course Eunice said she would stay. Then Mrs. Perry promptly spoke her mind:

"Well, then, Perry, do come. The arrangements for the night are all made, and I am sure you can do no good standing around in the way. I am almost tired to death. Una can call you if there is any change. But there will not be. I have seen such cases before. Come, before it gets any later; it is after midnight now."

Eunice felt that she could have quailed before the blaze of Perry's eyes, had they been directed to her, just then, but his voice was quiet enough:

"I shall stay with my mother, to-night, of course."

She was not subdued. Instead, she was angry.

"Oh, if you choose to make it as uncomfortable for me as you can, of course there is no one to prevent it; but one would think you might have a little consideration for your wife, especially when you can do no good. My nerves are not made of cast-iron."

His only answer was to take a lamp from the table, direct Mollie, who was passing through, to take it to Mrs. Harrison's room, and then say, "Good-night, Eleanor." Then he proceeded to wheeling an easy chair to his mother's bedside, and making Una as comfortable as he could.

"I don't suppose there is any necessity for this," he said, looking anxiously at her. "And I'm afraid it is too much to ask of you; but you don't know what an unspeakable comfort it is to have you beside her. It seems the place for a woman, and a woman who *loves* her."

"Never mind me," said Una, briefly. "I am used to night watching; I served an apprenticeship when father was sick, you know. How soon do you suppose Dr. Mason can reach here?"

That was the beginning of their night vigils together. Dr. Mason came the next day, and was doubtful, anxious, non-committal. Would come down again in a day or two and try to give a definite opinion. It might be a rapid case, and she might rally and live for weeks and months, even years; some cases did; it was impossible to tell. And then he went away and left them again in their consuming anxiety.

Meantime, Eunice was a tower of strength. Her apprenticeship in her father's sick-room, and in Aunt Ruth's house in New York, and in her mother's kitchen, had served her well. There was nothing that she could not direct about, from the best way of preparing the bed to the best way of making beef-tea and gruel. And she did not dare to go away, even for an hour. Not because Perry wanted her, as he evidently did; not because the cook and the chambermaid hung around her surreptitiously, asking for directions, but because of a pair of eager eyes that recognized her and followed her wherever she moved, and unmistakably spoke for the poor mute lips a pleading that she would stay. "You have always seemed to me like *my* child," she had said to her in a tender, yearning tone, only a few days before, and Eunice, thinking of it, flushed to her very temples, and staid.

Dr. Mason came again, and then gave forth his decree. She would live, he thought, through the summer, possibly much longer; she would, he hoped—was quite confident, indeed—recover speech to a degree—but motion! And then he paused and shook his head. Poor Perry! This was almost worse than death, and yet he accepted it as a reprieve, and clung to her, and smiled fondly over her, and whispered tender words in her poor dulled ear, and one sentence was, "Would she like to have Una stay with her all the time?" And the drawn mouth had tried to work itself into speech, and had managed, in a strange, uncouth way, but in a way that was perfectly intelligible to him, to signify that she would rather have her than any one else on earth. He did not know how fond had been the mother's hope that this would be her daughter. It was well he did not. These were hard days for him. He needed all his Christian courage to sustain him. Had Satan entered into the beautiful Eleanor that she stung so, in every direction? She called the house an apothecary's shop; said it smelled of all the herbs that ever grew, and that every dish in the house savored of gruel or beef-tea, and that people of refinement had a way of managing sickness so that the whole house wasn't redolent of it; and Perry bit his lip, and gnawed his moustache, and held his peace, keeping the utmost outward control over himself, showing by neither words nor tones that he was hurt to the core.

Meantime, when he was not present, and when, on rare occasions, Una was away from the sick-room long enough to be talked with, she had to bear the stings herself, and having neither love nor Christian principle to sustain her, she did not bear them very well; pride in herself and pity for Perry were the two controlling motives that kept her from absolute outbreak.

"What unbounded devotion!" she said to her one morning, the sarcastic smile that was so very hard to bear curving her upper lip. "It is almost a pity that it is not your own mother, and yet I don't know that you could improve the picture even then; and of course it wouldn't be as romantic nor exciting. On the whole, I believe it is better as it is."

"Mrs. Harrison," said Una, and her voice in its coldness startled even herself, but she spoke in the slow, unimpassioned tones that in natures like hers mean the white heat of anger, "I have borne a great deal from you, because this is a time of affliction and a house of mourning, and one who has been like a second mother to me all my life has no daughter of her own, and is dependent on me. But I warn you that I have borne all that I will. If you say to me again anything like what you have just been hinting I will appeal to your husband for protection, and tell him what his wife thinks of him!"

Now Mrs. Harrison was angry—more angry than she had ever been with Eunice Taylor before, and that was saying a great deal. If she had not lost all self-control for a moment she would not have said what she did.

"Tell him," she said; "tell him, certainly. Don't think to dare me by any childish spitefulness like that. Perhaps, since you are resolved on so dainty a bit of work, I may as well give you something to tell. I despise you both for a couple of weak-brained idiots. You are just suited to each other, and you should have married each other. There is that in Perry Harrison which requires coddling and mustard-plasters, and you have the element which is needed. I haven't. I shall never develop into the model wife, as you would have done. It is a great pity. In a novel, now, nothing would be easier than for you to give me a dose of poison and clear the way;

or you might elope with my husband—that would be more tragic in some views, and less common than the other. But I am not afraid of your doing either. Perry wouldn't think it right to elope, and he would never forgive you for murder, because it's wicked. So, my little cat, you can't scratch very hard. And really I'm sorry for you. I think myself it is a stupid sort of life."

During this half-insane harangue Eunice had stood as if rooted to the spot. What could she say or do ? Where fly, to be where she need never hear this hateful tongue again ?

The sudden and violent slamming to of the library door startled them both. Who was in the library ? Mrs. Harrison laughed.

"Shouldn't I have made a good actress ? " she asked, coolly. " I think I should have liked the profession. In fact, I was tempted in that direction once. I declare, I cheated you perfectly, didn't I ? "

And she laughed again. But Eunice was not cheated ; she knew that this was acting, and that the other had been genuine.

People in high states of rage, and people, too, without Christian principle to help them, can control the outward manifestation of it ; that is, if they have been trained to self-control. It is a matter of education. Eunice had been trained to it from her babyhood. She took up her glass of jelly and passed down the hall, precisely as if nothing had occurred, and she went through with the routine of that day as usual, many times, though, wondering who it could have been that slammed the library-door, and whereunto this would grow. She had lost all desire to shield Perry from a knowledge of his wife's character. She had just enough principle left to be sure that she would not voluntarily go to him with a story of outrage and insult. She was sorry, five minutes after she sent him that first note, which had been so entirely ignored by him, that she ever sent it at all. There was no danger of her descending to that level of attack again. But if he had heard, and should question her, and it should all come out, she would take no pains to spare him the knowledge of the character of the woman who was his wife. She had no business to be his wife; it was a great moral wrong; she did violence to his nature, to his sense of duty and to his highest convictions of life, every hour that she breathed. He ought to know it; he ought to know what a fool he had been. She hoped he did feel it to his very soul. And, as for making an effort to blind him, as she had lamely tried to do all the time, she would from this time forth speak to his wife exactly as she deserved to be addressed; she would not play the blind-folded idiot between them any longer.

These are just a few of the wild thoughts that rushed through her brain that night, as she sat alone watching beside his mother. The nurse was resting. Eleanor was in the parlor, from whence there echoed the faint sound of the piano. Perry was with her, doubtless. Una hadn't seen him that day. She wished at that moment that he would come in. His mother was in one of her heavy sleeps from which ordinary talking did not waken her. If he overheard any of that talk this morning, and would question her, she would not spare him, not she. He deserved the knowledge of his folly.

While she thought it over he came in, softly, without speaking. He came over to the bedside and looked at his mother. He was accustomed since her illness to having prayers at her bedside. Sometimes she was awake and heard; sometimes she slept. Usually Eleanor was with them; to-night she was not. Perry did not look at Una— did not in any way recognize her presence. He knelt beside his mother and clasped her hand in his, and then he prayed. What a prayer it was! Years and years afterward Una's nerves shook when she thought of that night and that prayer. Intense, solemn, tender, high-toned—not as of one who was in the depths of despair, and yet as one on whom a knowledge had fallen such as he had never before possessed. It might almost have been called a prayer of self-renunciation, of consecration, as from one who gave up himself, and his plans, and his hopes, and his happiness, then and there, from that time forth, and in doing it had gone higher and closer to the heart of God than he had ever dared to reach before, and so found that which the world not only could not give, but could not take away. Eunice had sat erect, with cold eyes and hardened heart, when he commenced, but before the service was concluded she had slipped on her knees, and, whether she prayed or not, she shed abundant tears. Rising at last he bent over his mother, who had roused some time before. He spoke tender words to her, low-toned and sweet, as one would speak to a sick child; then stooping, he kissed her, soft, clinging, lingering kisses, like a benediction, almost, and turned away. Stopping beside Eunice for just an instant, he held out his hand; she glancing up into his pale face an instant, dropped her eyes. There was in the clear, solemn depths of his earnest gaze that which shamed and awed her. He had struggled and suffered; those two traces she could see, but he had also gone up, beyond where she had any knowledge. He did not speak a word, but there was a bit of twisted paper in her hand when he went away. What was it? She hardly felt that she dared open it; it almost seemed to her as if he might have seen her wild, wicked thoughts and sternly rebuked them. She could not look at it now, the mother wanted her. She bent over her and received the sweet, trusting smile, and set about the tender little ministrations for her comfort, and waited until in the silence and hush of the sitting-room, where she had planned to pass the night, because the sick one so often wakened, and was restless and unable to fall to sleep without her. Then she took from her bosom that crumpled bit of paper and read it. This was it:

"Dost thou take this woman, Eleanor, before God and these witnesses, to be thy wife? Dost thou promise to love her, honor her, defend her, sustain and cherish her, in joy and in sorrow, in health and in sickness, in prosperity and adversity? Wilt thou be faithful to her in all things, and never forsake her, so long as ye both do live?"

"I will."

This was all. Not a line or word else of explanation or comment. Following that prayer it had a strange effect on Eunice, those simple, solemn vows, written out by a hand she knew so well. It was like calling on her to be a witness to a sacrament to take oath with him as to its solemnity and sacredness. All her rage died out, all her bitterness of feeling against him, for she knew now that the feelings had been bitter.

Straightway she went back with tenfold strength and power to her resolution made when he brought home a bride. Nor that, either: she realized fully that she couldn't shield him, blind his eyes—nothing of that now. They were very wide-open eyes, but she could keep, with him, those solemn vows—at least she could do it outwardly. She would show his wife all respect and deference. She would be—she would try to be— And there her exaltation broke down, and she cried bitter tears, born of youthful folly and of playing with edged tools.

It transpired very soon after that Perry was full of plans. He had consulted with Dr. Mason. He had learned that New York, and the constant attendance of that gentleman, might help his mother. He had planned with Eunice's father and mother, and with Eunice, that she and his mother should go to New York, to Aunt Ruth's, and board. That the payment for Eunice's services should be in actual hard dollars—a regular salary—sufficient to make her life far above the one of grinding poverty that it had been hitherto.

But what paid Eunice, or what kept her meek under the infliction of that brief, business-like talk, with money for its basis, was the memory of that prayer, and that slip of paper, which she kept, and also a certain curious little tremble of the upper lip, as he said:

"She can do without her son, Eunice, better than she can do without you."

And Eunice knew it was true, so long as "her son" must also mean "her son's wife."

So at home in her little room, packing for New York at midnight one night, she paused long enough to write in her journal this testimony:

"Oh, there are Christians! And Perry Harrison is a Christian, and Eunice Taylor is not."

17.

Though Dr. Mason came up to superintend the removal of his patient, Perry, with the devotion of a loving son, resolved to see his mother established in her rooms at Miss Brockton's.

"Of course you will only be there for a few days," the doctor had said, when they talked over the plans; "and, much as I would like to keep you out of the city entirely, I suppose I shall have to submit. But I tell you, my friend, that this clear country air is just what you need for the re-establishment of your health."

"*I* should think so!" said Eleanor, in her hatefulest tone. "The smoke of a factory village is acknowledged to be a complete cure for lung diseases!"

"You forget, Mrs. Harrison, that you people up here on the hill are breathing quite another atmosphere from that which they who live down in the village are taking in with every breath." Then, turning to Perry, he added: "I see how it is, and understand that you will not be quite easy about your mother unless you see her settled with your own eyes, and know for yourself that she is comfortably situated."

"That is it," returned Perry. "And it will be a little change for both my wife and myself. She has been waiting a long time for that visit to her mother."

"You need not count me in your plans," said Mrs. Eleanor, sharply; "I prefer to make up my own party when I go on a pleasure-trip. This being packed in with invalids and nurses is not to my taste."

Dr. Mason elevated his eyebrows slightly, but took no other notice of the lady's unfeeling remark, while Perry went on planning, apparently oblivious of her presence. But she was not to be ignored.

"See here, Perry!" she said, "I don't know what you can be thinking of! You talk of going away. What do you propose to do with me?"

"Why, I did propose to have the pleasure of your company; but, as you have declined to afford me that gratification, I suppose you will remain here. You will not be alone in a house full of servants."

Perry's voice had not a touch of anger in it, though it was strangely cold and dignified.

"I didn't marry the servants!" she said, angrily. "And I didn't expect to be deserted by my husband quite so soon. It seems a man is to cling to his mother, for all the law of the gospel about cleaving unto his wife."

"Now, Eleanor," said Perry, with a touch of vexation in his voice—not anger, but simply a vexed and pained feeling showing itself in the tone—"don't be unreasonable. You know that I ought to go; and more than that, I would be a monster not to want to go. And I really can not see why you should not go with me. I will stay, well, as long as the doctor here will let me. And then you might stop a few days longer, if you thought you would enjoy it."

"You are very kind; but I assure you that your condescension is quite uncalled for. I will not ask you to sacrifice your happiness; and, perhaps, as Dr. Mason puts it, your life in that way. And you quite forget that my mother is still at Newport, where I should be if I was not your wife."

"Eleanor!"

That was all. But the look in Perry Harrison's eyes warned her that she had stepped to the extreme of propriety, and it might not be well to venture farther in the presence of a third person.

How she shaped her plan of attack when they were alone did not appear, but when Perry saw Una again, he said:

"Una, can you do without me to-morrow?"

"Why, Perry," she began, then something stopped her, and he added:

"I speak truly when I say that I can not endure the strain upon my strength."

He did not say in what way the strain would come, but Una understood, and she answered:

"I know, it would be hard, and with Dr. Mason we shall get along all right. We will send a telegram just as soon as we get there. Yes, on the whole, I think that it will be better for you not to go just now."

What Dr. Mason knew or guessed he kept to himself. But this is what he *did*, when they met at breakfast that last morning, he having arrived in the early dawn of the autumn day. He said:

"Now, see here, young man. If you take my advice you will stay at home. You are not fit for the journey, especially such a trip as this will be, and I shall only have two patients instead of one, and, hurried as I am in these days, I can not take any more journeys out here. The truth is, you are worn out with watching and anxiety, and if you will take a little immediate rest it may save you some trouble."

There was certainly a grateful expression in Perry's eyes as for one instant they met Una's, as she added her word:

"Do, Perry, be persuaded to stay at home, and take care of yourself."

"He won't, and you need not think of it," said

Eleanor. "He has very peculiar ideas of his duty; and I am surprised, Miss Taylor, that you and he should differ."

It was the old insult, and for one moment Una's cheeks flushed. Then she swallowed her wrath, and answered, lightly:

"Perry and I have differed more than once in the course of our lives."

The doctor had evidently taken things into his own hands, and was making it to appear that his plans were being carried out, when, in truth, he was only trying to make it smooth for Perry. And this did not quite suit Eleanor, who wanted no help in the carrying out of her plan of keeping Perry at home, and she said, sharply:

"You need not trouble yourself to urge Perry to stay behind. If he will not do it for his wife I should think he would be too proud to do it for any one else."

But this was lost upon the doctor, who, with an "Excuse me, Mrs. Harrison," had left the table, even as she was speaking, and proceeding to the invalid's room was already preparing her for the farewell so soon to be spoken.

When Perry came back from the station, after seeing the party off, he shut himself up in the study, not seeing his wife until dinner-time. Then all traces of emotion had disappeared, and he was the affable gentleman exerting himself to be entertaining. But Eleanor was sullen, and would not be entertained. The more he talked the more she would not talk. He proposed a drive, but she was tired; she should think he would want to rest after all the tiresome life they had been living for weeks. For her part, she did not want to see anybody, or go anywhere, until she had time to appreciate the quiet of the house.

"Very well," returned her husband, speaking calmly. "If you are so anxious to be left alone I can not understand the force of your objections to my going to New York. You know very well, Eleanor, that I staid at home for no other reason than to gratify your whim."

"And now will you let me have a little quiet, to gratify another whim?"

"Certainly."

And with that he took his hat and walked out of the room and out of the house.

The summer, which was to have been so full of work, was gone, and September had come, and how little had been done! Yet, if he had not been so completely absorbed in his own sorrowful thoughts, the very sight of Joe Stone, whom he met coming up the hill, would have answered that lament.

Joe's step was light, and his open, honest face wore a look of conscious strength and power. Why, Joe had money in the savings bank! Joe read the newspapers! Surely that summer's work, broken and interrupted, had not been without results.

Mr. Harrison stopped in his walk to speak to the boy, with an enquiry as to how they were getting along at home, then said:

"Can you meet me at the lunch-rooms at half-past seven? I have a plan which I want to talk over with you."

Joe's eyes danced! Invited to lunch with Mr. Harrison! Could ever greater honor come to him?

"Thank you, sir, I'll be there."

Six months ago Joe would have wriggled and twisted, not knowing what to say, and perhaps ended by running away altogether.

"And you may bring your friend Dan with you."

"Thank you," said Joe, again, his eyes having another sparkle in them. Wouldn't Dan be glad!

Now Perry walked on with quicker step. Coming in contact with the bright, active boy had put new vigor into him. Partly that, and partly that he was now in a hurry. The appointment he had just made was a step toward carrying out a plan which came next in order as he and Una had talked it over months ago. Now there were other people to be seen before evening.

Going home to order his carriage, he found Eleanor was taking her nap, so that he could not carry out his intention of repeating his invitation to ride, for he well knew that it must be a very urgent matter that would reconcile Eleanor to being disturbed in her afternoon nap. So he went off without her, leaving a message with Mollie to the effect that he might not be at home to tea.

As may be imagined, the delivery of this message did not tend to increase Mrs. Eleanor's good humor. She was too proud to display her temper before the servants, but in a letter to her mother she poured out the vials of her wrath.

The days went by, filled with work done in furtherance of the designs he had formed for the help of the village people. There were new books and papers for the reading-room; the course of lectures; and, what interested the boys, the plan for a lyceum. To be sure Dan Baker said, with the most puzzled look imaginable:

"What in the world is that?"

But, when explained to him, he was eager and interested, and soon grew to use the word as glibly as any one. Perry sometimes thought it was the greatest undertaking of all, and feared that it would amount to the least. But, looking forward into the coming years, and seeing the growth of the crude efforts of Joe and Dan, and all the rest, he took courage, believing he saw promise of an ability to a development which he was making.

But the long letters which he had promised *himself*, as well as his mother, these were being crowded out. Not with the outside duties which he had taken upon himself, but by the constant demands made upon his time and strength whenever he came into the house. His wife claimed his every moment. No sooner did he seat himself in the library, and get as far as "My Dear Mother," than Eleanor would appear with some request, which, however trifling, must have immediate attention. Perhaps she only wanted to send a message down stairs to the cook, sweetly adding :

"Perry, if you would only have some bells put up in this old shell, as well as some other modern conveniences, it would seem more like living."

And when he returned she wanted a yard of ribbon, and Mollie was so very busy, would he just go down and get it right away? Then, would he read aloud? Or, if his throat was unusually bad, she insisted upon his listening while she read one of her favorite authors, which were scarcely to the taste of a scholarly man.

To his, "Now, Eleanor, I must finish that letter; mother will be anxious to hear from us," she would reply :

"Oh, let the letter wait; no news is good news; one day won't make any difference; and this book must be returned to-morrow. Now, do listen"—he still insisting he ought to write—"Oh, now, Perry, you are positively unkind. You know I never enjoy anything alone. I should think you would have some consideration for me. Your mother has some one whose sole business is to amuse her. But, of course, I am but a second person in your thoughts."

"Now, Eleanor," said her husband, "don't be foolish. That sounds a little like the complaint of a spoiled child."

And, resigning himself like a martyr, he laid aside his pen and gave up the afternoon to the whim of the woman who, because of her selfishness, was burdening his life."

"Never mind," he said, "I can write to-night," never suspecting that the woman had already planned to fill up that also.

"I had a note from Miss Wilbur this morning," she said, as they were at tea. "You were not here, so I took it upon myself to decide the question. She wants us to spend the evening there, and I sent word we would do so."

And so to the Wilburs they went. And the next day it was a trip to the city, and so on, day after day, there was always something to keep him out of his study, and prevent him from writing only short, hurried letters to his mother:

This is what Eleanor Harrison said in a letter to *her* mother:

"Now we have got rid of those two women perhaps I can have my husband to myself. As for his writing long letters to his mother, to be read by that girl, I won't have it! It is just as bad as it would be to write to her, and I won't have that! Perry's mother is just the one to help it along. I will see if I can't play a little against them. I will keep Perry so busy that he shall not have time for writing sentimental letters. Those two simpletons shall not carry their point that way. They will make a fool of Perry if I do not prevent it. Why, I actually believe that girl fancies Perry thinks he has made a mistake in marrying me! I should think his devotion to his wife would convince her of her blunder. Why, he actually gave up going to New York as an escort for his mother because he fancied that I would miss him. They all made a great fuss about his want of affection for his poor, dying mother. But it had no sort of effect upon him, and he staid behind in spite of them. I will say, I have the most devoted husband in the world; that is, so far as his throat and his mustard-plasters will let him be. And now that they are out of the way, I fancy I shall be able to manage him and the mustard, too. It is all nonsense, this petting and dosing. A little vigorous letting alone, when he gets in one of his down spells, will be better than mustard. I am going to take matters into my own hands. And as for his writing long letters for that girl to read, he shall not do it—not if I can help it."

18.

EUNICE'S LETTER TO PERRY AND ELEANOR.

NEW YORK, May 13, 18—.

Dear Friends at Home:

You two people ought to write oftener to your mother. I know you have a great many cares in that bustling place, with a large family to look after, and all that sort of thing! But, for all that, you shouldn't neglect your mother. Her poor drawn face quivered pitifully when I had to tell her there was no letter to-day; and yesterday it was only a postal. I don't mean to be cross, but I have been feeling a little indignant at you all day. Now please reform. Your mother is better. I can see quite an improvement, and I'm sure Dr. Mason feels a good deal encouraged. If she had nothing to worry about, she would get along faster; but, Perry, I can see that she worries about you. She imagines that, because you don't write long letters to her, you are therefore not able. If you *were sick*, I am not sure but the might of her mother-love would enable her to rise up from her sick-bed and go to you. I don't believe it is a Christian duty to neglect such a mother. There, I didn't mean to say another word on that subject!

I'll tell you who is real good to her—almost like a son—your brother, Tom Haddington. Did you know he was here? He has been boarding with Aunt Ruth, by spells, all winter. That I suppose you knew, though I didn't. And he is taking quite a long spell at it now. It is a fortunate thing for your mother. He comes up to see her every day, always with a flower, or a bud, or an orange, or some sweet-smelling offering. She watches for him, and follows him wistfully with her eyes when he departs. Perhaps as much as anything, she enjoys the prayers that he offers at her bedside. He *does* pray as though he were used to it, and believed in it, and rejoiced in it; very few people pray in that way, you know. I think such praying must be helpful to one who is sick. He is very thoughtful, never forgetting to come, for a few moments, as soon as she is able to see him in the morning, and again just before her room is closed to callers at night; this, beside the bright little calls made between times. In fact, Perry, possibly your brother-in-law will usurp the place you have hitherto held in your mother's heart. How should you like that?

He is rather good to most people except me.

I hope Eleanor will forgive me for saying that about her brother; but he has been ugly to me, and I feel like having so much revenge. I'll tell you about it. He came to me last evening, and said he and Aunt Ruth had been plotting against me. They were of the opinion that I had too quiet and pleasant a time up in that sunny south room, from morning till night, with nothing to do except to be cheery to a loving and patient invalid; that I must yield my place to Aunt Ruth, for the evening, and be taken out to breathe a little of outside life, that I might be the better able to appreciate the sweetness and rest of my retreat; and considerable more high-sounding stuff. I was very willing to agree to the plan, inasmuch as your mother fancies Aunt Ruth very much, seeming to really desire her presence; and as for Aunt Ruth, she has taken one of her insane and intense fancies for the invalid, and would go down on her knees to serve her. I had a plan also, and it needed Mr. Haddington, or some other masculine, to help me carry it out. The moment he proposed my going out with him that evening, I saw my way clearly.

"Make it to-morrow evening," I said, eagerly, "and I shall be delighted. There is a place to which I very much want to go, to-morrow."

He looked so grave over that that I hastened to assure him that it was not a theatre, or any other disreputable place, that I wanted to attend, but a church.

"I want to hear Dr. Rogers," I said. "He was my father's pastor ever so many years ago; indeed, he married my father and mother, and I have always wanted to see and hear him. I noticed by the morning paper that he was to preach in Brooklyn all day to-morrow, and, if you can take me in the evening, I shall be able to please my father with an account of his sermon."

I wish you could have seen the young gentleman's face as it looked when I had ceased speaking! It was as grave and disturbed as though I had proposed marriage to him then and there.

"I'm very sorry," he began, hesitatingly, and then stopping in distress.

"Why, never mind," I hastened to say. "Of course you may have other engagements. I meant if you had no other plans I should like it; not, of *course*, if it interferes. I dare say some of the boarders will be going over, and I can accompany them."

"It isn't that," he said, instantly, as if he were afraid I would give him credit for a motive that did not exist. "The trouble lies in reaching there."

"Reaching there?" I repeated, in bewilderment. "Why, don't the ferry-boats and street-cars run as usual?"

"I presume they do," he answered, his disturbed look deepening, if anything, while Aunt Ruth, looking from one to the other of us, smiled sardonically. "But the difficulty, Miss Eunice, lies in the fact that *I* do not ride on street-cars, or ferry-boats, as a rule, on Sundays."

"In the name of common sense, why?" I asked, in downright and genuine perplexity, for this was a form of extreme religiousness with which I had never come in contact before. Of course it is because street-cars do not run in Nassau, for, even while I write, I feel instinctively that you, Perry, would be taken in the same way, was there the slightest provocation. But I didn't think of it then, and was honestly bewildered.

"Why," I protested, "how could people get to church if they didn't ride in the street-cars, at least, to say nothing of the ferry-boats?"

"As a matter of argument," he answered, composedly, "I presume I could prove to you that it is not a question of reaching *church*, but a necessity which is supposed to exist for reaching the particular church of one's choice. There are churches within easy walking distance of the majority of the people who frequent street-cars. But what if there were no other way of attending public service on the Sabbath, except by breaking one of the express commandments of the

Lord in regard to the Sabbath-day—what would it prove, Miss Una?"

But I was too much vexed with him to argue, you may be sure. Did you ever hear of such an absurdly inconvenient conscience? I wonder how such people manage to live in this wicked world? I told him he ought to be translated, and he answered, quietly, that he lived in restful expectation of that event. One dab I made at him and missed. I had heard, only the day before, that some of the very wealthy gentlemen of the city had to do with street-railroad stock, and, from a conversation that I had overheard, I imagined him to be one of them; so I said:

"I should think if it was such a wicked thing to ride on street-cars on Sunday, it would be almost as wicked to grow rich from the proceeds of other people's riding."

"In which I entirely agree with you," he said. "I can not conceive how Christian people make it seem right."

I didn't make much by that argument, you perceive; neither did I get to hear Dr. Rogers. I assured your polite brother-in-law that I could not think of allowing him to sully his conscience for *me*. But I needn't have said it in the hope that he would be mortified; instead, he simply bowed, and said:

"Of course a Christian has no right to violate

his conscience to please *anybody*," which was a polite way of saying, "Don't be disturbed, I haven't the slightest intention of going."

I attended church in the evening from sheer self-weariness, and a desire to do something; and I put down my wrath and went with Mr. Haddington, because he asked me, and because there was nothing else to do, or no other way to go. We heard what he pronounced a powerful sermon. It was about forgiving one's enemies. He proved conclusively that no one had a right to live and breathe the air of heaven who cherished enmity in his heart, or something like that. So, if you two people have any enemies, you must forgive them before you say your prayers to-night. I forgot to say the text was, "If I regard iniquity in my heart, the Lord will not hear me." Wicked people have no right to pray, it seems. That is one comfort. My conscience needn't trouble me any more for a neglect of that duty, as it is clearly not a duty for me.

There! this letter must close. I meant it to have been a long one, containing much more about your mother, but Mr. Haddington, who is sitting with her, has just called to me that she wants me, and, before I can return, it will be mail-time. So I will wait until to-morrow for further particulars. Meantime, this is far more than you deserve; and I have said nothing about my boys! I shall write to them; tell Joe Stone so. Good-by, UNA.

[FROM EUNICE'S JOURNAL.]

This evening I sent a letter to Perry, which contained a few grains of truth, swimming in a sea of deceptions. It was a wicked letter! I enjoyed every line of it. How Mrs. Eleanor will wince over my somewhat elaborate description of her aristocratic brother's attentions to poor little me, who am now nothing but a hired companion for her husband's mother, doing what a daughter and son ought to do for her. I made much of Mr. Tom Haddington; his attentions and his conscience; yet I did not say what I thought. I did not tell them that I honored the man from the very depths of my soul for his firm, grand adherence to right, or to his views of right, even when I knew very well he would do a good deal to please me. What a trial to Mrs. Eleanor. Her brother stooping to please me! I should think that to her would be almost worse than to have her husband on friendly terms with me. I didn't tell the truth about that sermon, either; it *was* a powerful one, and it was to those who are not Christians as much as to others—more so, perhaps. It made me feel strangely. I have been unable to get away from it ever since. I have always had a feeling that I could be a Christian whenever I chose, and that I certainly would be one sometime; I could not be separated from my father and mother for an eternity. Yet, now it seems to me that I never can be, not if that preacher's theories are correct; for there is one woman in this world that I have no desire to forgive, and if I had the desire I haven't the power. *I can never forgive Eleanor Harrison.* That looks *awful*, put in black and white. I did not know I was so wicked. Yet I feel in my soul that it is true. I *can not* forgive her. More than that, I can't *want* to. She has stabbed me too often and too sorely. I could forgive her slighting way of speaking to me; I could forgive her insolence in speaking of me or in writing about me, but her slow shipwreck of her husband's life, and the cold and cruel hand with which she holds him away from his mother's dying bed are acts not to be forgiven. She is his wife, and if she had been to him what she ought to have been I believe I could feel, oh so different, even though I know now, what no other soul will ever know, that she ought never to have been his wife. I am the one whom Perry ought to have married! That looks strangely, written here, before my eyes. What would become of me if other eyes than mine were ever to see it? But it is true. I could have been to him all that a wife ought to be; I could have helped him, mentally and physically; yes, and in time, spiritually. *She* never can; or, worse than that, never will. And for her utter disregard for his feelings, and aims, and aspirations, I hate her, even more than I hate her for myself. If to be a Christian means to forgive Eleanor Harrison, and to look upon her with endurance, even to *love* her, as the Bible phrases it, then I can never be a Christian, for I can never do it, *never*. It would be an easy enough thing to be a Fatalist—that is, if I knew what Fatalists are or what they believe; perhaps I know as well as they know themselves. But how is it possible for people to suppose that the little things of life are ordered by an overruling Providence, a Providence that knows the end from the beginning! Why my whole life is an utter refutation of such a theory. Why should God, if he took the trouble to care anything about me, have thrown my life in unison with Perry Harrison's from my babyhood, linking it closely with his up to the time when, without planning of mine or knowledge of mine, it had grown to be part of me—necessary, so I thought, to my very existence, and then snapped the thread, and, instead of putting the ocean or the Alps between us, setting us side by side, for me to endure insult and misery, and never be able to lift a finger to break the chain? Where is the wisdom or the love in that? Doesn't he know what I could have been to Perry Harrison? Then he knows less than an ignorant, sinful girl? Doesn't he care? Then he is not the tender God who plans all things for good. Or, caring, can not he help it? Then he is not God at all. What *can* one think? I am weary with thinking. I wish I need never do any more of it. Yet, what faith some people have! Still, when I think of it, it is the faith of people who have not been tried. After all, what does Perry Harrison know about trial? His own sickness is the extent of his trouble, and bodily sickness is not by any means so hard to bear as some other things. He has told me a dozen times that he sees the hand of love in that. What if he understood his wife as well as I understand her, instead of supposing her to be all purity and grandeur? Then there is Tom Haddington. A grand man, indeed. But why shouldn't he be? What has he had to make him otherwise? A son of fortune and of luxury, the hardest trial he knows anything about is to wait on his mother to the door of the opera, and sit in the carriage for half an hour before it closes, waiting for her, because his conscience, which really, in him at least, needs to be translated his *inclination*, will not permit him to attend. Intellectually he is above the opera, and he thinks it is his conscience. As for Mr.

Romaine, the very quiet of his face tells that the road of his life has been as smooth and level as the floor. Such people have no difficulty in believing that their lives were planned for them. But why was mine planned for me in such bitter by-ways?

Now, here is another change. Just as I was getting interested in those boys, struggling to help them—really eager to do so—making plans for their advancement, suddenly I must be taken up without plan or desire of mine, and set down here a hundred miles away from them, and put in such a position that I can do nothing to help them. The only piece of work for others that I ever undertook, from an honest desire to help along people who were nothing to me, and it is whisked out of my hands. Why? Any one can see that I was doing them good; any one can see that I was needed there. Where is the wisdom in this planning?

Oh, Eunice Taylor, what would your blessed father think of this wicked writing! He shall never see it, nor know of it, nor of the bitterness of my life! Dear, precious, self-sacrificing father! He would have planned life so smoothly for me, if he had the power. Well, meantime, I have had the exquisite pleasure of writing to Mrs. Eleanor as though I were her very sister. I have advised and scolded. I have proved the familiarity of my friendship with her brother Tom, and made her feel thoroughly and helplessly exasperated, I believe. For that bit of exquisite pleasure that has fallen to my lot, let me be thankful.

Now I must go to Mother Harrison. *She* loves me. And oh, how dearly I love her! She is Perry's mother!

19.

FROM PERRY TO HIS MOTHER.

NASSAU, Sept. 28, 18—.

My Dear Mother:

Don't, I pray, think me a forgetful or undutiful son, though my letters have not been as prompt as we could both of us wish. I have been very busy, and, while I am quite as well as usual, a little extra exertion always uses me up. What have I been doing? Very little, when I come to think it over, but someway the time has been pretty well occupied. For one thing, we have had company almost constantly. When there has been a lull, we have had to pay visits, and you know how exhausting it is to me to do much in the line of visiting. But Eleanor has so many unpaid calls on her list that it seemed best to undertake to return some of them; and she likes to draw her friends around her. Yesterday I went out in quest of a girl to take the place of Molly, who has gone away for a while; someway, she and Eleanor did not get on very well together. I suppose that Molly has lived here so long that she seems presuming sometimes to one who is a new-comer, and unaccustomed to the ways of the house. Anyway, it seemed best for the happiness of all of us that Molly should leave; and, as Una's mother is not strong, and misses her daughter's helping hands, I have arranged for Molly to stay there until you all come home; and, as I said, I was out all day yesterday trying to find a substitute. I found a stout German girl, but I think I shall not care to intrust the cleaning up of my study to her clumsy hands. When I can not stand it any longer, I can send for Molly to come over and fix me up.

So much as to domestic affairs. I am afraid that I shall make bungling work of keeping you informed as to our housekeeping successes and failures, though it may be easy to record successes! Eleanor hates housekeeping, and knows as little about the management of a house as a child. But you must not be worried. I was not altogether the loser in those years of my life that I was forbidden the use of books, and shut in from active out-door amusement. I do know considerable about household matters, and, if necessary, I am not sure that I should not be able to act as housekeeper! Do you remember the cake I made on your birthday, long ago? However, I will say that these things are not to my taste.

And, while I can truly declare that I do not rebel at the life I am compelled to lead—for I know that my time is in the Father's hands, and He makes me His instrument of work here—still there come hours when all the brightness of the career which I had marked out for myself, in my university days, spreads itself out before me, making the shadows of the present only deepen by contrast. Living in the busy world, grappling with the questions of the hour, in a hand-to-hand fight, having physical strength to match mental energy—how I should have gloried in it! It seems now, looking on from afar, that I might have done work that would tell! And yet, "He leadeth me," and I can rest in the belief that all thwarted schemes—all failures—are but God's hedging in for other purposes, and even our mistakes he will overrule for good. I think that the results of our mistakes are the hardest to bear. We can lay the blame nowhere off our own shoulders, and, put it as we will, the best we can say is, that if we had made use of the light given us, we might have seen the right. And yet God, in his wonderful mercy and love, makes use of our blunders to raise us up toward himself. We ourselves may do something in the midst of disadvantages. Sometimes splendid victories are won by the retrieval of blunders. It is a good general who organizes victory out of mistakes.

And is it not a wise man who uses his own mistakes as stepping-stones to something higher? We have seen something of this already in the working of our little enterprise here among our people. We made some errors in our planning, but out of them grew better things, and I am hopeful as to final results. Una's boys are doing finely, and, though they miss her, it may be that a little absence will only strengthen her hold upon them. Joe Stone flourished a bulky letter at me this morning, as I went down town, so I conclude that you will be in receipt of the latest news. Miss Wilbur makes a very good teacher, and she told me, last night, that it was her first taste of the luxury of helping somebody! So you see that every extremity of ours gives God an opportunity to do a new thing for us. Louise Wilbur to the front, in Christian work, will be an advance which will surely tell all along the line!

Eunice, you must not let my mother worry about me; I am really quite well. Eleanor says that she is going to burn up and throw away all the medicine in the house, and make a new man of me out of the necessity of doing without tonics, etc. What will Dr. Mason say to the new regime? If I were only rid of the troublesome pain in the side, and had a little more strength of muscle, I should be good for half a century of work. But, lest the time be short, I must be busy. We have delightful weather, and I think that we will go to Redwood, for a day or two, soon. Daisy writes that Aunt Phebe is not well, and I would like to see her again. So, if all is well, we will run up for a short visit. It will be a taste of a life quite new to Eleanor, for ours is not the real country after all. We must go farther back among these hills to find the old open fireplace, the five o'clock breakfast, and the twelve o'clock dinner, which are Eleanor's especial abhorrence. But these, with the nine o'clock bedtime, we shall find at Uncle Nathan's.

I almost wish that we were going to-day. That desire grows out of a bit of cowardice on my part. There is to be a lecture at Frasier Hall this evening, and Eleanor is anxious to hear the man, who is said to be very eloquent, but is a notorious infidel. I said to Eleanor, this morning:

"I would not go where *you* would be insulted, or my mother, much less can I go where I know that my best Friend will be blasphemed."

But every one does not see it that way, and the man's attractions, in a scientific point of view, are so great that he draws crowds, and among them are many Christian people, who mistakenly think they can walk through the slum and not be contaminated. Not even by my humble presence will I countenance such a man. And, if we were out of town, I should not have the pain of refusing to accompany my wife, as she wishes; but then, again, if I ran away, I should not have the consciousness of being perfectly straightforward.

There is the dinner-bell! Mother, forgive your boy, and don't let Tom Haddington usurp my place. God bless the boy! I know of no one with whom I would sooner share your love. Una, thank him for me, for all his kindness to her and to you.

Very lovingly, your son, and brother,

PERRY.

The letter finished, folded and ready for the mail, Perry went down to dinner. Eleanor was there before him, though she was not remarkable for promptness.

"Well," she greeted him, "I did not know but you were going to turn yourself into a letter! I hope that precious epistle, which you have spent the morning over, is not as long as your face. I declare, Perry, I am truly thankful that I am a married woman; you do write such frightfully long letters! Sometimes it would be two or three days before I reached the end of one of those you used to write to me me when I was in Europe!"

Perry laughed; perhaps it was a trifle forced, but it was his policy to understand Eleanor's sharpness as pleasantry, until he was perfectly sure it was something else.

"You are relieved from that infliction now, though it may be at the expense of a heavier one!" he said.

"I had quite a long letter from Tom this morning," said Eleanor, "and I wrote one to mother. I thought I might as well do that as anything, knowing that I should not get a glimpse of you so long as the house contained a sheet of paper. About how many quires did you use? I told mother I was writing a long letter, because I never expected to have a chance at pen or paper after this, for you had taken to sending whole reams to your mother."

Then they fell to discussing plans for the evening, and so filled up the dinner-hour. As Perry was going up-stairs, half an hour later, Eleanor said, calling after him:

"Perry, there is a letter on my dressing-table which you may like to read. Just step in and get it. I'll be up to the library by and by to talk it over."

"All right," returned Perry, passing on up the stairs, never suspecting that it might be all *wrong.*

The letter which he found was not Tom's, as he had supposed, and he even ventured to look around a little for her brother's letter; but there was only one in sight, and he concluded that Eleanor had been proposing something to her mother which she wished to discuss with her husband, so he seated himself in his library-chair and settled to the reading of what was almost as long a letter as some of his own. Parts of it ran like this:

DEAR MOTHER :— You must look after Tom! That absurd boy will ruin himself in spite of us, if we do not have a care! I declare, I thought when we got that girl off to New York with Mother Harrison we were going to have peace. But it is worse now she is there. She writes to Perry *for his mother*, and manages to put in a good deal of her own affairs. It would appear, from her story, that Tom is devoting himself to Mother Harrison with a more than filial self-abnegation, and of course he is constantly coming in contact with Miss Taylor. Mother, we must not let the boy go on so.

Here Perry smiled in spite of himself, as Tom Haddington was five years his sister's senior. Her assumption of superiority was somewhat amusing. The letter went on:

Now, mamma, I succeeded in thwarting that girl's plans once, and I will do it again; she shall not entangle my brother. I am not so devoted to my husband's family, nor to my husband, either, that I would not risk something to save Tom. There! Was that a wicked thing to say? Well, mamma dear, you know that Perry Harrison only gave me half a heart, and, although I will own that I think he did it honestly, supposing that it was all he had, and I don't think that he has found out his mistake to this day; yet I despise him for it! And I — well, I was fond of him, I suppose, in my way; but I am not one of the sort to marry for love, and I should never have married him had I known about this Miss Taylor before our engagement. But I would never have it said that another woman came between us, so I married him, rather than be the victim of a broken engagement. But it is a fact that Perry has made one grand mistake, perfect as he pretends to be — the mistake of having married a woman who knows him better than he knows himself, and who means to use that knowledge to punish him for his folly. Of course Miss Taylor owes me a grudge for supplanting her in my lord's regards, and is mortified and angry that she fails to make him hate me, and now she is going to try to spite me through Tom. I am silly to give the matter a thought, I know, and you will laugh at me; for of course Tom understands his position, and knows that he can never marry Eunice. Still, it annoys me, and I wish you would look after him a little more closely. I shall be there myself in the course of a few weeks to manage things. I am determined that I shall not stay cooped up here much longer. There is so much nonsense talked about sea air and city atmosphere being bad for Perry, and everybody is supposed to be only too willing to sacrifice themselves for his benefit. Now, I never did sacrifice myself for anybody, and I shall not begin now. And Dr. Mason—what an old humbug he is! And Mother Harrison and all the rest may hold their peace, for I will not endure this prison life forever.

Now, mamma, don't shake your head and sigh over me. I assure you that we are a model couple. I have heard it remarked, "How perfectly devoted Mr. Harrison is to his wife," and, "How adoringly the young wife looks up to her husband," and all that sort of stuff. So you see, mamma, that you need not fear any scandal. Both Perry and I will have the good sense to keep any little differences we may have quite to ourselves. Perry understands that I am not accustomed to dictation, and acts accordingly, and he *is* always ready to sacrifice himself to my whims, and I let him. It is no more than fair, having been cheated, I am going to make the most of what I have.

It is fortunate that I never formed the habit of showing my letters to my husband. This would hardly bear inspection, would it? I just wonder what would be the result if Perry *should* walk in and read over my shoulder what I have written! But he won't. He never did such a thing in his life. It is some consolation to feel that one's husband is a gentleman.

Perry Harrison had no thought, until he reached this point of the letter, that it was not intended for his eyes. It was a succession of cruel stabs, but he thought they were all meant to reach him. With them had come into his own heart such a revelation as made him turn pale and sick. That day in the library, when he listened to the heartless words of his wife spoken to Una, the truth had only half-dawned upon him. But here it was, so plain that he wondered how it was he had been so slow to gain this knowledge.

There was more of the letter, but with the conviction that it was not the right one, he folded and returned it to Eleanor's table, and in a state of bewildering thought wondered what he should say. The future was too black and heavy to look at just then, and he sat there with just this thought, What next? when Eleanor glided in, with a letter in her hand.

"Why, Perry," she said, "here's Tom's letter in my pocket! Did you hunt for it?"

"Not much; but I found one which I supposed was the one you wished me to read. It was a letter to your mother that was lying upon the table."

For a moment a look of utter consternation swept over Eleanor's face. Then quickly recovering herself, she said, laughing:

"Why, Perry! *Have* you been reading that piece of nonsense?"

"Not all of it. I concluded that it was not the one you wished me to see."

"Oh, I don't care; only I fear you did not appreciate the humor of it. Mother and I always had a way of talking and writing nonsense in a sort of tragical way to amuse each other, and as we understand it so, no harm comes of it."

"Eleanor, *I* understand it, perfectly. You need give yourself no uneasiness in regard to the matter."

With this remark, spoken in his usual tones, Perry passed out of the room, just turning back to say:

"I believe you wished to talk something over with me. I shall be at your service in an hour; or we can talk as we drive this afternoon."

Standing there where he left her, utterly dumbfounded, Eleanor thought: I wonder what would make him forget to be polite! Of this letter to her mother she was thoroughly ashamed. Not for worlds would she have him know her just as she stood revealed there. She felt that, laugh it off as she would, henceforth he knew her as she was; and that when he said, "I understand," he *did* understand.

It did not take her long to recover herself. Such people never waste time in taking up a position. Having determined upon her course, she went quietly to her room to make an elaborate toilet, for they had planned to call upon the Wilburs, and the Wilburs were people for whom even Eleanor Harrison thought it worth while to be particular.

As for Perry, now all was clear to him. The fearful mistake he had made stood up before him in all its shame and horror. And this woman whom he had made his wife, whom he had looked upon as pure and womanly, was she indeed false and wicked? Never again could he call her sarcasms and whims pleasantries. And she, for whom he would have sacrificed so much, had, with the utmost coolness, declared herself willing to sacrifice him if he stood in her way! It was an hour of fearful shame and agony—the agony of remorse—for Perry fully realized that he had not been blameless.

When Eleanor appeared, ready for the proposed

ride, she found her husband waiting upon the steps. He helped her in, took his place beside her with his usual manner. If Eleanor expected a scene, she was disappointed; but she ought to have learned by this time that her husband was not the sort of person to act in a scene.

Ten days later Perry wrote in the old journal:

The fearful revelations of the past few days have been like a succession of whirlwinds passing over my soul. At length I have settled into a calm. It can be endured, this life which I must henceforth lead. But it is a bitter thought that my own folly and wrong-doing have brought sorrow upon us all; for that Eleanor suffers I can not doubt. And Una! Oh, God, why was I so blind! Why did I not know that Eunice Taylor was more to me than this woman whom I have made my wife? For I know now that it is true that the love I gave her, calling it "brotherly," was deeper and stronger than all other loves. I know now that I must pay with my own happiness the life-long penalty of my wretched mistake. And if that were the whole of the price I could bear it. But she, too, must bear the sting of my unfaithfulness—she whom I had loved and cherished all my life, until I was bewildered and fascinated by the beautiful Eleanor. Of all wretched things in this life, can there be any worse than a loveless marriage? And this is ours! In plain words it is just *that!* God help us both!

Two days ago I wrote to mother and Una, and I remember I said something about mistakes, and what good might grow out of them. But what of the mistakes that are fatal! Will all our lives be miserable failures because of this? Our vows were "until death," and, with God's help, I will be a faithful husband; and by and by there will come peace, and then not very far away will be the end. Since I have began to see things as they are, I have said a thousand times, "Fool that I have been!" How could I ever have blundered so miserably? When I was lying so near to death, at Uncle Nathan's, it was Eunice Taylor, and not my promised wife, who came to me; it was Eunice who was so anxious to have me become a Christian; it was she who is to-day like a daughter to my mother, and who should have been my wife. But it is too late now, and the work before me is to make the best of what is; to bring, if I can, something of symmetry out of the wretched, misshapen thing that I have made of the gift which God gave me to fashion and shape into his likeness as a Christian. There is but one thing left to do, and that is to bear this burden patiently, and to help the others to bear it, making it lighter for them when I can, and, looking ever unto Christ, wait quietly for the end; not in idle waiting, but, with what strength I have, doing his work.

20.

Amidst all the apparent tangle of affairs, and apparent mistakes, and real heartaches, things moved steadily toward one accomplishment, which probably the eye of God saw, as he saw all things else; and he knew the end, and caused the wrath of man to praise him, and decreed that the mistakes should work out fruit to his praise.

Still, to those who were looking on, it *all* appeared a mistake. Eleanor Harrison, bewildered—not to say frightened—by the utter silence of her husband, and detecting in his manner toward her a certain passive endurance of her society, rather than pleasure in it, was not the least miserable of the people whose lives were woven into each other. She sent her miserable letter, not without adding to it, on the same evening of her ride with her husband, the following postscript:

"Mamma, what do you think! Perry saw my letter, after all! I wouldn't have had it occur for a thousand dollars! Not that I mean much of anything, of course, except about Tom. I'm in earnest about that, and there is real danger. The girl has a sort of fascinating way about her, that attracts just such thoughtless people as Tom, and passes for talent. But it is so horrid to have had Perry reading all this stuff! I would burn it now, instead of sending it, only I want you to see just how horrid it is, and tell me what you think. Of course I was vexed when I wrote it, that girl's letters exasperate me so! Perry is good about it, just as he is about everything. If he were not so uncomfortably good, there never would have been any trouble. I never intended to marry a saint. I wanted a comfortable sort of sinner, like myself; and Perry Harrison certainly stood very well in that character when I promised to marry him; but now I might as well be the wife of a home missionary, and be done with it!

"Now, I'm running on again, so as to have some more to repent of! Just read this letter, and tell me what you think of me—to ease your mind, you know; and then burn the letter, so that no more evil will come of it. That horrid German girl is shouting at me from the foot of the stairs! I shall teach her better than that. It was through a blunder of mine that Perry got hold of the wrong letter. He is much too perfect to have read it, except by accident.

ELEANOR."

Was it only another mistake that the silly mother, to whom a daughter dared to write such wicked letters, instead of burning it, carried it around in her pocket, sighing over it with all her heart, weeping tears occasionally over portions of it; for where her daughter was wicked, she was sometimes only weak. And at last, three weeks after she had received it and answered it, receiving no reply, and fearing she hardly knew what, suddenly drew it forth one evening, and, with a half laugh, half sigh, handed it to Tom, who had run down from New York to see how she was, with the remark:

"Here, Tom, I ought not to worry alone. See what a life Eleanor is leading, and tell me whether there is any truth in her fears that you are being entangled, too. I'm sure I hope one of my children will have sense enough not to disgrace his mother."

"What do you mean?" Tom asked, vaguely, frightened by her hints; but he took the letter, and retired with it to a side-table.

He read it slowly, carefully; and yet, pausing over, even *spelling*, every word, it could hardly have taken him as long to master the contents as he sat, holding those daintily-written sheets before his face.

"Well," his mother said, at last, speaking sharply, for his silence made her anxious. "What do you think? It surely isn't in Sanscrit, that you should be so long in deciphering it!"

"I think," he said, speaking slowly, and coming toward her as he spoke. "I think that my sister would be ashamed to have me read that letter. For the atom of self-respect that she may have left to her, I trust she need not know that I saw it. As to the rest, I hardly know what I think. I had trusted that, if Eleanor were not a Christian, she at least was an honorable woman; but it seems I was mistaken. If you want any message to her from me, mother, tell her never to dare to write Eunice Taylor's name to me, and never to let me hear of her speaking her name in any dishonorable or unwomanly way, or she will have to answer for the consequences."

And, in a white heat of anger, he strode from the room. Then, indeed, that mother cried. She wanted high-toned propriety in her daughter, and she wanted a brilliant marriage and lofty prospects for her son. And now, from his manner, she was almost certain he was getting entangled with that *Taylor* girl!

You will be able to tolerate Eleanor Harrison better, when I tell you that this mother of hers was actually as much disappointed in her son as she was in her daughter! With such a mother, what could be expected of the daughter? And yet the son was one of earth's noblemen!—no, I mistake, earth had nothing to do with it. He was one of the princes of the royal house. He was on terms of the closest intimacy with the King.

During these days, what about Eunice Taylor and her thwarted life? She made two entries in her long-suffering journal, bearing date but two days apart, and you shall read them both:

October 11, 18 —. — I have held my pen for full five minutes, I should think, in doubt whether to yield to my inclination and write here, or let the poor white page go, unmarred. Yet why should I not get rid of so much bitterness as will stick to its pages?

I am a very wicked girl. I see it more plainly than any one else possibly can, unless it is God himself; and sometimes it seems to me as though even he could not know the depths of wickedness in my heart, or he would leave no place for me on this earth.

All this I can say to myself, but I can not let any one else know it. It has to do with matters that can not be told.

Almost every evening, for the past two weeks, I have been at prayer-meeting; led there, in the first place, by the persuasion of one who seems to have such a longing for my soul that he can not let me alone; led there, afterward, by a strange sort of power, that I can neither describe nor understand—a power from which I seem unable to get away, and of which I am afraid.

They have been wonderful meetings; I never knew anything like them before. I have had a queer sort of longing that I might enjoy them for Perry. What manna they would have been to him! I can dimly imagine it. As for me, it seems to me that they have led me close to the very door of heaven, only to show me that it is barred against such as I. Instead of it being the easy thing I had always imagined it—to be a Christian—I find that, to me, it is an impossibility; and that, not from any fault in the provision, but because of the hardness of my own heart, I have been led to feel, in a measure, how great a thing it must be to have that wonderful Christ for a friend. But he is not *my* friend; he looks at me with mournful eyes, and can not accept me. There is a barred gateway between him and me, and not even he can remove the bolt.

His, "I say unto you, love your enemies," clear and emphatic as it is, just shuts me out of heaven. I can not, *can not* do it! I can not even *want* to forgive, and love. The idea of *loving* Eleanor Harrison is actually horrid to me! Almost I feel I would rather be lost, body and soul, forever, than to do it, even if I could; and

I *know* that I can't. In every possible way has she injured me, and that without the slightest provocation; even when I was trying to struggle against my worse self, trying to endure her, and to help Perry, by keeping him blind. The very effort to do it has made me despise her more; beside, it was for nothing; I did not succeed. I believe in my heart that she makes his life miserable, though he does not know her, as I do, else he would despise her too. Sometimes my heart is so awfully wicked that I long to make plain to him just what she is, and see him turn from her in scorn and loathing. I could do it; sometimes I am afraid that I shall. Almost the desire consumes me. It came to me, last evening, in meeting—came, right in the midst of a wonderful sermon, from that wonderful text: " Father, forgive them, for they know not what they do." Oh, it was sublime forgiveness! But that is just it. It was God-like, because he is God, and I am only a poor worm of dust. Beside—that *awful* beside —*she knows* what she is doing. She is setting about it deliberately, with ends to accomplish. I can never, *never* forgive her; and, while I write it, I realize fully that, by that statement, I am bolting the door of heaven against me. She can not enter there, and this is sin, awful sin, and I can not help it.

The entry closed abruptly, and Una ran down stairs, suddenly possessed with the belief that she must get away from herself and her tormenting thoughts for a little, or they would drive her wild. A strange life she was living. Trembling on the edge of a great, and, as she truly phrased it, an awful decision. Deliberately turning away from the loving, forgiving Saviour, and refusing to forgive a frail sinner like herself. The hardness of her heart amazed herself. There were anxious hearts in the house for her. Mr. Romaine had said all he dared to her; but he constantly presented her before his Elder Brother, pleading for her soul. Tom Haddington had a consuming anxiety for her that almost unnerved him. He could not help but see that she was passing through what might be the solemn turning point of her life. For all he could know, the Lord, who was knocking so loudly and so patiently at the door of her heart, might pass by, and never knock again. He knew there was some strange obstacle in the way, he could not conceive what. He could not help in any way, and he was overwhelmed with the sense of pain and responsibility. He wrote to Perry, but he had received only a constrained and bewildering answer. Since that view of his sister's letter, he began dimly to realize what some of the weight at her heart might be; began dimly to understand that it was something with which a third person could not meddle, and which nobody could help but God; and to God she would not go.

When she suddenly left her room to get away from herself, she went to the parlor, and there she found Tom Haddington.

"I didn't know you had returned!" she said, giving him her hand, her face lighting with pleasure. In her present sore state of heart, his persistent friendship was a salve.

"I am but just returned," he said.

And then the next sentence was utterly unpremeditated; it had been the last thing that he had meant to say:

"Una, are my sister and Perry Harrison an ill-mated pair?"

Eunice drew herself up proudly. Even his *brother* she felt had no business to question.

"You should ask him," she said, haughtily. "If you really think that is a proper question to ask, he certainly would be likely to have more definite information on that point, than ought to be expected from me."

"Don't," he said, simply; "please don't, Una; I am in sore trouble; I thought it possible you might help me."

Instantly the flush of indignation passed from Una's face, leaving it deadly pale, and the hand that she laid on his arm trembled visibly. Yet she managed to keep her voice somewhat steady.

"Is it Perry, Mr. Haddington? Is he in trouble?"

"In *awful* trouble, I'm afraid; trouble that I can not help him with—that there is no help for this side of heaven."

And then Tom Haddington did what was so strange a sight in him, that it controlled Una's terrible excitement. He dropped on the low sofa near where he stood, and wiped great hot tears from his manly eyes. There was no getting away from some revelations after that. He did not tell her about that horrible letter, he did not mention her name in the most remote way; yet, somehow, he made her plainly understand that he was deceived—and disappointed in his sister, and that the husband of her choice knew how false was the heart he had taken to his home forever.

Eager question and answer followed each other, until both suddenly felt themselves to be revealing secrets that did not belong to them. Una paused in the middle of a sentence, and the startled glance of her eyes revealed to Tom that he had been hearing words, concerning his own sister, that must overwhelm him with shame and pain.

"Poor Romaine!" he said. "If he knew of this, he would surely be amply revenged."

"What do you mean?" Una asked, startled

out of propriety again. "What can Mr. Romaine have to do with this?"

"Nothing, thank God. He, at least, has escaped."

And then again he felt that the sentence, left unexplained, compromised Mr. Romaine in a manner that was hardly right. So it was, in a few sharp, pain-fraught sentences, revealed to the amazed Una that Mr. Romaine was once a man of great wealth and high position, and was the betrothed husband of Eleanor Harrison. But he lost his fortune and his promised bride at almost the same time.

"Does Perry know of this?" Una asked, eagerly.

Tom Haddington winced.

"No, he doesn't; but so surely as I am a man of honor, he would have known it had I not firmly believed that Eleanor had utterly changed, repented, in lowliness of heart, and that her entire heart was given to Perry Harrison, and that the other was a mistake."

They were interrupted by the coming in of other boarders, and it was well that they were. Each felt that more had been said than it would have seemed possible to have said to each other about these things. Una went back to her room. She was not afraid to be alone now. Strangely enough her excitement was calmed. She was utterly stilled. It seemed to her that there had been an earthquake, awful indeed, swallowing up much that was bright and beautiful. But, for all that, the air was clearer. Two things thrilled her—in a sense, hushed her. Mr. Romaine, the man whom she had set down as one for whom life had always worn an unruffled calm, had been through dark and bitter waters, and had come out with the peace of God written on his forehead. Evidently he had forgiven Eleanor Harrison, utterly.

But there was a greater thought than that. Perry Harrison, bound by hopeless ties that only death could break, obliged to live beside, talk with, minister to, a woman utterly false, not only to him, but to her sex, and to all ideas of right and honor, was yet sustained, controlled, patient; she knew *how* patient. His letters to his mother breathed of rest and trust, and spoke always carefully, even tenderly, of Eleanor! How paltry her causes for anger looked, beside this accumulation! Strange leading she was having!

When Eleanor Harrison wrote that bitter letter, she had no conception whereunto it would lead. The Lord knew. The " wrath " of one of his professed servants was being made to praise him. Since her life would not honor him, her sin should.

It was only two days afterward that Una wrote this in her journal:

"Midnight! I have been reflecting whether or not to tear out that last page. I have concluded to leave it as my private monument to the dear Christ's enduring love. How almost blasphemous it seems! I dared to compare my wrongs with *his;* and, though I did not mean that, it seemed as though I thought my own were heavier! And yet he waited and called and coaxed, and, at last, after weary tossings and almost shipwreck, Eunice Taylor consented to enter into peace. And oh, what *peace* it is! "Bless the Lord, O my soul." Surely I can forgive and pity and love all the world. I can pray for Eleanor Harrison, miserable, misguided, unsaved woman that she is. I am sure the loving Lord pities her. I am sure he would have even her come into rest.

"A blessed thought has come to me. Perhaps He will use me as his instrument to bring her in very deed to himself. Oh, I will try for it. I don't know what I can do, but perhaps I can do *something*. They are coming here next week, Perry and she—coming for Mrs. Harrison; then we will go home. Oh, mother and father, what a heaven of a home I will try to make for you! Oh, my class of boys! I will teach as I never taught before! I presume I shall have to come down from this high state to common living. But to-night I am lifted up. The earth, and all it has, or might have, or, rather, might *have had* for me, has receded, and heaven draws near. I say to my soul: 'Soul, it is only for a little while; alone here, and with burdens to bear, not by any means so heavy as those of some others, but yet heavy. Only a little while, and then the sunshine of the Father's home.'

"'Bless the Lord, O my soul; and all that is within me, bless his holy name.'"

21.

ELEANOR TO HER MOTHER.

Dear Mother:

We have just returned from a three days' visit to some of Perry's relatives up in Vermont. We found a batch of letters awaiting our return, among them yours. Perry wanted to stay a week, but I could not endure the sort of life. I found myself in a nest of saints; Perry and Tom are bad enough, but those up there are of the Puritan stamp. Mercy! I did not draw a free breath while I was there! The only relief was a certain Aunt Jane, of whom Perry is not over fond; so I imagine it was a positive relief to get over there where I could say wicked things without feeling the reproving looks of the Puritan maiden—Priscilla ought to be her name, but they forgot themselves and called her Daisy. My! How this husband of mine reveled in religious talks and prayer-meeting talks while we were there. I did not suppose that so much could be got inside of three days. I thought that I should suffocate, but, being on good behavior, I succeeded in not shocking the Puritans more than a dozen times. It was a positive relief to get back. But your letter, and the one which Perry had from his mother, have stirred up all my wickedness. Yours was such a mixture of scoldings and pityings! And you know that I never would endure scolding, and pity rouses me to a pitch of fury. So please, mamma, don't scold and don't pity. But Mrs. Harrison's letter —or, rather, Eunice Taylor's letter—is the one that vexes me most. Perry gave it to me to read, and took himself off to sing a psalm of thanksgiving, I suppose. Such a fuss as everybody is bound to make over that girl! The letter was only remarkable for the absence of any mention of Tom's name, except a reference to something he had done for Perry's mother, and one other thing—the designing young lady announces, in a very meek way, of course, that she has, as she expresses it, "found the way of peace." Now, of course I have no objections to the girl's turning out a saint, but it is extremely inopportune. Don't you see, my dear mother, that so long as she made no pretense of saintliness, we were comparatively safe as regards Tom; but now the misguided boy will think she is an angel. There is just one bit of comfort to be got out of all the pile of letters, and that is one from Dr.

Mason, wherein he says that Perry may come after his mother next week. Propriety, having decreed that coming from New York a bride, I should not return in the space of a year, more or less, unaccompanied by my husband, will not go further, will it, and say that once there under his escort and protection, I may not stay as long as I please, if business calls him home? My newly-made saint will find she can not defy me, and once with Tom I think I can manage him. I shall take care that Perry does not see this letter, though I think it is a very good letter.

ELEANOR.

Now, by way of contrast, read this from Perry's standpoint.

NASSAU, Oct. 20, 186–.

My Dear Mother:

We have just returned from our visit at Uncle Nathan's. I would gladly have staid a week, but Eleanor was so lonely and homesick that I came away to please her. That house is like a little haven of rest. A weary soul finds there such loving care and tender leading I could scarcely tear myself away; yet, as I left no directions for letters to be forwarded, knowing Una would telegraph if you needed me, it was as well to come home. I found Una's last letter and one from Dr. Mason. I opened his first, and read the joyful news that I may have my dear mother at home again. Oh, mother, it has been so sad and lonely here ever since you went away. My heart went out to God in thanksgiving at the good news. We have already commenced our preparations, and will, I hope, be with you the first of the week. Will you please tell Aunt Ruth not to trouble herself about rooms, as Eleanor has expressed a preference for an up-town boarding-house, and there is no special reason why she should not be gratified, except what may be a selfish one, my own desire to be constantly near my mother, and my great partiality for Miss Brockton's home-like arrangements and cream biscuit.

Mr. Harrison was careful not to state what had been the reasons given by his wife for not wishing to go to Miss Brockton's. But perhaps Una understood better without the reasons being given than Perry did with them, for, be it remembered, Una was, thanks to Tom Haddington's revelations, wiser in some respects, as concerned Perry's wife, than was Perry himself.

"There's one thing, which may as well be settled in the outset," said Eleanor, as they were arranging for the trip to New York, "I am not going to stop at Miss Brockton's, and you may plan accordingly, or leave me out of the planning."

"Why, Eleanor, won't it look strangely?"

"What look strangely?"

"Why, for us to go elsewhere. Both of us have been in the habit of stopping there, and mother is there, and Tom and Una—"

Perry unintentionally coupled the two names, and this roused Eleanor almost to fury.

"Exactly! And do you think I want to stand by and see my brother made the dupe of that designing girl? Indeed I will not! I could never breathe in the same house with her. But that is not the worst of it: Miss Brockton has lowered the reputation of her house to such a degree that *I* don't care to go there."

"Eleanor, what *do* you mean?"

"Nothing; only I do not choose to be mixed up with the class of people one finds there nowadays."

"My mother, for instance?" said Perry, somewhat stiffly.

"Oh, now you need not get up on stilts! I will acknowledge that the presence of an invalid in the house would half spoil the good time I propose to have while in the city, and so long as she has her nurse we can do her no good. But, as I said, I won't be mixed up with such persons as that Mr. Romaine. I don't see why he should push himself into a first-class establishment. Miss Brockton ought to know that she will be the loser by it."

"Well, I don't know," returned Perry, with a twinkle in his eye. "It is almost two years since Mr. Romaine became a member of Miss Brockton's family, and her establishment continues full. It takes people a long time to find out into what disrepute the house has fallen!"

"Well, Perry Harrison, it makes no sort of difference how you laugh or what you say; I will *not* go to Miss Brockton's if Romaine is there. You know how I dislike him; and you knew it when you invited him here last spring. Of course I had to be decently polite in our own house. I wonder he had the audacity to come!"

"Very well," said Perry, wearily, as if the whole matter was troublesome. "Have it as you like; only remember this: I shall consider it my first duty to attend upon my mother, because she needs my care, and because her comfort is the real reason of my going to New York, and all else is a secondary consideration."

Mrs. Eleanor was forced to be satisfied with this concession, and, with much inward chafing, and some outward expressions of disgust, she set about her preparations for the visit.

"I expect a gentleman here this morning to talk over some plans for altering the arrangement of rooms, so as to accommodate mother and her attendant," said Perry one morning at the breakfast-table. His wife looked up in surprise. "Has it not occurred to you," continued Perry, "that as it is now there is no convenient place for two people below stairs?"

"I confess it had not occurred to me," returned Mrs. Harrison. "May I ask what you propose to do?"

"I do not know that my plans are practicable," replied her husband. "But I would like to do this; move the library into mother's old room, and cut a doorway between the old library and the sitting-room, and fit up those two rooms for my mother's use."

"I don't see any necessity for all that trouble," said Eleanor. "Why not let the nurse occupy the little store-room that opens out of your mother's room?"

"For several reasons. In the first place, my mother is attached to the sitting-room, and it is convenient to the dining-room; whereas, it would be too far to wheel her chair from her old room three times a day. And, besides, the little room you speak of is too small, and, being sunless, unfit for a guest."

"Do you expect that such a cumbersome thing as a wheel-chair is proper for a dining-room, asked Eleanor, in her sweetest tones.

"Certainly, when there is a *lady* in it," replied Perry, in tones which matched hers in smoothness and evenness. "I presume that it will often happen that mother will take her meals in her room, but I wish to arrange it so that she can do as she pleases in regard to the matter, and I see no other way of fixing it."

"Do you expect that Molly will be willing to undertake the task of waiting upon your mother?" asked Eleanor.

"I presume she will do it gladly, if we can not do better," returned Perry. And then he added, without any apparent hesitancy, though he fairly dreaded the effect of his words: "Of course I do not know whether or not Eunice will accept the proposition; but I have the consent of her parents that she shall continue to act the part of a daughter to my mother. It will be a life of close confinement for a young girl, but of course you will relieve her now and then."

"Don't build any hopes upon me—I was not made for a nurse," returned Eleanor. "It is my advice that you bring from New York a regularly trained nurse, instead of trusting to an inexperienced and manœuvring young girl."

"Eleanor, you are my wife, and therefore entitled to my loving consideration; but you must never again speak in that way of my friend, Miss Taylor! If my mother wishes, and Eunice will consent, she will continue her attendance, and the library will be properly fitted up for her use."

Eleanor Harrison's wits had plenty of work. For the next few hours faithfully she studied up her plans to thwart this scheme of her husband's, and to frustrate what she was pleased to term "the designs of that girl" as regarded her brother Tom. Her plan for the first developed itself in part at tea-time. She was apparently in the best of humor, and under the spell of her fascinations Perry almost forgot that there had ever been any trouble—that there had been a mistake.

"Perry," she said, sweetly, "it seems to me that we can get along without Miss Taylor, if we have Molly. I know your mother is attached to Una, but don't you think that I could win her love, and learn to care for her as tenderly?"

"Perhaps you might," replied her husband, too much surprised to think clearly, therefore the more easily duped. "Still, as you are so unused to the confinement of a sick-room, and know so little about nursing, I fear it would be too great an undertaking."

"Oh, you forget Uncle Arthur, and the years that I waited on him, and humored all his whims! Dear me! What haven't I endured from him?"

"We might get along," said Perry, thoughtfully. "Still, I am inclined to think that Una knows my mother's ways so well, and is so used to her in her present state, that it will be best to carry out my plan if we can, at least for a time, until you and I take some lessons," he said, smiling.

"Well, perhaps so," returned Eleanor. "But I am in earnest; and you won't mind, will you, if I ask your mother to let me be her nurse? I really think I ought."

To go back to Perry's letter, from which we have digressed. It went on, after discussing various family matters:

And now, dear Sister Eunice, what should have been first in my letter, comes last. But there is a song of thanksgiving in my soul, whatever my pen may write, whatever my tongue may say, and wherever my steps may tend. The sister and confidant of my boyhood, the friend and helper of these later years, has taken up the new song, even the song of salvation! And there is a little house down the street where there is rejoicing. As your father led in the prayer-meeting last evening his voice had in it such a triumphant ring that everybody must have been lifted up above fears and distractions. My joy had so overmastered me, choking my voice, that his strong, clear utterance astonished me; and sitting there listening to him, I learned something of the visible effects of the exaltation of a pure soul whose faith in all these years has never failed nor faltered. But, as I shall see you both soon, I will not write more. We expect now to remain about a week. Eleanor did think of staying longer, but a new idea, which she wants to work out, has brought about a change in her plans, and I presume we shall all return together at the end of a week.

PERRY.

Little did the unsuspecting Perry know of the ideas which Eleanor was trying to work out!

[FROM PERRY'S JOURNAL.]

October 20. — I have been trying to write to mother and Una, but I have found it impossible to put into the letter anything of my real feelings. I am afraid the letter will seem strangely cold; but how could I say more, when my soul is so stirred? It has taken all my strength to quell the tumult which has been raging within me during the last three days. It is well that we did not go immediately to the city. I shall have time to get used to the new state of affairs —to put down the rebellion of my heart. I thought I had conquered myself, but sometimes there comes a fearful realization of my wretched mistake, and all the hard battle has to be fought over! No, not so; thank God there are some things forever settled! All the wretched doubts of God's goodness and overruling providence, all darkness as to the path of duty, are swept away —swallowed up in the sea of infinite love and light. But the *pain* and weariness, that sometimes is a sharp agony, these are not yet conquered. It seems a strange providence that has so interwoven our lives—lives which, it would seem to us, ought to run far apart. But my mother can not do without her son, neither can she be quite comfortable without her who should have been her daughter; and I see no way but this which I have proposed, unless Eleanor's newly-developed love and tenderness for my mother shall ripen into the fruit of careful nursing.

But what a Christian Una will make, bringing the activity of her old life into Christian life! When her earnestness becomes Christian earnestness, her zeal Christian zeal, her tenderness and love Christian tenderness and love, all the noble developments of her character consecrated, will make her a rarely-beautiful example of perfect Christian womanhood!

While it only needed this to make the wretchedness of my fatal mistake stand out in all its horrible proportions, and mock me with a vision of joys that might have been, yet, in my soul there is rejoicing. I write truly when I say that, above and beyond all, I rejoice that another soul is redeemed from the bondage of sin. I see stretching out a long line of work, right here in Nassau. Those boys! *Now* she can work for them! She will be a power here—in the evening school, in the Church and Sunday-school, and everywhere. Nassau could not do without Una Taylor now!

Thank God that my poor blundering life has not turned her heart against Christ, as I sometimes feared. Indeed, so greatly has this thought oppressed me that I could not speak to her, nor do anything to put others in the way of helping her. But God be praised! he has not needed me in the work! And now may he do for her abundantly out of the riches of his grace! And oh, my God, help thou thy servant!

Then, a day later, this record:

"There *is* 'a peace that passeth all understanding!'"

22.

The different elements composing the lives that at present are woven into each other, met next in New York. Not, indeed, in the same house, by reason of Mrs. Perry Harrison's determination not to be trammeled by the "first-class fanatics who congregated there." A mixture of motives led her husband to yield to her in this matter. First, because she desired it, and there seemed no special reason to the contrary beyond the look of the thing; and, secondly, because his sensitive spirit began to have a shivering dread of putting his wife in contrast with the earnest lives among which he should be thrown, and realizing the impossibility of assimilating them. He had a strong, abiding determination to do his duty, well and faithfully; but he saw no reason why he should make that duty harder than was necessary. Therefore, when the first embarrassment of explanation was gotten over, he had strong satisfaction in feeling that the contrasting elements of his life were two miles away from each other; and often, when he was under the shadow of the one, he could be away from the pitying eyes of the other.

Their stay in New York was to be short, although it was the season of the year when most people were coming instead of going from the great city. Yet the invalid was so much better that she began to have an eager longing for a sight of the dear old home which had been her abiding-place for forty years, and it was judged best to gratify her. Already, however, had Mrs. Perry's newly-formed plans for deposing Una come to grief. Having boldly broached the matter herself to her mother-in-law, and by reason of that lady's inability to make herself understood having had the argument all her own way, she went to her husband with a glowing description of her success. But there were those who, by patient care, could understand the signs and the strangely-spoken sounds of the poor, twisted lips; and a little of the old spirit of the strong, self-reliant woman shone out that evening as she made her son comprehend that Eunice had *promised* to stay right beside her as long as she lived. Glad was Perry to hear this, but his wife was indignant, and attributed it to the poisonous influence of a designing girl. Meantime that girl was struggling with her newly-acquired sense of right and duty, and the undisciplined heart that rebelled fiercely against the covert sneers and open insults of her beautiful enemy whenever they came in contact. This was often; oftener, indeed, than Perry had planned: for, by reason of her determination to watch over and save her brother, his wife was willing and eager to accompany him.

They were together one evening in the back parlor, which was indeed a sort of family sitting-room, where none but the special favorites among Miss Brockton's boarders were invited to enter. There were present Perry and his wife, Mr. Romaine, Tom Haddington and Eunice Taylor. Miss Brockton had volunteered her services to care for the invalid, and give Una a breath of rest. Which arrangement was specially gratifying to Una, from the fact that Mrs. Harrison continued to exert a sort of spell over the somewhat fierce nature of Aunt Ruth, from which much was hoped. Already had the genius of the Christian religion begun to influence Una's acts. Having found a wonderful and ever-present Friend, she began to desire that others might be drawn to him; among them Aunt Ruth, for who needed him more than that lonely old woman?

"This rain interferes with many apparently very nice plans," Tom Haddington was saying. "Our time is growing so short it hardly seems as though we could spare an evening."

"Why, Tom," said his sister, " do you mean to have the end of the world come right away, that you talk about there being so little time?"

"I was referring to our friends," Tom said, coldly. He always spoke coldly to his sister nowadays. Then he turned to Una:

"I wanted to take you to the Ninth Street prayer-meeting this evening. It is a young people's meeting, and it is conducted on a somewhat novel plan. I fancy it might have answered some of the questions that are troubling you in reference to 'those boys' of yours."

"Oh, then, I wish I might have gone," said Una, eagerly. "Those boys do trouble me. I mean I can't plan how to interest them in things that I specially desire to help them with now."

The tone of familiar friendliness with which she addressed the elegant Mr. Haddington, without a touch of reserve in it, and apparently without the slightest sense of having been specially honored by his notice, stung his proud sister in a way that none of those present could understand, by reason of their having been educated on a different plane from herself. She spoke in her most supercilious tone:

"Really, Miss Taylor, I shouldn't think the boys in that evening school need trouble *you*. As a regularly employed attendant on a sick woman I should think you could have little time to devote to their interests. Your duties will be likely to keep you very closely employed. I was thinking yesterday that mother would need some plain sewing this fall, and it will be just the thing to occupy you in the long evenings. I shall set about arranging as soon as we reach home. If I have really to settle down in the country, and be the mistress of the establishment, I may as well plan for the interests of all concerned. So I am quite convinced, Miss Taylor, that since you are to be under my jurisdiction I can keep you busy without reference to those boys."

It was a long sentence, told off rapidly and with distinct design toward one object, the opening of Tom Haddington's blinded eyes to the fact that he was actually giving a good deal of thought to a girl who occupied the position of servant in *her* family and was subject to *her* orders. That it showed very little knowledge of her brother's nature is not to be wondered at. People who all the time think from such totally different standpoints as that brother and sister occupied, can hardly be expected to understand each other. As for Una, she thought of it afterward, how strange it was, that the strongest feeling in her heart at the moment was pity for Perry Harrison. And truly he was to be pitied! What was he to do? How shield his wife, and at the same time not insult his friend? Mr. Romaine turned flashing eyes of inquiry on him, and Tom Haddington's face was working strangely. Perry gave them little time, however, for thought. His voice was low and clear:

"Una, I beg you will forgive my wife. She is a new-comer among us, comparatively, and can not understand the relations that have always existed. She does not know that you are the dear and honored friend, not only of my mother, but myself, and that we all understand the position you occupy to be one which you take out of pity for one who has always loved you like a mother, and who clings to you in a way that can not be put off. That *I* thank you for it, in a way that words will not express, I think you know."

Then Eunice found her voice again.

"What nonsense!" she said, gaily. "Mrs. Harrison knows I'm doing my best to take care of her mother, and that I do it for pay—hard, unromantic dollars—and heartily enjoy the creature comforts that can be bought with them. Of course I acknowledge my obligations to her as mistress of the house, and am as ready as possible to do anything that I can to help in any way."

But Perry was not through. He did not smile, did not even glance gratefully toward Una.

Truth to tell, just then he could not have trusted himself to do so. He had more to say. His voice was still low, but with a sort of ring in it that meant unalterable decision:

"Eleanor, you are to understand from this time forth that the position which Miss Taylor occupies in our house is that of a guest of my mother. She is under no control save that of her own unselfish heart. She is at all times to be deferred to, and planned for, and treated as my mother's guest. Moreover, it is my mother's house, not mine, and I believe that my mother's desire is that you shall not be troubled with the management of affairs, but that Miss Taylor shall select such helpers as she needs, and arrange the affairs of the house to suit herself. Of course we are at liberty to board elsewhere, if we so desire, and I am not sure but it would be the best arrangement we could make: but that we need not discuss now, only I see it is necessary to make plain to you what I thought you understood, that the home is mine only through the courtesy of my mother."

"Dear me!" said Mrs. Perry Harrison. "Then Eunice is housekeeper, is she? That *is* a notch higher in the estimation of some people, though I never could understand what difference it made," which was her way of admitting to herself that she was foiled.

Una wrote this in her diary the next evening, not that same one :

I can pray for her; I can do it with all my heart. Last night I was burning with anger; not so much for her treatment of me, because she overreached herself—she went so far that it was absurd—but because she so disgraced her husband, and that, too, before her brother. How could she do it! I felt then as if she were so far beneath me as a woman that I could not even pray for her. But to-day it is different. I have been reading two wonderful verses—just two—out of the Bible. It is all my heart had room for this day. First is that far-reaching-one: "Forbearing one another, and forgiving one another; even as Christ forgave you, so also do ye." That, in itself, settles all feelings of wrath and indignation, even all feeling of heart-burning. But I did not realize how strangely wonderful that forgiveness of the Lord was, till I turned to the reference in Isaiah, and behold it read: "I gave my back to the smiters, and my cheeks to them that plucked off the hair. I hid not my face from shame and spitting." Over that verse I cried great, hot, burning tears; and all the hardness of my wicked heart seemed to weep itself out in those tears. After that I could and did pray for Eleanor Harrison with all my soul. And I have a feeling that the cry went up, even unto heaven. How plainly I see now why I was led as I was; why I had to leave my poor little half-work, down there in Nassau, that I mourned over so much, and come here. I came to find my Christ, my pardon, my peace. I came to find how to work and how to live; for I will confess to you, Journal, that living was getting to be very wretched business to me. Now I feel as though it could be borne, and as though I could do good, strong, cheerful work in the name of my Lord. A real, intense life of joy from the human side is evidently *not* to be mine. Instead, I have *peace*, and the Lord can use me where he may. Perhaps, after all, peace is higher than joy. Day after to-morrow we are going home.

It was the morning before the Harrison party were to start for home, leaving Mrs. Perry behind them, she having changed her plans and determined to make a long visit in the city. This was not in accordance with her husband's wishes, for he distrusted her, and shrank from himself; and yet he could find, as yet, no way to controvert it. He neither could nor would stay himself, having resolved that duty to his mother demanded that he should see her as carefully and comfortably arranged as possible. He stood looking from the side window of Miss Brockton's back parlor, gloomily contemplating the rows of brick and stone that shut out earth and sky. Looking at them, but not thinking of them at all, he was, as usual, thinking of his wife. Her last determined plan had been to attend the private hop given by an old acquaintance, and her last defeat had been the utter refusal of her husband to accompany her. He could not see that even duty to his wife led him to countenance all the plans that he knew were in order for the evening. His brother-in-law came into the room, and presently joined him at the window. Both gentlemen remained utterly silent for several minutes. At last Perry spoke:

"Tom, have you any influence over Eleanor?"

"Not enough to keep her from dishonoring her family to-night," her brother answered, bitterly.

"Then you have heard of her plans? Did she tell you?"

"Mother did. Mother thinks that both you and I are wickedly obstinate. She doesn't know how to account for the change in *me;* and yet she is a Christian, Perry, and so is Eleanor. What makes the difference in people?"

To this Perry made no sort of answer, unless the perplexed "thinking-aloud" tone in which he said, "I don't know what to do," could be called an answer.

"It is ridiculous!" said Tom, warming into vexation. "I wonder that Eleanor's sense of propriety doesn't deter her. In our circle, at least, young wives have not been in the habit of attending such places without their husbands. Perry, has it never occurred to you that Una Taylor has a singularly quick brain? Possibly she might have a plan."

Perry winced visibly.

"I can't appeal to Miss Taylor for help!" he said; and then he went abruptly from the window and the room.

Yet help was coming. Not through Miss Taylor; not, at least, in any way she had planned or prayed for. But it was decreed that Mrs. Eleanor Harrison should not make public the difference of views between her husband and herself by appearing at the private hop that evening. She was in her room at the Winston Place boarding-house, indulging in a survey of some of the most bewildering of her toilets, deciding for the evening, when there came an imperative ring at the door, that instantly seemed to her to have somewhat to do with her. She opened the door and found herself asked for, and in a few moments more was reading the following note:

"Let the bearer of this bring you to mother's room as rapidly as possible.   PERRY."

In a very startled and somewhat subdued way she obeyed the summons, being quite rapid for her, but not so rapid that *one* did not reach there before her. She found the whole house in confusion—servants running hither and thither, some of them crying; her husband locked in Tom's room, refusing for the moment to see even her; Una pale and quiet, trying to collect her thoughts and give much-needed orders; and on the bed, in "mother's room," a pale, cold form, with a smile of angelic sweetness hovering over her lips, that had already lost their drawn, earth-pained look, and spoke of infinite release.

Even Mrs. Perry Harrison saw the impropriety of attending a hop that evening! Yet she was not greatly changed. It takes more than death to change the life-currents of a soul. The very next evening, as the sad company were carrying out their programme of going home with mother (a programme not changed, save that the mother for whose comfort they had so tenderly planned traveled apart from them in the ice-car), Mrs. Perry Harrison said, speaking in a low tone to her brother, and yet not sufficiently low that Una did not distinctly hear every word:

"Tom, what is the use in having that Taylor girl in the drawing-room car? There is plenty of room in the other cars, and her occupation is gone now. I don't see any need of her being crowded in as one of us."

If she had wanted to help her brother along in his march toward one consuming desire, she could not have planned better. He gave her a withering look from under his heavy eyelashes, and then, instantly deserting her, turned to Una.

"Miss Una, take this chair; it will be better shielded from the smoke when the window is raised. Perry, on the whole, I think I will go up with you. I may be of service to you in some way." Then he seated himself in the chair next to Una's, and wheeled it around so that he could have a full view of her face, and a fair chance for conversation.

"I am very glad," Perry said, simply.

As for Mrs. Perry, she was very angry, and turned her back not only on them, but her husband; which he, poor motherless, worse than wifeless, sore-hearted man, cared little for. Indeed, it was, in a sense, a relief. He had had deeper wounds from her than that.

There were times when he shuddered over the feeling that if she would but turn her back on him forever, so far away that a watching world, and, what was infinitely worse, a watching conscience, would excuse him from ever going after her again, it would be almost heaven to him. Is there any help for a soul when marriage vows have become such galling chains as that?

23.

It was evening when they reached Nassau—a dark, rainy evening, toward the middle of November; and can any one conceive of anything more dreary than a November rain? All the afternoon the heavy rain-drops had splashed against the car-window with a dull, aching sound, and with the darkening of the day Perry's grief seemed to grow heavier, until it became almost unbearable. It was such a different home-coming from that which they had planned. The contrast was almost crushing. Instead of the precious mother, living, to care for, with the hope of her further restoration, there was only the worn-out body to lay away beside the husband of her youth. Sometimes, during that long, dreary ride, it seemed as if he could not bear it, and an unuttered wail went up to heaven, a cry for release from the thraldrom of life—a thraldrom which it seemed to him could only end in death. He sat near his wife, attentive to all her wants, but never speaking except when necessary.

Mr. Haddington and Una carried on a low,

serious conversation, which angered Eleanor, because of the familiarity which its tone evinced.

The Harrison carriage was waiting for them at the depot. Una allowed herself to be placed therein, though Eleanor plainly intimated that some one ought to be there to walk home with her.

In her feverish anxiety to be at home, Una peered out into the darkness for a first glimpse of the house, and presently said, in a low tone:

"Mr. Haddington, I think we must have passed my home, though I can not discover any light. Won't you speak to Thomas?"

Low as the words were spoken, Eleanor's quick ear caught them, and she roused herself to say:

"Why, to be sure! We must have passed. I presume your father and mother are sitting by the kitchen fire, and that is the reason we do not see the light. It is quite chilly." And, drawing her wraps closely about her, she added: "Perry, Miss Taylor wants to stop at home, of course. It can't be far back to the house. She may as well get out here, and save Thomas the trouble of driving back."

Perry leaned forward and spoke to Eunice.

"You promised to stay beside her to the end. There will be some things to do in the morning, and she would have wished it to be your hands that should linger about her at the last. I thought you would stay by us until all is over, so I ordered your trunks sent up with the rest."

So Una put aside the intense longing to see her father and mother at once, and prepared to bear for a little while longer the sneers and slights of the haughty Eleanor. But as they stopped, and the lights shone out, she saw, with a glad bound in her heart, her father coming down the steps ready to lift her from the carriage. Giving her a glad but quiet greeting, he whispered:

"Your mother is in the dining-room."

Mrs. Taylor explained that they had come over in accordance with a telegram from Perry, to see that everything was in order for their return.

Eleanor was indignant.

"Just think," she said, "the whole Taylor family quartered upon us! The way *some* people presume to make themselves familiar is insufferable!"

It was at this juncture that Tom found one of his opportunities of being "of use" to Perry, in hiding from the notice of others the disturbance which Eleanor was inclined to make, and which, but for his management, must have been seen and heard by everybody in the house.

Perry, worn out by fatigue and sorrow, was persuaded to leave everything to his friend, and take some rest; and his wife, silenced by a few decided words which Tom felt called upon to speak, concluded to follow his example.

Poor Eleanor! She felt that she was being defeated. Her plans for putting down "that girl" had failed in every instance. Not because Una would not be put down, but because she was so intrenched in the love and respect of her friends, and her own determination to act up to the promptings of her conscience, that she could not be affected by Eleanor's cruelly-aimed blows. And Mrs. Perry was forced to acknowledge to herself that her sarcasms had not the slightest effect upon Tom. She had planned for Una's discomfiture, and, behold, her scheme became a bridge upon which Tom walked over hindrances straight to Una's side. Plainly she must adopt some new line of procedure. One thing was certain—her brother should *never* marry that Taylor girl if by *any means* she could prevent it! Eunice should not triumph over her in that way! Ah, if she could have known how far from Eunice Taylor's heart was any thought of triumphing over her enemy. If she could have believed that in these days, when her own heart was so full of hatred, that the despised friend was praying for her, was sending up to heaven agonizing prayers that into her heart and life might come that peace which so filled the days and nights of the petitioner; if she could have known this, what would have been the effect upon her own undisciplined heart?

The next morning Una was standing alone beside the cold form which in life had been so dear to her, when Eleanor came into the room. Speaking in her sweetest tones, she said:

"I wanted to consult you about a little matter. I suppose that here in the country it is customary for *all* the family to go to the cemetery. Of course in the city it is different. I should not think of it, but my brother thinks I ought. But what I wanted to say is this: I presume there will be quite a number of the relatives and family friends who will return here to dinner, as many of them have to ride some distance, and will need some refreshment, would you be willing to see that dinner is prepared and served at five o'clock?"

"Certainly I should be *willing*," replied Una, "but I think that Molly has received instructions from Mr. Harrison in regard to that."

"Yes, I know. Of course Molly will do most of the work; but you understand that it will be necessary to have some responsible and competent person to take the oversight of things after we are gone, and it occurred to me because of your position in the family heretofore you would be the proper person."

"Certainly," replied Una, with paling cheeks.

"I am at your service; command me in any way you choose."

If Eunice Taylor had spoken the thought that was in her heart she would have said, "Who has the best *right* to follow this cold clay to its last resting-place, this woman who has no love for her, who, because she is her son's wife, usurps the place, or I, who loved her only next to my own blessed mother, and whom she loved, I verily believe, as she did no other woman on earth?" And bitter, burning tears fell, which were not all for the loss of her friend. But this last scheme of Eleanor's was doomed to failure, and that through Mr. Haddington's thoughtfulness.

"Perry," he said, in Eleanor's presence, "I think that Miss Taylor should have a place among us this afternoon. Your mother had no more devoted friend."

"Why, of course," replied Perry, "It had not occurred to me that it was necessary to speak of the matter. She is *one of us*, assuredly."

"So I told her; but she had an idea that she would be needed to look after things down stairs."

"What could have put that into her head? I told her this morning that Molly could attend to everything. The love between those two was like that between mother and daughter, and no daughter could have been more faithful."

To the outside world it was but natural that when they gathered for the last sad and solemn rites of burial, Eunice Taylor should have a place among the relatives and dearest friends. Indeed, it would have been a cause of wonderment and remark had it been otherwise; for everybody knew the intimate relations which she sustained in the family, and none knew of the fires that were raging under the calm, outside life that was being lived by those who were apparently as one family, mourning the loss of one dear to each.

Tom found himself so useful to Perry that he had remained, and even after the funeral he had staid on, scarce knowing why, only that Perry wished it. They were sitting together, Perry, his wife and Tom, Una having gone home, feeling that her work in that house was now over; that henceforth she would have little occasion to go over to the Harrison mansion. "That chapter of my life is over and ended," she said to herself. "Someway, it seems as if everything were over. I don't know how I can take up the thread of a new chapter, I am so tired."

"But Eleanor was saying:

"Perry, I suppose we ought to give Miss Taylor something, in consideration of her services. Of course she has received compensation for her work; still I think they will expect something more." As her husband did not reply immediately, she said, "Don't you agree with me?"

Then he roused himself to say:

"In some things I do, and in some I do not. Miss Taylor's work was a work of love; no money would have induced her to endure all she has suffered had she not loved my mother; and she would have done it without pay, if that had been possible, so that I do not agree with you in thinking that she expects anything more. But if you mean that we owe her a debt of gratitude which we can never pay, there I agree with you, and certainly think that a token of our appreciation of the good she has done us would not be out of place."

"Well, I suppose that is only another way of putting it," returned Eleanor. "I am more practical, but it amounts to the same."

Tom Haddington thought it amounted to something quite different. But he said nothing, and Mrs. Eleanor went on:

"I will tell you what I was thinking of. You see it does not take me long to get down to the practical details of a plan. Would it not be well for me to select some of your mother's dresses—there are some very handsome ones—and perhaps some laces? I think Miss Taylor would prize those things more highly than anything which we might buy. There is that set of mink furs; those would do nicely for her. The reason I spoke of it now is that I heard her talking of buying a set before we left the city, and perhaps she will secure some if we do not attend to it immediately."

Had it not been for the sadness of Perry's lot and his own deep sympathy for him, Tom Haddington would have laughed outright. But as it was, he only became absorbed more deeply in studying a picture upon the wall opposite him, all the while listening for Perry's reply to this absurd speech.

"Well, Eleanor, that may be a good idea. But you and I must remember that nothing is ours. Mother's lawyer will be here in the morning, and then we shall know the contents of mother's will."

Eleanor bit her lip, and covered her discomfiture as best she could.

Just then it was not pleasant to recall certain sentences in a letter which she had that day written to her mother. These were the sentences:

"Mother Harrison's jewels are magnificent! And of course, as the daughter of the house, they will fall to me. Am I not a fortunate woman? Especially, there is a dainty enameled watch which I have always coveted, with a chain and diamond pin. And she had quantities of old laces, which will make you fairly wild when you see them, as you will, for I can assure you that I mean they shall see the light when I come into possession."

There were other matters touched upon in this letter, as in the next quotation:

"It will be very lonely here now, as the weather grows more dreary. I do not know how I shall endure it, and I do not mean to. If we can not go to New York, then I am going to persuade Perry to go to some other city and board for the winter; and if I fail in that we will have some gay friends here to spend the winter. Someway I am determined to have one more taste of pleasure before I die. Just now we are all mixed up. The Taylors have stepped in, and are running the establishment. To be sure they all went home last night after the funeral, but Mother Taylor came over this morning to help put things to rights, she said. I do hope we shall settle down to something soon. Such a disturbed life as we have led almost ever since we were married. Well, I shall miss Mother Harrison; she was a cheerful woman, and very interesting, and presided over the establishment with great dignity, though she liked to manage people and things rather more than was to my taste; but she seldom interfered with me—never, in fact, unless Perry was concerned. Then, she never seemed to remember that her son was a man grown, and capable of deciding questions for himself. Poor fellow! He is almost sick. He is so unreasonable in giving way to his grief. I have not indulged him in any conversation about his loss, for you know I have no patience with sentimental outbursts, and I think the best way is to draw him away from his sorrow as much as possible. To that end, as soon as we can make arrangements for a prolonged absence, I think we will get away from this place. Tom lingers still. He seems to be on very friendly terms with Eunice Taylor. I did not encourage his staying, but Perry has taken up the idea that the fellow is useful to him, though for the life of me I can not see what he does. But I don't think Perry Harrison could live unless he was indulged in his whims; and one can never know what new one he will take up. It would be a comfort as well as convenience if one *could* be prepared, so as to circumvent him now and then. I am almost in despair about Tom. All I can say has not the slightest effect upon him. He will persist in his fancy for the Taylor girl; but I will make one more effort to upset her plans. I think I have an item of news for her which will be something of a damper upon her. And now that Mother Harrison is gone I do not know of any conceivable excuse she can have for coming here. But there is Miss Brockton's. That woman will do all she can to help the matter along, and the next thing will be for Eunice to spend the winter there. I wish Tom would go to Europe. Can't you persuade Uncle Arthur to go to Florida, and take Tom with him? Tell Uncle, from me, that he ought not to spend another winter in this climate. Something must be done quickly."

Perry's mention of his mother's will had caused Eleanor to reflect that perhaps, after all, things might not be entirely at her disposal; and so it proved. Especially was she chagrined to hear the coveted watch disposed of in this manner:

"And to my beloved friend and adopted daughter, I bequeath my Geneva watch and chain, with a diamond pin attached."

And, besides this, there was a small legacy. Of course Eleanor thought that Mother Harrison was incapable of making a will, and they ought not to think of carrying out such absurd bequests. But she was quickly silenced by Perry, who said:

"Eleanor, if my mother had directed that every one of her possessions should be buried a hundred feet deep in the earth it should be done;

and I think that Dr. Mason's name as one of the witnesses of this document should be a sufficient evidence of her mental state at the time."

And then my Lady Eleanor set about making the best of that which she could not help; and very soon she found her opportunity to turn the matter to advantage, as she thought. Miss Wilbur came to pay a call of friendly sympathy. Eleanor, knowing that Tom was in the back parlor, took occasion to dwell upon Mother Harrison's affection for Una, and to say how very glad she was for the girl because of the money left her. "It was so opportune; it would be such a help to her in making up her bridal outfit."

To Miss Wilbur's expression of surprise at this indirect announcement, Eleanor said, with seeming confusion:

"Well, perhaps I ought not to have mentioned it. Please do not speak of it. But Mr. Harrison's Cousin Daisy pointed out the gentleman when we were in Redwood. You know Una was up there a year or two ago, and it seems that she captivated a young Redwood farmer. She has a very captivating way with her; don't you think so?"

Now, so little confidence had Tom Haddington in his sister that, if she had come to him with this story, he would not have believed it. But he said to himself, "What possible reason could she have for inventing it to tell Miss Wilbur? She could not have known that I was here. Perhaps I ought not to have staid here, but it never once occurred to me that I was committing an impropriety."

And with this thought Mr. Haddington let himself out through the side-door, and walked down street to find Perry, answering to his sister's call as he passed the front parlor that he would return with her husband. He carried with him a suspicion that he could not wholly reason away, and which rankled and gave him a most uncomfortable feeling.

But his sister was not yet through, though the next thing she did was quite unpremeditated. Miss Wilbur's call was a long one, partly because she waited to see Mr. Harrison, and while she was there Eunice came in.

"I find," she said, "that I left some of my belongings here, after our diligent search for everything."

Then she and Miss Wilbur fell into a talk about those boys, Miss Wilbur wondering if Perry would give her another class, now that Una had returned to her boys.

Just here Eleanor's evil genius helped her to a sudden thought.

"Why," she said, evincing more interest in her husband's schemes than was her wont, "I should not wonder if Perry would give you his class. Some one will have to take it when we go away."

"Why!" said Miss Wilbur, "are you going away? That is too bad! We can't let you go!"

"I do not know how long we shall be gone, nor just when we shall go," replied Eleanor. "It depends upon other people a little, as journeys do when there is a wedding in the case."

"Pray tell! who is going to be married now?" exclaimed Miss Wilbur.

"Well," and Eleanor put on an air of hesitancy which was not all assumed; she could not quite bring herself to utter a bare-faced falsehood, and was trying to word her sentence so as to make an impression, without making a false statement directly, " I suppose that my brother's engagement to Laura Myers has been talked of so long that it can scarcely be called a secret, yet it has never been publicly announced, neither am I authorized to announce it," she said, laughing.

"We understand," returned Miss Wilbur, nodding merrily to Una, who began at once to recall a thousand little things which corroberated this insinuation of Eleanor's.

Well might Eleanor Harrison, looking at it from her standpoint, congratulate herself upon her morning's work. She had not made a single false statement, and yet she had awakened suspicions which might possibly accomplish her purposes without further interference on her part. To be sure, she had a sort of disgusted feeling that she had descended very low to take such means to bring about her ends; but then she reflected that the matter was important enough to make use of any means allowable. And after all, she had only recounted some bits of gossip which, put in the right light, were likely to serve her purpose well.

Meantime the sad-hearted husband went about feeling the sorrows of his lot pressing more and more heavily upon him, until it seemed as if his very life must be crushed out. If he had hoped that his wife would be softened and subdued by the nearness with which death had come; if he had hoped for sympathy, or even her tender consideration, he had hoped in vain. Her own comfort was as usual her first thought. If her wishes were attended to, she was always the most amiable of mortals—the most fascinating of women—but the disarrangement of her plans, even though it was by the hand of death, could not be borne patiently.

The one all-absorbing thought of Eleanor Harrison's life was a thought of *self*. It is astonishing to note how this passionate love of self shuts out all consideration for others, and leads one even to dishonor. And as Perry learned more of his wife's character, the low estimate which she put upon truth and honor was to him a most painful thought. This woman, whom he had taken to his heart, believing her to be all that was pure and lovely, was willing to descend to petty persecutions, and daily exhibited traits of character from which he turned with loathing and disgust. And yet she was his wife! He would be true to his vows. This he said over and over, humbling himself before God in bitterness of soul.

No records were made in the Journal in these days of fierce trial, no words could describe what he was passing through; but this verse, written upon a slip of paper, and thrust between the leaves of his memoranda, tell wherein he found his strength:

"Though I walk through the valley and the shadow of death, I will fear no evil, for thou art with me."

24.

If anybody ever went back home after a long absence, with a vivid sense of responsibility, and a strong determination to accomplish a great deal, that person was Eunice Taylor. She had plans and schemes innumerable. Her home, her father and mother, her boys, her friends in every direction came in for a share of her planning. So much to do—so much that *she* could do. There was a sad side to it all. There was no Mother Harrison eagerly and intelligently interested in every new enterprise to talk it all over with. And Eunice did not yet realize how she should miss her, although she thought she did. But she was just now in the mood to be lifted up, even over the sadness. Her life seemed to her to be one of self-abnegation, of self-surrender, and it was fitting that this friend, too, should be given up.

I am afraid during these first days Eunice took a sort of sad pleasure in her self-sacrifice, dwelling with a certain feeling that might almost be called satisfaction, on the desolateness of the life stretching out before her. No special friend! *One* special friend lying in the grave, and one special friend further removed from her than though the grave covered him. "For then," she said to herself, drearily, "I should have the right to think about him."

And it did not seem to occur to her that certainly she was thinking about him most of the time, whether she had the right or not. Indeed, these two people, if the truth must be told, were in danger of considering themselves very interesting martyrs, and of making the most of their martyrdom in what seemed a perfectly decorous way, to be sure. It is a dangerous experience when two people deliberately agree that, though solemn and insurmountable barriers divide them from each other, they still were made, and originally intended, for each other, and that, therefore, they have the right to get what comfort they can out of the waste of life that remains.

Eunice Taylor had clearly accepted the situation. She reasoned with herself after this fashion: "If Perry were happy and at rest, I should have moral courage enough, and pride enough to make myself forget even his existence, if I chose. But he has made a frightful mistake, and now there only remains for us to do right, and get what comfort we can out of it."

So she planned for the school. She would consult Perry about this and that and the other thing, and see that matters shaped themselves just according to his taste. He should not be disappointed there at least. She found herself constantly wondering if Perry would like this and approve of that, and determining within her mind to strike out in a dozen new ways that would require his help and advice. All simple, innocent plans enough, valuable in themselves; destined, if carried out, to do a great deal of good, and destined, also, to give her almost unlimited opportunity for seeing and consulting with Perry Harrison.

So pure and innocent were all these plans; so entirely on the side of what she believed to be duty, that they did not interfere in the least with her determination to pray and watch for the change in Mrs. Harrison, that she believed would make a different woman of her; and yet, it must be confessed, that she had no more faith that the change would come, than she had that any other well-nigh impossible thing would happen to her. The promise involved in the "*Believe* that ye receive, and ye shall have," she certainly could not claim. As for Perry, his life by no means looked so bright to him as Una's did to her. He was weighed down under a heavy load of pain and sorrow. He felt, both physically and mentally, unable to cope with the dreary monster that life seemed to him to have become. He was interested, indeed, in all the plans for work, but not with that absorbed interest that he had once felt. A pall seemed to him to have dropped over everything, and constantly he had to struggle with the desire to do the only easy or inviting thing that there seemed left to do—drop all effort at self-control and self-nurture, and lie down on a sick-bed and let life drift away from him.

During these days his source of comfort and strength, humanly speaking, was found in Tom Haddington, who lingered, despite the need he felt for going, because he was anxious over his brother-in-law's state, and saw that he was helpful to him. Also, to be frank, that was not the only reason why he lingered. He was entirely frank with himself. He knew that it was pleasanter for him to stay in the vicinity of Eunice Taylor than it was to stay anywhere else in the world. The little plan about her approaching marriage with a Redwood farmer, that his sister had concocted, fell to the ground by reason of his straightforward nature. After revolving the matter for a few days, he cut it short by the frank question :

"By the way, Perry, is Miss Taylor soon to marry?"

"To marry!" repeated Perry, wheeling around on him in the library, and looking amazement, consternation and annoyance in the same second. "Who on earth would you have her marry?"

"It might not rest with me, you know," Tom answered, with heightened color. "But I heard the report, and thought you would be likely to know."

"It is utterly false," Perry said, haughtily, as if he had been personally aggrieved. And Tom, looking at him with grave, pitying eyes, said no more, and felt that he had learned more than he meant to.

Meantime Perry struggled hard against the feeling of despair, where his wife was concerned, and tried to reason himself into a braver, stronger state. Yet his prayers for her were much like Una's—hopeless and spiritless. What would the All-wise, All-pitying Lord do to help and keep these two children of his, whose lives ran so closely together and yet so far apart?

Perry had his help first, and, as was fitting, it came through the friend who was becoming so dear to him. They were talking, he and Tom, about a young man in whom Perry had, for a year past, interested himself.

"I don't know," the latter said, wearily, just at the close of the conversation, "I feel rather hopeless in regard to him. I can't think of anything that will be likely to touch him. He is in a dangerous way, and, he seems to me, to be in a very hopeless way. I confess that I am discouraged."

Tom surveyed him thoughtfully, as one who wondered whether it would be better to speak or keep silent. At last he said:

"Do you know I don't like to hear you speak in that way, my brother?"

"In what way?" Perry asked, smiling a very tender smile. Amid all the soreness of his present relations there was one bright spot in the thought that his marriage gave him a right to claim brotherhood with this young man.

"Why, that you can't think of anything that will touch that man, and that you are discouraged. It seems to me to limit the power of God. Don't you think, my brother, that God can touch his heart, if he wills to do so, and don't you think that he waits to hear your prayer in this matter, and that though he may see fit to keep you long waiting, he will assuredly answer in *his* time?"

Certainly, this was not new doctrine to Perry Harrison. Had he been questioned in regard to his belief, he would have most likely expressed his views in language very similar to that which his brother had used. Yet it suited the Lord just then to pour a sudden flood of light on this thought, insomuch that it seemed to him like a new revelation. He had no answer for Tom. He was silent for several minutes, but, when he turned his face that way again, it glowed with a brightness that of late had been entirely strange to him; even then he only said:

"Thank you."

And Tom Haddington went away feeling that the Lord had spoken words of meaning to his friend. It wasn't of the young man of whom they had been speaking that Perry thought, when left alone. It was of his wife. Had he not in his heart believed that she was hopelessly hardened and indifferent? Had not his prayers for her seemed to himself like leaden weights, dropping down into dust as soon as uttered? Had he not said to himself that he knew of nothing which could reach her? Now, suddenly, there flashed over him the remembrance of the omnipotence of the God whom he served. What mattered it that *he* did not know how to reach her? Christ did; and just then and there it came to him—the hope, nay, more than the hope, the *belief*—that Christ would have her for his own.

From that hour there was a new power for living and doing breathed into Perry Harrison's discouraged heart. As the days went on he carried out many of his plans with eagerness, and arranged for more work in every direction, and threw himself into it. But the consuming desire of his heart became the conversion of his wife. For that he prayed with all his soul;

about that he thought wherever he went, and whatever he was about. It colored all his words to her, and all his actions. He was in a constant eager state of expectation. He looked for something very surprising to come to her and rouse her. His faith had not yet reached high enough to remember that God has no need of great or surprising ways of doing things; but it had reached high enough to give him faith that, in *some* way, the work would be done. The natural result of such praying and such living followed.

What is the natural result? Well, there are several, but the one of which I now speak is the fact of the impossibility of praying daily, hourly —I might almost say constantly—for a person, without having spring up in the heart a tender, patient, unselfish feeling for that person, that shall pervade all conversation, and color all association. And when that person is a man's wife, bound to him by sacred ties that, in the sight of God, he has no right to sever, the feeling grows until it may safely be called a high and holy form of love. So, although the early passionate love that Perry Harrison believed himself to have felt for his bride had died a violent death, there came in its stead this tender, patient, persistent, unselfish love, that would not give her up, that would not turn away from, and, as far as possible, forget her, but would be, in every word and in every thought, true and patient. In short, there came to Perry the knowledge that this matter of loving is not a blind chance, as so many, even Christian, people seem to think, but that God's hand held it, and his power could manage it. I can not tell you how it rested this tossed soul to feel that even his mistakes were in his Father's keeping, and that that Father was bound in honor to bring good out of them.

Now what of Eunice? Who will help her? For truly I tell you she was in danger. She had come to that dangerous place where she believed that it was impossible to help thinking of, and planning with, Perry Harrison, in a way that it is not good for any woman to think of, and plan for, another woman's husband. The most prosaic and wearisome of all helps came to her, a blessing so utterly disguised that she wept bitter tears over it, and wondered why, and why, until her brain reeled. Into the midst of her eager working and planning came a morning when, on attempting to rise, she could only groan miserably and fall back on her pillow, with a sense of weakness and pain as new to her as it was unwelcome. So utterly unaccustomed was she to sickness that, through all the day, she patiently fought the symptoms, feeling assured that she would conquer by the next morning. And it was five long, miserable days before she succumbed to the fact that a slow, prostrating fever had her in its grasp, and she was not to get away—at least, not until it had taken time to wear out her strength and powers of endurance.

A miserable invalid was Eunice Taylor. She was willing to work; no matter how hard the drudgery, she believed her strength equal to it—at least, she stood ready to try it. But to lie still and be waited upon—to have the doctor come, and count her pulse, and look at her tongue, and give his unpalatable doses, and his more unpalatable advice—to have her mother go up and down stairs twenty times in the course of one forenoon to minister to her necessities—to have the father, whose hard life she had meant to help in so many ways, grow daily paler and more anxious over her—these required more fortitude than Eunice felt she possessed. Still it would do no good to say, "I can't." This was work from which she could not slip away, and excuse herself by an apology of unfitness. Her class had a substitute; a stout girl in the kitchen did much of her work; her plans, most of them, went on, with Perry's help; but nobody was to be found who would take her place on that bed, and stare, day after day, at the pattern of crooked lilies on the wall-paper. How could she help wondering and wondering why she was not allowed to work, just as, in her own estimation, she was ready. All this did not take place immediately after the home-coming; indeed, the bustle of the holidays was well over before Eunice found that she was sick. But the sickness—the first violence of it being spent—still lingered, in that hopeless, dreary way that so many invalids understand; no worse, and apparently no better, day after day.

All her life-long Eunice remembered the misery of those days. She saw nothing of Perry. Either his prayers, or his new hopes, had opened his eyes to the belief that it would be better for his wife, better for himself, to see as little of Eunice as possible, and what he did not know how to manage her sickness came in and managed for him. He did not forget her. His remembrance took most practical forms. The stout girl in the kitchen came by his recommendation, and was sustained by his purse, and not a day passed that substantials and delicacies did not appear at the little house across the way from the great house.

Every day he was careful to learn just how she was; but, although the days grew into weeks, and the weeks into almost two months, and Una was sitting in state in the great arm-chair that used to be *his* mother's, and had been sent over specially for her, he did not come near her. There were days, at first, when this was very bitter to Una; then there came days when she was very indignant; then there came days when she felt that he was wise and she was foolish, but that she must still continue to be foolish; that there was no help for her except in death; and she weakly and feebly prayed to die, not really meaning that, much more then she had meant some other prayers of hers, but too weak and desolate to know what she did mean. At last she happened (?) upon a sentence in an old book written many years ago, the writer of which had for years been sleeping in his kindred dust; and these were the words she read: "Shall a soul suppose that its plans and aims and prospects are all mapped out for it by the divine hand—each little thing it shall do, each little way it shall go, except that great and wonderful thing, the love of the human heart for another human heart? Shall it believe that that experience is a matter of chance? that God has nothing to do with it? that he can not control it? that, if it love unworthily, it must, therefore, continue to love unworthily through all time? no help? that, if it love unwisely, the unwisdom must continue? that, if it allow itself to love a wicked man, it must forever love that wicked man? What folly is this! Shall not He who formed the human heart be able to control and guide its passions, if that heart be but willing to submit to His guiding?"

There was more of it, but Eunice dropped the book, and lay back on her pillow and cried; not for sorrow, either, but for joy.

Here was help—a great and mighty Helper. Not unworthily was her love bestowed. But unwisely? yes, since the object of it had said of another woman: "And, forsaking all others, I will cleave only to *her*." Thus much Una had, some weeks ago, begun to realize, but she was still in the meshes of the folly that there was no help, no escape. She had not forgotten her Almighty Saviour. She still depended on him for salvation—for heaven; but she had ignored his messages: "Lo, I am with you alway," "Let not your heart be troubled," "I will give you rest." Unconsciously she had adopted the absurd platform that a love like hers was wrong, and that she must continue its victim! She never forgot that day when light broke upon her darkness. It was curious how rapidly she recovered after that! rapidly, as compared with her long days and weeks of no progress; but the work was slow enough. March, with her blustering moods, was almost passing out from them before Una appeared, wan and pale still, despite the crimson wrapper, in the little parlor, and was pronounced able to see one or two friends.

Afterward—years afterward—it struck her as a strange thing that the last person from the outside world with whom she had talked on that evening before her sickness was Tom Haddington, and the first person who opened the door eagerly on her, that first afternoon that she was down-stairs, was Tom Haddington, with a tiny bunch of hot-house violets. She remembered vividly the first words she said to him:

"I didn't know you were in town. When did you come?"

And then in the very next breath:

"How is Laura Myers?"

"I'm sure I don't know," he answered, wonderingly, to her second question. "I haven't seen her for three months, and I don't happen to remember that I have heard any one mention her name. Is she a special friend of yours? I didn't know it."

Then Una's cheeks were suddenly red; her own question began to seem so absurd to *her*. And then, feeling that she was blushing, and feeling vexed that she should, she blushed harder than ever. And Tom came and laid the sweet-smelling spring beauties in her lap, and stood before her, smiling.

25.

ELEANOR TO HER MOTHER.

Feb. —. This is our wedding anniversary, as you may remember, though, in that case, you are more thoughtful than any one in this vicinity. Indeed, people *here* have time for only one thought, and the topic which is so all-engrossing is, of course, Eunice Taylor; no other person has power to move the sluggish pulse of this quiet town. Miss Taylor is sick—has been for weeks, and it is almost amusing to see the interest which centers in that sick-room. Every hour in the day we have bulletins telling of the patient's state, and as these do not vary greatly in their report they cease to be of special interest. Seriously, I suppose the girl is quite ill, and I am not so much of a barbarian as to want to have her suffer. But I can't help thinking that some good may grow out of this confinement. If she were well we should have Tom dawdling about, and now I hope that he will get over his fancy before she gets well; and there is likely to be plenty of time, for the physician says she will not recover very speedily. And now I suppose it is true that her sickness is the result of her too close attentions upon Mother Harrison. They ought to have known better than to let a young girl take such a responsible position; but some people will do almost anything, and run almost any risk of health and life, for money. As usual, my husband is very kind, doing everything that can be done for the Taylors, and it is no more than right that he should. I understand how he feels, for she was a faithful attendant, and did more for Mother Harrison than any stranger would have done, and of course he feels he owes her a debt of gratitude. If money could pay such debts (dear me, I wish it could) she would have been paid a hundred times over. I am glad that I have not such a grateful disposition; I should not like to be forever in one's debt. But so long as Perry feels that way he will have to go on paying in installments.

Well, as I said, this is our anniversary. Perry has not spoken of it, and I will not remind him of the fact, so I presume we shall spend the day like all other days. What a year this has been! I wonder if all the years to come will be like it! I never expected to settle down into this humdrum sort of life. It might suit some women, but it is not to my taste. I suppose that Eunice

Taylor would have considered it the height of bliss to have lived in this aristocratic old house, and taken up the work which one might find to do here. On the whole, I don't know but it *was* a mistake that Perry did not marry her. I know she thinks so, and I know, too, that he *has* thought so; but of late he seems changed. If it were not for his conscience we should get on splendidly. It used to be his health; but he has outgrown that. I believe he would risk his life for me. He seems to have forgotten that he ought to be careful. Actually, I have to be careful for him! But that conscience of his is a most inconvenient article to have about one. As for managing *that*, I have given up in despair; it is altogether beyond me.

But, mamma, it is not a very pleasant thought for any woman that her husband in his inmost heart has felt that another should have had the place he has given her; and, though I believe that he is trying to put that other out of his heart and out of his thoughts, sometimes I just hate them both. And this is the worst of all, that he should have forgotten what day this is! You know that I never was sentimental over birthdays, and all that; but I believe in a proper notice of the first anniversary of one's marriage, if only for the looks of it.

Well, I am going to ride; so good-by until after dinner.

Later.—Well, mamma, I shall have to take it back! Dear me, I wonder if I shall have to take more things back! I went to drive, as I said; drove over to see Miss Wilbur, and came around by the river road, so that it was past dinner-hour when I reached home. Found Perry waiting in the dining-room.

"I am sorry you have been kept waiting," I said, just as coldly as I could speak, for I had been nursing my indignation all the morning.

"It is of no consequence," he said. "I have only just come in."

I ran up stairs, not because I cared about keeping him waiting, but because my drive had given me an appetite. But I did not come down quite as soon as I intended. On my dressing-table lay a package, addressed "To my wife," with two dates, one a year ago and the other to-day! He had not forgotten, after all! And that was why he sent Thomas into the city last night and again this morning. Then I had to dress for dinner; my driving costume would not do at all with such jewels as that box held! I just wonder what the man did with his conscience when he spent such a sum for diamonds for his wife! And, mamma, I have not seen such a look on his face for six months as he wore when I came down to dinner with them on. Now don't imagine that we rehearsed a scene. Nothing of the kind. We are not of that sort. He said, simply: "How do you like them?" and I replied, "They are magnificent! Thank you." And then we ate our dinner.

I suppose it would have been proper to have sentimentalized somewhat over the day we celebrate, but we are neither of us hypocrites enough for that. He wanted to please me, and I was pleased, and that is all there is about it. And while I am so comfortable about Tom I can not help being happy. I am sure I have all I wanted when I married Perry Harrison. I never pretended to have married for love. I wanted the name and position which he had to give, and if he chose to fancy that his love with it was something to set that off, why, I never disputed him.

This congratulatory mood in regard to her brother continued until that March day when she was surprised by his reappearance in Nassau. She sat moodily looking over the last magazine when he returned from his call upon Una. She had been roused to a pitch of fury by seeing him turn his steps in that direction an hour before, and had scolded Perry as if he were to blame, and finally driven him off to his room, where he paced the floor, not fighting the old battle over; in that old struggle he had so far won the victory that he had ceased, even in his secret heart, to think of the past as a mistake and to mourn over it. All the ruins of the past were but a foundation upon which to build anew, and the earnest, wrestling prayers of the present were for his wife. Daily he humbled himself before the Lord that his faith might rise to take hold of that infinite love which he longed to have encircle her. It seemed to him that morning that she was farther than ever away from God and from him. Seldom had she been so bitter and sarcastic in her remarks. Never had his patience been more tried; never had he come so near utter despair; and, with her taunting and even insulting remarks ringing in his ears, he could only take his position squarely upon the promises, and, resting in the certainty of their fulfillment, wait God's own time, which was nearer than he in his most exalted moments dared to hope.

Eleanor's mood was not improved by what she was able to draw from Tom as he passed through the sitting-room.

"Well," she said, "so you have come back! I began to think that you were going to spend the day! Did you and Miss Taylor settle the destiny of nations?"

"Not exactly," he replied; "we were only interested in individual destinies."

He was passing through to the next room, but she recalled him.

"Tom, it is no secret, but you may not be aware that Eunice Taylor was, and is yet for aught I know, in love with my husband, and that her illness is in a great measure owing to her disappointment. Of course it is just as well to put it that she was all worn out with the cares of last summer; but we all understand it. Now if you want to marry her you may. I have told you the truth. I presume, however, it will be all the same to you. I don't pretend to understand the code of morals which you and Perry and some other people have adopted."

"Thank you," said Tom, his face flushing, then paling. "Your warning comes too late. I do not need any information as to Miss Taylor's past history. And please to understand, Eleanor, that disparaging or insulting remarks about her will be considered as personal. And another thing do, I beg of you, take care how you speak lightly of your husband's character, even to your brother."

And he went out, leaving Eleanor angry and ashamed. For once she was thoroughly ashamed. She suddenly realized that it was no light thing to speak thus of her husband; and however much he might endure from her, spoken to him, it was a different matter when she cast suspicion on him by talking to another. She knew Tom would not tell him, but what if he had overheard! Someway, all her plans and all her hopes as well, seemed slipping away from her. Tom would marry Eunice Taylor—that was evidently a settled matter, in his own mind at least. They were all linked together against her. Someway, she felt shut out. Tom was positively cruel to her. She could not see why he need be so cross. He had not been at all as he used to be since Eunice Taylor went to New York. Of course she had prejudiced him against her. It was a hard, bitter lot; but sometime she would have her revenge out of it! Tossing her book away, she went up stairs, reappearing, an hour later, in all the magnificence of her last new toilet.

"Perry," she said at his door, "I am going to the city on the train. If you choose to drive in for me this evening you will find me at Mrs. Clarke's. Otherwise I will come back at nine o'clock."

"Why, isn't this a sudden start?"

"Somewhat. But what do you think, will you come for me?"

"Certainly, unless something occurs to prevent. I will be there at seven o'clock. Goodby."

He looked after her with a longing, wistful expression, which did not escape Tom's eyes as he stood by listening to the conversation.

"Unceremonious, I declare," he said, laughing, "when I have only a couple of days to stay!"

Perry looked grave as he turned to resume the conversation which had been broken off. He at least was enjoying his brother-in-law's visit. They dined together, and then went out to walk and talk, and so passed the afternoon.

Meantime Eleanor was trying to get away from herself, though she did not know that. She walked rapidly down the hill to the depot, and found herself too early by fifteen minutes. It was not a pleasant place in which to wait, that dingy little sitting-room. But there seemed nothing better to do, so she seated herself on one of the benches, gathering her flounced train up out of the dust, and prepared to endure the discomfort of the next quarter of an hour.

Two girls were walking about the room, with the unrest of girlhood, eagerly picking up items which might interest them for the moment. On a table in one corner was a quantity of papers and tracts. And Eleanor remembered just then that she had heard Perry and Eunice discussing the propriety of that arrangement, and she had laughed at the idea, and said it was like all the rest of their plans, pretty enough to talk about, but of no practical value. People who wanted that sort of reading would supply themselves, and others would not be caught by that bait. In their progress around the room the young girls came to this table, and, leaning over, began reading snatches from the papers. Eleanor paid little attention to them, indeed, she was not conscious of listening at all, nor did she know until afterward a single word they said; but, when she was seated in the car, these words flashed upon her. She had heard them time and again, but never did they come to her just as they did in that hour. And years afterward she could hear that fresh, young voice repeating, "Thou art tried in the balances and art found wanting." With a startling emphasis they came to her, as if spoken by an invisible voice. There was a whole sermon in the words, and never in her life had she been so affected by any sermon. Tried in the balances! Suddenly all her past life seemed thrown into the descending scale, which sunk lower and lower, and, alas, she had nothing with which to balance it! Found wanting! The words rung in her ears, until it seemed as if they were borne on the wind. She had been censuring others, while her own life was an utter blank —wanting! Overwhelmed by the thoughts which flooded her brain, she was half a mind to take the up-train and go back home from the first station. But, finally considering that she was "nervous," decided to go on.

"I declare," she said, "I stay cooped up so

much that even this little trip has all unnerved me. I shall be unfitted for going out at all at this rate."

Reaching the city, she first tried shopping as a remedy for her low spirits. But someway silks and velvets had lost their attractions. Laces were only a vexatious puzzle. And, after making a few purchases, she sought out her friend, Mrs. Clarke, hoping that in her cheery home she would get brightened up.

As she waited a few moments for that lady's appearance she said to herself: " My heart is as heavy as lead. I don't see what is the matter with me. I never was so troubled by anything as I am by that verse, and I have heard it a thousand times. Dear me, I wish I could forget it."

Mrs. Clarke was full of chatter about the things which usually interested Eleanor, but to-day she could not get rid of the weight which rested upon her heart.

Presently callers came; one lady was on her way to a religious meeting, and full of eager interest in it.

" You ought to go to the meetings," she said to Mrs. Clarke. " They are wonderful. I never heard such preaching. Yesterday afternoon the text was: 'Will a man rob God? Yet ye have robbed me. But ye may say, Wherein have we robbed thee? In tithes and offerings.' And in the evening it was: 'Thou art tried, and art found wanting.'"

Eleanor started as if she had received an electric shock. Those words again! How they followed her! The lady went on:

"You know Mrs. Gage. She has been a church-member for years; but this morning she came into the meeting and said that she had been led to look into her heart and life, and she saw that, tried by the word of God, she was found wanting, and it was now her purpose to give herself anew to Christ in a full consecration."

As the talk went on Eleanor felt as if she must stop her ears; it was distracting to her; she could not think connectedly, and she wondered how she was to get through the afternoon. And when her husband drove to the door an hour earlier than the appointed hour—full of apologies for coming so early, and explaining that there was likely to be a heavy storm—she met him with exclamations of delight, and would not listen to their hostess' urgent invitations to wait for an early tea.

"No," she whispered to Perry, "I want to get home."

"Haven't you had a pleasant time?" he asked, as they rode away.

"No; it was just horrid!"

Her tone was so strange that Perry asked, anxiously:

"Are you ill?"

"Thank you, I am perfectly well; but I think I am stupid. I guess I got chilled going down," she replied.

"Your brother and I have had a good visit," said Perry. "I tell you, Eleanor, Tom is a wonderful Christian."

"Well," she replied, almost petulantly, "it is well to have one in the family. None of the rest of us make any pretensions to being remarkable in that line. For my part, I never saw the need of making a fuss over one's religion. Mine is good enough for me."

"Oh, Eleanor!"

That was all he said in reply to her, but there was a world of tender yearning in the tone, and Eleanor felt it. And here was another thing that she could not get away from.. That was just the beginning of a fierce conflict in Eleanor Harrison's soul. Oh, the restless, weary tossings of days and nights that followed! Days and nights within which there was no rest—no light! "Found wanting!" Why, her life had been one continual nothingness—she had absolutely nothing to put against the folly and dissipations of her life, her envyings and hatreds, and all the rest of the long array of sins which all at once stood out in all their ugliness. Of the fruits of the Spirit, what had she wherewith to prove her right to the Christian name she bore? She had been so secure in her religious profession, and now thus suddenly to find it turning into a shrunken and lifeless thing, with no weight, and to have nothing to put in its place, plunged her into despair. Turn which way she would, she saw only condemnation written. She could find no rest for her weary soul. In vain she tried to occupy middle ground. She could not bring herself to a full personal consecration. To her mind that involved so much that was impossible, and she tried to make compromises with her soul. She would be more patient and gentle. She began to realize how utterly selfish she was; how unwilling she was to make sacrifices for others, while demanding of them constant yielding to her wishes, and she resolved to begin a life of unselfish devotion to others—her husband first—and then she would extend her loving ministrations to those around her. But in vain; she could not rid herself of the ringing sound of that word which followed her, and thrust itself in and spoiled everything she undertook. What was the use of doing anything, if always there be something "wanting?" What should be put in the balance? It was one morning at prayers that it came to her, in two words which Perry read. She did not remember the connection at all. Her ear caught the expression, and suddenly it all rushed upon her that here was what she needed, "*Christ's righteousness!*" With this to throw into the balance she would never be tried with that miserable result, "found wanting."

26.

A shadow darkened the doorway of the neat little back parlor where Eunice Taylor sat, sufficiently recovered now to trifle with a bit of sewing, or read a little, or take short walks around the room, as her fancy might please. She glanced up, expecting to see her mother, or perhaps Aunt Katy—a kind old friend near at hand, who had been by turns nurse, and watcher, and cook, and all the time a faithful friend during the long illness.

"Why, good afternoon," she said, slowly, an accent of surprise as well as of doubt how to receive her caller showing in her tones, for it was Mrs. Perry Harrison, in faultless afternoon toilet, standing before her.

"Come in, please," and she half arose, as if she would give her visitor a seat.

"Oh, don't get up," Eleanor said, gliding into the room, and coming close to the crimson chair. "How ill you look! No, I mean how well, compared with what one might have expected after such a long sickness. They told me you were greatly changed. How long is it since that afternoon when I saw you last? Does it seem very long to you? Oh, dear!"

To what did the exclamation apply? And what had occurred to make Mrs. Harrison nervous? Positively this was the first time that Eunice had seen her since the day before she was taken sick.

Among all the callers who had penetrated to her sick-room since she began to grow better, and among all the less intimate friends who had called since she came down stairs, Mrs. Harrison had not been counted. For the sake of the public, and the desire she had to have Perry's relations with his wife appear well before that public, Eunice had been sorry. For herself she rejoiced. In her weakened state she had dreaded meeting her persistent foe. Her cheeks grew red, and she felt nervous over meeting her this afternoon. Why had she come? Some unpleasant errand must have brought her. It did not appear for some time why she had come. She was strangely silent, lapsing into long pauses, when her face, from the grave, troubled expression that rested on it, was a study.

Eunice watched her with a puzzled air, the nervousness gradually passing off. Mrs. Harrison was somehow somewhere changed. What was it? Nothing definable, nothing tangible—a subtle, mysterious, positive something.

Breaking a longer pause than usual, which had followed an attempt to be civil and commonplace in her inquiries and expressions of sympathy, Mrs. Harrison said, suddenly:

"Eunice, suppose you wanted to begin life all over again—just as if you hadn't lived it at all, or wanted to forget that you had—how would you begin?"

What a strange question!

"Why," said Eunice, hesitating, and laughing a little, "I think I would just *begin*. I might not be able to forget, you know; but I would play that I did, and go ahead, doing the best that I could."

To herself she said: "I surely ought to be able to give advice on that point. Don't I want to begin at the beginning, and forget everything? I wonder what it is that she wants to forget?"

"But I mean," said Mrs. Harrison, and her fair face flushed a deep red, "suppose one's life had been a deception from beginning to end; suppose one had deceived one's self first, in a measure—well, yes, largely, and then had deceived others more—one's very best friend, you know—and, indeed, everybody; and suppose one were dreadfully, *awfully* sick of the life of deception and sin, where would one commence?

"Mrs. Harrison," said Una, laying down the bit of needlework she had been holding, and turning astonished eyes on her guest, "what *can* you mean?"

"I mean more than you can possibly imagine. And I don't know why I am telling you, except that it seems to me I must tell somebody. Eunice Taylor, you think you know me; and you tkink I am only a cold, selfish woman, without any heart or conscience. I'm a good deal more than that; I've choked my heart, and stifled my conscience, and my worst enemy need not have wished me a more miserable life than the one I have been leading. Now I want help. It seemed to me as though perhaps you could give it, and I have come to ask you. Once, away back, ever so many years ago, I believed I was converted. For a little while I kept up the farce of being religious, or what passed for the name; but finally I came to believe that there was nothing to it *but* name; that I had as much as anybody else, and the people who pretended to have more were hypocrites or fanatics. My mother was a church-member, and that, among other things, confirmed me in my views. Well, I wouldn't if I could go back and tell you about all my miserable life; it would make you sick again. Yet I have resolved to tell you this afternoon some things that I never meant to tell to anybody, in order that you may help me. Once I was engaged to a man whom I respected and loved.

He lost his money, through what seemed to me a piece of folly, born of religious fanaticism. He called it common honesty. We quarreled and separated. That is a long story, but I put it briefly, because I do not like to talk about it. After that I became engaged to Perry Harrison. I never loved him. I respected him, and his money, and his old name, and his education, and all that sort of thing; and I didn't believe I was doing anything so very wicked, for I thought I could make him happy enough. He was a gay young man when I knew him first, and would have been satisfied with a gay life such as I was willing to lead with him. But it all turned out so utterly different from anything that I had planned. You know what sort of man he became; but you don't know how nearly I have come to hating him for it, nor what an awful life I have lived; not realizing, either, that the awfulness was of my making. I didn't love my husband, but I resented his not loving me, and I believed myself an ill-used creature, who had a right to get what she could out of a wicked life; but I hauen't been able to get anything out of it but utter misery. I believe I have been nearer suicide than many a one who reaches that depth at last. Now, Eunice Taylor, why am I telling you all this? I have as nearly hated you as it is possible for a sane woman to hate another woman;

and yet, you see, I am coming to you for help. Don't speak yet; I have more to say. I have had an experience, lately, different from anything else in life. I have found that I never was a Christian; that there *is* Christianity; that there is a *Saviour*, and that he can and has both *saved* and forgiven me."

"Thank God!" said Eunice, in a low, awe-stricken tone.

"Thank you for that," Mrs. Harrison said. "It makes me feel that I have come to the right source for help. I believe in my soul that God sent me to you. I did not mean to tell you all the miserable story that I have been pouring out; I meant to have been utterly silent about some portions of it; but I have grown so awfully sick of deception, in all its forms, that there are times when it seems to me it would be a relief to cry the whole story out to a gaping world. Now I am coming to the place where I want your help. How much of this miserable story ought I to tell my husband? I need not tell you that I have learned to respect him as few men can be respected; and I need not assure you that I mean to try with all my soul to repair some of the misery of the past. But will it repair it, to go over those sickening details, a hundred times more sickening than you can imagine, and make clear to him where I have stood?"

For the first time since her excited story began she paused, and waited eagerly, one might almost say hungrily, for Eunice's reply. What could she say to her?

"You ask me such a sudden and such a solemn question," she said at last, "that I ought not to answer you hastily. I don't know what to say or to think. You have overwhelmed me."

"I know; you are sick, and I ought not to have come; but I couldn't help it. I'll tell you one other thing, and then the depths of my degradation will have been reached. That man, the one with whom I quarreled, and whom I sent away from me, has always been, and is to-day, the one man who is more to me than any one on earth; and, up to three days ago, I could have said than any one in heaven. I have tried to hate him; I have struggled hard; I believe I have succeeded in acting to him as though I *did* hate him. But, well, I haven't, and it is impossible. Now, is it ever going to be *possible* to get away from this feeling? And is this a thing that, in order to be true, I must confess to my husband?"

Now, Eunice began to have a glimmer of the way she had been led, and the reason why. Was it that she might help this struggling, tempted soul? Why not? But, in order to help her, she must be as frank as herself. Could she be? If she couldn't, what had the Lord Jesus a right to think of the prayers that she had offered for that soul? Her hesitation was brief.

"Eleanor," she said, leaning forward and laying her hand on Mrs. Harrison's arm, and addressing her by a name that she rarely used, "you have reached ground now where I can indeed help you. What one has experienced one's self one can know to be true. You *can* conquer that feeling; God both can and will help you. He is faithful who promised, and will not suffer you to be tempted above what you are able to bear. He can take away the love you ought not to feel. He can give you rest of soul, just where it ought to rest. Eleanor Harrison, I know, for I have been down to the very depths of that degradation of which you speak—lower down, perhaps, than you have been. I know what I am talking about, and I *know* he who made the heart can hold its loves and its hates in his hand. I wonder if you understand me? Remember, I say, I *know* it to be true."

"I understand," said Mrs. Harrison, speaking in a low tone of suppressed excitement. "I understand you fully. I thank you, and I thank God for your words. They help me as no other words could."

"As for the other question," said Eunice, strangely calmed now, the very force of her effort to say that which cost her pride so dear seemed to have hushed the tumult in her heart, "I must think of that; I may be wrong, utterly wrong. But it seems to me now that it can do no possible good to lead your husband through all the misery of such revelations. He has had enough to bear. Surely you might spare him where you could. No, I would begin right here, it seems to me. Eleanor, he knows enough. Why, you have shown him in a thousand ways that you do not love him. If you can begin to show him that you respect him, it will be dearer to him now than anything else can be ; and I feel sure that the respect that you can bestow, and that, as a Christian, you will grow to feel for him, will be a truer basis than that of mere human, unhallowed love. Now, as I said, this may be wrong advice. I can not tell. I am startled and almost frightened by your story, and yet I pity you as I could not have pitied you but for some things that I have felt. And I will help you, oh, how I will help you! I feel now as if I could."

"You have told me the truth," Mrs. Harrison said, rising, and drawing her wraps around her, "and that in itself has helped me. I was almost forced to come to you. I don't know what I shall do or where I shall commence ; but I know I must commence a different life with my husband. He *has* borne a great deal. I'll make what amends I can."

She came over close to Eunice's chair, and touched her arm with a gentle, caressing sort of movement. Another woman of different mold would have bent and kissed the girl. Mrs. Harrison only stood close beside her.

"Una," she said, at last, using the name she had almost never used, "you have had a great deal to bear from me. I believe you are great enough to forgive me. Can you let me be your sister, I wonder?"

There were tears in Una's eyes, and she could not trust her voice to make any answer; but she did what she had not supposed it possible to do to Mrs. Perry Harrison—she raised herself to a level with the fair, haughty face, and left a tender kiss on her cheek.

It was long since she had written in her Journal—not, indeed, since her sickness. I think she felt satisfaction in writing in it occasionally, because it merely received the revelations that she made from time to time, without regard to the strange changes of opinion which she chronicled, and without demanding wearisome explanations as to how she reached that state of feeling. So she wrote just what she wanted to express, utterly unintelligible though it must have been, viewed from the Journal's standpoint.

April 18—. Poor Eleanor Harrison! What a fierce, undisciplined heart she has! What struggles she will have to make! What struggles she has made to crush her better self! What an infinite compassion to wait for her, and call after her, and receive her at last as His child, even though she had professed to bear His name, and was a false witness for Him all the time! What a Saviour! Surely no human heart will dare to stand aloof and unforgiving after that! I *will* help her; I feel sure that I can. Don't I know something of the struggle? Don't I know the heights of grace that our Lord is willing to bestow? What strange leadings! Fierce lives! We need none of us have had them, if we had been willing to be led, instead of insisting on leading ourselves. And yet the Lord would not let us make shipwreck. He will save us all. He will give us work, I verily believe, to do for him. He will even crown us each with jewels at the last. What wonderful forgiveness! Surely there is no sin that a child of his ought not to learn to forgive in another. She asked me if I could be her sister. I had to do it. It was an awful humiliation, but for the sake of her soul's peril I had to do it. I had to be entirely frank. I believe it helped her. Yes, I will be her sister. Perry, my brother, I will be your wife's faithful, patient, helpful, forgiving sister. So help me God.

More writing. Eleanor wrote a letter that night to her mother. Perry waited for her in their dressing-room, and watched the swift pen move gracefully over the paper, and marked the flush on her cheek, and wondered, with a heavy sigh, what she could be writing; and whether it was another letter that ought to blush to see the light of day. Thus ran the letter:

Dear Mamma:

I want you to do something for me. I want you to gather every letter that I have ever written to you since I was married, every scrap, and burn them all. Do it just as soon as you get this letter. I want you to burn every single word; and I wish I could in some way burn the remembrance of them from your heart.

Mamma, a great deal of what I have written you is false. Indeed, almost everything I ever wrote you or told you I believe has been false. I am a living lie! I have been, but oh—well, mamma, I do not know how to tell you anything about it, for I feel sure that you would not understand. You are a member of the Church, just as I have been; but still I *know* that you will not understand the change in me. I can not tell you about it, but it does seem to me that I can *live* it. I would give all the money I am worth in the world if I had not written you those letters. I have insulted my husband, and he is grand enough for me almost to fall down and worship him instead. And some of the very times I was writing to you I felt that he was.

Mamma, he is waiting for me now while I am writing, and it makes me nervous. I will break right off here. Perhaps next time I can write more coherently. Only, mamma, be sure you do just as I say.

"Tom," said Mrs. Haddington to her son, as he dropped in one morning to receive her commands, " I really think you ought to go down to Nassau and look after Eleanor. I believe she is losing her mind. I received the most utterly incoherent letter from her last night that you ever heard of. She says I will not understand her, and I'm sure I don't. Just read it, and see what you think."

It was a very reluctant hand that reached out to receive the letter. At first Tom Haddington was tempted to say that he would not read it; that he had tolerated enough of his sister's letters. But, on second thought, it seemed necessary to be prepared for anything she might do. So he held the dainty perfumed note in disdainful fingers and read. But when he handed it back there was a light in his eyes and a ring in his voice that made his mother wonder.

"Instead of losing her mind, mother, I should say that she was at last coming into the possession of her sense. 'Clothed, and in her right mind.' The God of miracles still lives."

"I believe you are all of you insane together, and I wish I knew what to do with you."

Thus muttered his mother as her son turned, with apparently a new-born, eager purpose, and hastily left the room.

27.

It was a strange, sad comment upon the relations existing between this husband and wife, that Eleanor could go to Eunice Taylor, whom she had so hated, and could write to her mother, whose Christian life she felt had little depth. She could speak to these two of the change which had come to her, yet she could not summon courage to tell Perry of this new experience. Twice during the day following her interview with Una her hand was upon the knob of the library door, but even then she turned back. She had an intense longing to make amends for all the wrong-doing of the past; she longed for his forgiveness; she felt that she could go down on her knees to him and beg him to forgive her for all the fearful wrongs she had done him. But she knew that he would scarcely understand the depth of her sorrow, unless he knew all.

"He would not hate me quite, even if he knew everything," she said to herself; "and God knows I have no wish to deceive any one. And yet, as Una said, he has suffered enough already, and I may spare him now. But how shall I prove to him that I am trying to begin all over? Will he not think it all another piece of acting? If he really knew me as I have been he might well think so."

It was positively a sacrifice for Eleanor not to lay open to her husband's gaze the horrible, black gulf of sin and falsehood and deception through which she had dragged, and from which she had been lifted by the surpassing love of an infinite Saviour. She had such a desire to have all clear between herself and Perry, and such a longing for help and sympathy, that it was hard to be silent. It was a sacrifice to save, not her own feelings, but another's, and beyond this longing for his forgiveness there was growing up in her heart an intense, eager desire to stand by her husband's side in his work for the Saviour, who had held her back from utter ruin, who had given her grace to turn forever away from her sin and folly. She did not realize how utterly opposed to Christian work were all her habits of thought, her tastes, her associations, everything which had hitherto made up her life. Only to *begin*—to get a sure footing beside Perry and Tom and Una, and the battle would be won.

Well had Una written, "Poor Eleanor Harrison! What struggles she will have to make!" Would she find it easier to put into her life that which she could not put into words? Would they, Perry and Tom, understand? Well, if they did not" (and a thrill of joy animated her whole being as she thought), "There is One who knows, and he will give me the opportunities I seek."

For one who had been for years a church-member Eleanor knew little about the Bible promises; but she knew that somewhere were such words as these: "Call unto me and I will answer thee, and show thee great and mighty things which thou knowest not." And she resolved to ask Christ to show her what to do, where to begin. It was not like Eleanor Harrison to make much of the inner life at the expense of the outer. The heart cleansed, the sources of action purified, her desires and hopes took practical shape. To undo the wrongs, where this was possible; to build up anew upon the ruins of the irreparable; this was her hope and eager desire; these were the opportunities she sought. Even the smallest details of her course she would repair just as fast as she could. She had begun by requesting her mother to destroy those miserable letters, and now she waited to be led forward—waited, and yet it was not a restful waiting. She was too much accustomed to having things done without waiting. All her life she had been exacting and impatient of delay, and this was only one of the many forms of selfishness against which she must hereafter struggle.

The spring came on early that year. The March days had only just gone by, with their blustering winds, and the weather was warm, the birds were singing, and the grass already began to take on a greenish hue; and Eleanor, unable to settle to anything in-doors, went out to walk off her unrest. She was really and truly resting in the love of Christ; she felt that henceforth there was no doubt about her belonging to him; and now she wanted something to do for him— she was eager to "witness" for Christ. The lesson of patient waiting was hard for her to learn; but our Lord, who knoweth our frame, will not lay upon us heavier burdens than we can bear, neither will he give us harder lessons to learn than we can, by the aid of the Spirit, conquer.

And so it was that some little work was given her to do that very day. As she passed through the dining-room on her way out she saw the new girl, which was the seventh since she sent away the faithful Molly, making bungling attempts at putting the room in order.

"Oh, dear," she said to herself, "what a distracting looking room! How will Perry ever swallow a mouthful of dinner! I am sure I don't know what to do! I wonder why we have such wretched times getting servants that are efficient. There was Molly; she was a splendid housekeeper, I will own that, if she had but known her place. I don't think we have had a decent meal since she went. But I couldn't put up with her ways."

Couldn't you, Eleanor Harrison? Well, who could put up with *yours?* It was just that thought that came to her, and she blushed to remember how she had sent away this old-time servant, who seemed necessary to the comfort of the household. Eleanor must have been strangely humbled when she could have said, even to herself that perhaps she was somewhat to blame. The truth was, she knew actually nothing about housekeeping matters, and Perry sadly missed the comforts and the perfect order to which he had all his life been accustomed. Eleanor had not seen Molly for months, and had no knowledge of her place of residence. Was it chance that led her to stop at a street corner, undecided which way to go? "It looks pleasant down that way," she thought, "and I have never been there." So she turned into the narrow street, and had gone but a few steps when a voice broke upon her ears.

"Were you coming to see me, Mrs. Harrison?"

It was Molly, who rose from her stooping-posture among the flower-beds, and turned as if she would pass into the house to receive her visitor. Eleanor hesitated a moment before replying. Then she said, laughing:

"I believe I was, though I confess I did not know it until this moment. But I won't go in; it is so sunny I would prefer to talk here."

Fifteen minutes later Molly entered the house, and, speaking to a white-haired woman who was sewing in the cosy little front room, said:

"Mother, I am going back to Mrs. Harrison's."

"Is that a wise thing to do?" said the mother.

"I don't know, but I promised Mrs. Harrison. I don't know what possessed me, but she had the words out of me before I knew it. Someway she seemed different. I can't tell how, but more like the dear mother. Maybe the spirit of that precious woman has someway entered into the young woman. I don't know what it is, but she is different."

"When do you go?" asked the mother.

"This afternoon," was the reply. "She said she wanted me to get tea; that it was a surprise that she was planning for Mr. Perry. She said she knew he had missed my ways about the house."

"Well," said the mother, "you can do as you think best, but I should think you had enough of life with that woman at the head."

"I shall try it, anyway," returned Molly, with decision.

As for Eleanor, quite elated over her work, she hastened home, thinking how she would enjoy Perry's surprise. She managed to detain him in the library until the tea-bell sounded. They went down together.

"I really believe that our newest experiment is going to be a success," said Perry; "this certainly looks like it, though it has taken her some time to show her skill."

It was certainly an improvement upon the recent order of things. Fresh table-linen, glittering silver and glistening glass, smoothly-cut slices of bread evenly arranged upon the plate, pinky slices of cold meat without any ragged edges—everything in perfect order, the delicious aroma of properly-made tea pervading the room. All this was accredited to the slatternly girl who had of late served up such nauseous dishes.

Eleanor enjoyed Perry's surprise and evident pleasure; and he, noticing her manner, was puzzled by it. Indeed, he had more than once been puzzled within the past few days. Eleanor's moods were always varying, but of late, though not so varying, they had seemed new and strange. In response to his remark upon the change for the better in the table appointments, she only said she hoped it would last. But there was more than that in her face, and he waited to have it explain itself. Presently the trim and familiar Molly appeared with a plate of Perry's favorite muffins.

"Ah!" said the gentleman, "this explains it. Do you always take hold of the work when you make a visit?" he asked.

"Oh, Molly is not visiting us," replied Mrs. Perry. "She has come to stay, for a time at least."

"That's it! Well, it will seem like living again. But Eleanor," he continued, as Molly left the room, "do you think it a wise thing to do? Will Molly be more yielding than formerly, do you imagine?"

There was a bright color on Eleanor's cheek, as she answered with an embarrassed laugh:

"Well, Perry, I don't know as to that; but I thought that perhaps we had both learned something, and if we should each yield a little the points of contact would soon wear smooth."

"Well, arrange it as you choose. Only I would not like to have the old story repeated," returned Perry, and Molly's reappearance put an end to the talk upon that subject, but to Perry his wife was becoming more of a puzzle than ever. Could it be the proud, haughty Eleanor who talked of mutual concessions, and this, too, in connection with a servant? What had come over her? Even in her most gracious moods she had never been like this; she had never been known to acknowledge herself in the wrong in the slightest degree. He grew anxious as he remembered that for days a change had been coming over her. Could she be ill? Was it physical weakness that had depressed her spirits? Or was she pining for a change? True, she did not seem sad to-night, only quiet; there was a gentleness that was almost sweetness in her tones, which was different from the smooth, even, society manner usual with her. Different, in that they sounded like heart-tones. But Perry, blind and deaf, did not understand them. He thought her lonely and homesick, and read in the softened manner a sort of patient submission to the inevitable.

And that evening, long after she slept, he paced up and down the library, his brain racked with varying plans.

"Can I *never* make her happy?" he thought. "Will she not see that I am trying to atone for the wrong I have done? Unconscious though it was, it was a wrong such as a woman like Eleanor would find it hard to overcome. Perhaps we ought to go away from here; she has never been happy here, and now there are so many unpleasant associations at every turn of the old place that, hard as it is, I am almost ready to turn my back upon it, for her sake. God knows that I would make almost any sacrifice for her."

It was true. The sacrifices which had been met at first from a sense of duty had become the willing offerings of a loving heart. It was not the worshipping love of youth, nor yet a hoping, trusting requited love; but a tender, pitying love, that would draw its object within the circling love of God. With even such a love, deep, earnest and self-sacrificing, Eleanor Harrison might well have call herself blessed.

It was with this longing for the power to make her happy that he planned and prayed and fought, with the temptation to lie down in despair, for there were times even yet when answer to his prayers seemed afar off—when he felt that he could scarcely endure the waiting—as if they must have help for the life that they were leading; and this was not more upon his own account than upon hers, for he knew that his wife was not happy; that he had utterly failed in his efforts to help her to bear the sorrow which had come upon her as the result of the fearful mistake into which they had fallen. He would take his wife and go away; it would be better for all. Una was recovering, and yet he had not seen her; not that he dreaded the interview upon his own account. He felt that the love which he had been fighting against was conquered. He knew now, out of his own experience, that the grace of God is sufficient even for the retrieving of such mistakes. He did not fear to meet her; she would always be to him as a dear sister; but he was not sure of her state of mind. She was weak, and still confined to the house. But, sooner or later, he knew that they must meet; and, while he believed there would not be the slightest cause for it, he feared that if they were to keep up the old habits of intimacy Eleanor's hatred and jealousy would again be aroused, and it would seem very awkward not to meet on friendly terms, the two families had so long been united in close intimacy. It would be hard to leave his people, for he had grown to think of the interests of the village people as his own. But that might be managed; the school, the lunch-rooms and other enterprises had become so well established that they might be left to the care of some one else.

"Duties never conflict," he said, "and it seems to be my evident duty to try to make my wife happy."

And with this conclusion he planned an extensive summer tour, which he laid before his wife the next morning. She listened until he ended by saying:

"Now, Eleanor, if we carry out this programme, either as a whole or with modifications, you will want a few days in the city soon."

She replied by asking:

"Perry, is it on my account that you have planned this?"

Always truthful, Perry answered:

"I certainly had my wife's pleasure in view, though I expect to enjoy the trip myself."

"But you would not go except for me," she persisted.

"I should not go except *with* you," he replied, laughing.

"That is dodging the question. But I think I understand you, Perry Harrison," she said, laughing, too. Then, soberly: "Don't think I would drag you away on such a chase as this. We will stay at home this summer, except for a few weeks, perhaps, if we can make up a pleasant party for the mountains. I know you will gain strength faster than you will if you go on this journey. And, besides, how can you leave your work here?"

"I thought you would like it," Perry said. He was too much surprised to say much, and a little grieved that the scheme which he had at the expense of his own inclination laid before her should not meet with her favor, for he could not yet realize that she was making a sacrifice for him.

"I would like it," she replied, "only I—well, Perry, need we decide at once?"

"Certainly not; take your time."

And Perry, looking into the face that met his gaze so frankly, thought how very fair was this woman, whose life was linked with his own, and there rose before him a vision of what their life might yet become. It seems strange, sometimes, how opportunities come to us when we really seek them.

That afternoon, as they were at tea, a note was left for Perry, which seemed to disturb him.

"Is it anything serious, Perry, asked Eleanor. "You look troubled."

"Not very; only Miss Wilbur says she will not be able to meet her class this evening at the hall, and I don't quite know where to look for a substitute."

There were a few moments' silence, then Eleanor spoke. In those few moments there had been a fierce conflict going on in her heart. All the instincts of her nature revolted at the thought of coming in contact with the class of people whom she fancied were accustomed to meet in that hall. And then she had so opposed the whole scheme. Her pride whispered to her not to follow out her impulse—that it would be too humiliating. But her new resolves thus put to the test triumphed, and she said, hesitatingly:

"Perry, could I do it?"

The stupid man look puzzled, and said:

"Do what, Eleanor?"

"Why, teach that class."

"Why, *would* you?"

"If I could. If you think I would do for once. I thought it would save you trouble, perhaps."

"Thank you."

That was all he said, but the look and tone made it mean much. Still Perry was puzzled.

Would these two ever understand each other?

28.

EXTRACT FROM EUNICE'S JOURNAL.

May 4, 18—. How the days go by! Actually it is a year to-day since that spring morning when Tom Haddington came up from New York all unexpectedly, because he had been here so short a time before, and—well, what a fool I was! During all this year I haven't written in my Journal; I have been too busy and too settled. I don't believe people write in journals unless they are unsettled and unhappy. I'm not sure I believe in journals; at least I don't believe in mine. I never read a sillier, and, in some respects, a wickeder book! I mean to burn mine, or lock it up in the largest and deepest trunk I can get to put in my new garret. The garret is immense, Tom says. I have been running through it this evening—the Journal, not the garret—trying to determine whether there is any record in it that I want to keep; if there is anything my descendants might like to read. If there isn't, what was the use of my writing it? Now, possibly, there will be people living a hundred years hence who might enjoy reading it, simply because my hand wrote it. But the question is, Would I enjoy having them? There are some tender words about that dear saint, Mother Harrison. Those might be helpful to young Christian lives. There are some strong words of my dear father's, that might be helpful to anybody. But the mass of it is rubbish; my cheeks burn with shame while I read it! Such unutterable stuff about Perry Harrison! A good deal of it before he was married, and some, infinitely worse, afterward! Could I bear to have any young, pure-hearted girl—my grandchild, say, or Perry's great-grandson—read that terrible revelation of folly and sin? And yet, wouldn't my mistakes be helpful to them, possibly? Don't people often see things with blinded eyes, when, if they would look at another life that has been lived, and see the same lines of trouble made smooth, and crookedness made straight, by the infinite love and the infinite patience of a Friend who never makes mistakes, and never changes, and never dies, wouldn't it be helpful? At least I shall not burn my Journal to-night. But it doesn't seem to me that I can let Tom see it, ever. It is too silly, where it is not too wicked.

The idea of my ever fancying that I ought to

have married Perry Harrison, especially after he *was* married! I seem for a time to have ignored that important fact. But, even before that, how I could have fancied such a thing seems incredible to me. Perry is a dear, good friend; a better brother it wouldn't be possible to have. Tom says he is the grandest Christian man, in some respects, that he ever knew. But—well, he isn't in the least like Tom, and I know that Tom Haddington is the only man on earth whom it would be possible for me to marry.

How glad I am that Perry has never known the folly and the sin of which I have been guilty! Being true and brave and strong-hearted himself, it has never occurred to him that I could be otherwise. He need never be humiliated by knowing it. Yet I am glad that Tom knows all about it, and equally glad that I did not have to tell him. He says he thinks he has known all about me that could be told by human being, and a great deal that couldn't be told. Ever since he first knew me, and all the time that I was being a blind simpleton, he was grand and patient. I thank God for such a friend. How wonderfully have I been led! What a horrible mesh of tangles would I have made of the web of life could I but have had the weaving it! And yet there was a time when I deemed myself wise enough to have planned it all, and done much better work than was done for me. Well, the infinite patience of God is beyond conception to one who has not tried it to the utmost, as surely I have done.

Do you know, Journal, you are to bid good-by to Eunice Taylor this very night? Surely you must have had enough of me; at least *I* have. To-morrow before this time I will be Eunice Haddington! That is a remarkably pretty name. Eleanor has pleased herself by writing it in a delicate running hand on some of my handkerchiefs. Eleanor has done everything for me. Who could have supposed that the day would come when I should be proud to own her for a sister? There is change for you! Not all in myself, either. Who would recognize in her the Eleanor Harrison who came a bride to the old homestead? How fast the Lord can work when he takes a soul in hand to transform it to suit his pattern! Eleanor is an intense anything. So of course her intensity shows in the new life as it did in the old.

There is Tom; I hear his step in the hall; he is coming to see about trunks, and really they are not half packed. Good-night, old friend, and good-by. I don't believe I shall ever feel like looking at you again.

EXTRACT FROM PERRY'S JOURNAL.

May 4, 18—. God bless my sister Una. How beautiful is the life that is opening before her! What an idiot I was not to see long before how the tide was drifting! The Lord knew. If, as a Christian, I am more thankful for one blessing than another, next to the gift of a Redeemer, it is the guiding, over-ruling hand of God that fills me with joy. There is no tried, tempted soul, however fierce the waves of temptation or pain may roll over him, but may, if he *will*, rest quietly covered by the shielding hand. "God is faithful, who will not suffer one to be tempted above what he is able to bear; but will with the temption also make a way to escape, that we may be able to bear it." That is true, *true.* Let me set my seal to the absolute *certainty* of help from the blessed Lord, in all our needs and sorrows and terrors. He more than keeps his promise; he gives more than simply grace to endure; he sets one on the heights of peace.

Let me record my gratitude here for the way in which I have been led. Looking back I can see that the way was a wise one; that his tender mercies were all around me; that he had in view my present as well as my future in the way in which I have been led. I feel very grateful for the help this Journal has been to me. I shall keep it for a future help. Looking over it humbles and subdues me, and at the same time helps and rests. There are records of defeat, it is true, but, blessed be his name, there are also records of victories. There are pages that I will need, some day, to paste together, in order that by no mistake shall human eye behold them; and there are pages that might possibly help some struggling soul, at least the mute companionship and enduring patience of the book has helped me, and I shall keep it as a friend.

Eleanor and I are going over this evening to say good-bye to Una Taylor. She will be Mrs. Tom Haddington to-morrow. I record with gratitude the fact that I can say, with clear voice and sincere heart, thank God for that! They are suited to each other. I think, aside from their two selves, no one sees this more plainly than Eleanor does. What gracious things the Lord can do for a soul when he abides within! My Eleanor grows; underneath her are the Everlasting Arms. There are things that she thinks I do not know; I mean she shall continue to think so; it is best that she should, for the present, at least. One of these days, when we have both gotten so near to heaven as to be able to smile together over past human follies, we will talk it over, perhaps, and make all things plain to each other. Indeed, it may not be until we both have entered heaven, and then I do not know but it may all have sunken so utterly into nothingness as to be not worth talking of, for then we shall realize that nothing but love remains. Love for Christ first, and next the love that he sanctions and blesses, and *no other*.

One other thanksgiving let me record, before we say good-by to Una. My Saviour, my Helper, my Healer, I thank thee that thou didst give me Eleanor Haddington for my wife, and didst teach me to cleave unto her until death do part us, and didst give me the hope and confidence that death itself *can not* part us; that the bond between us need never be broken. May we, as we each day draw sensibly nearer to each other, be drawn nearer to thee, until ourselves shall be utterly lost in thee. Amen.

It is the experience of human beings generally that they so promptly become accustomed to a new order of things as to forget in a few weeks that any other condition of affairs ever existed. At least if they do not forget they cease to comment—even to think of it—except at rare intervals, when some special occasion forces the contrast on their attention.

At the Harrison homestead the year of peace that had followed the sadly tossed and disappointing life which had been lived there, had so calmed the inmates that, as I say, except on special occasions they had already ceased to think of that other and trying time. There had been several weeks of bewilderment to Perry, when, in the stupidity of his heart, he struggled to plan new things and new scenes for his wife, and she gently refused to be planned for; and at last, bent on discovering what it was she wanted, and how they could better their life, he prisoned her in his study one evening and tenderly, patiently, persistently questioned, until in a burst of tears his haughty Eleanor had melted before him, and told the story of her new hopes and plans and aims, and begged his help and his patience. And he, looking down upon her in amazed bewilderment for a few moments, had suddenly exclaimed, with a ring to his voice, and an intensity of feeling that she had not expected:

"Bless the Lord, O my soul, and all that is within me bless his holy name!'

Since which time that tune, in some of its changes, had rung in his heart. And yet they rapidly, after the manner of mortals, settled into the new order of things. It was amazing, when one looked back, to see how soon it became the most natural and matter-of-course thing in the world for Mr. and Mrs. Harrison to go together to the evening school, to arrange together some new plans for the reading-room, to call together on certain ones about whom Perry had been anxious. Nay, according to her eager, restless, nature, she went ahead of him; she brought all her fascinations to bear on the factory boys and girls. It became an ordinary occurrence to Perry to come with a perplexed face and say:

"Eleanor, what shall we do with Maynie Phillips? I am worried about her." Or, "Eleanor, Will Bates is in trouble. I don't quite understand the circumstances. Can we get at them, do you think?"

And then would follow a consultation, during which Perry's brow would clear, and his voice would have a relieved ring as he said:

"That's a capital idea! Oh, Eleanor, what a helper you are!"

It took, too, but a short time to become accustomed to the fact that a remarkable change had come to the feelings with which his wife and Una viewed each other. During Una's remaining days of invalidism Eleanor was daily at the little house across the way, and on the first evening when she asked Perry to accompany her, and he saw Una for the first time since her illness, he felt the change that had come to both. Since that time the old habits of running back and forth from the Taylor house to the Harrison house had been resumed; only in these days it was Una who consulted Eleanor, or Eleanor who consulted Una. The long and frequent consultations that had been the habit of years between Una and himself were over. The habit had been broken in upon by illness, and was never resumed. It was very rarely indeed that he saw her alone now. It was not that either shunned the other, but that both were so full of their plans and their work; and their work began to lie so much apart, that the need for consultation seemed to be gone. Una did not go into the school again; the village people thought she was not well enough, and Eleanor had taken her class. But Una knew that it was not worth while to resume a routine which must so soon be broken in upon.

They stood on the steps one day, chattering, Una and Eleanor and Perry. Una had her hat in her hand, and was just going.

"Oh, Una," Eleanor said, "wait a minute, please. I want to get that list I made out for you. The directions where to find the places are all written out. You can't mistake. I've given you ever so many errands to do, but I couldn't help it."

"She is going into town to-morrow," she explained, in answer to her husband's inquiring look, "and I want some things for the class. I can't go myself, because those two girls of yours are coming this afternoon to learn leaf stitch."

Then she vanished.

"Una, do you remember that I once told you that you two could be great helps to each other?" Perry asked, as they waited.

"And I was skeptical," answered Una, smiling. "I was a simpleton in those days, and Eleanor was not what she is now. We are both changed, and life has changed."

"I know," answered Perry, gravely. Then, smiling: "Besides, Eleanor tells me she asked you to be her sister, and I judge that you consented to it."

A vivid blush overspread Una's face, and she looked down in utter confusion.

"I did not mean," continued the wicked Perry, that you depended solely on her asking. I assure you I think you have ample reason to consider yourself heartily invited to the relationship." Then his tone changed again. "God bless you, my sister! I thank God for you. I am glad that you are to be, more truly than ever, my sister. And I thank God that Tom Haddington is my brother."

There was peculiar emphasis thrown into that last sentence, as if he desired to call her attention to the event that had made Tom Haddington his brother, and then he instantly spoke of something else. It was all the talk that these two, who recognized that they had been fools, and had had been saved from shipwreck by unseen hands, allowed themselves to have about their past.

Neither did Una and Eleanor refer often to that passage in their history when they had come so near to each other as to lay bare their hearts for each other's gaze. They were neither of them women to whom this was an easy task, and such do not frequently tear open old wounds. Once Eleanor referred to it. It was the evening before the wedding, and they were together in Una's room, giving last touches to the preparations. A little silence had fallen between them, broken at last by Eleanor's question:

"Una, did Tom tell you about Mr. Romaine?"

"Yes," Una answered, and then hesitated, as one who did not know what next to say. Presently she added: "It did not surprise me; I wonder that he has not gone before. I think he is just fitted for mission work, only one would have thought that he would have found enough to do in this country."

To this Eleanor made no answer. She was evidently not in a mood to discuss the respective claims of home and foreign missions. At last she said:

"I am not sure, Una, that I can make clear to you what this is to me. You remember what I told you once, and how you answered me? Well, your words were true; there is help with God; his mercy and his forgiveness and his patience are infinite. I have tried them all; sometimes it seems to me I tried them to their utmost limit. He has given me not only pardon, but peace and rest. And yet, Una, there is a pain that it seems to me even God can not take away. I have wrecked a human life—I mean so far as earthly happiness is concerned. Isn't it strange? While I have found a friend, who is every hour of my life dearer to me, I, who alone am to blame, have been received into the fulness of earthly happiness; and he, who was the victim only, not in any sense the sinner, is the sufferer?"

"Are you sure?" asked Una, turning toward her with tender, pitying eyes. "Can there be any real suffering where a soul is so entirely at peace with God as his is, and where one is so utterly given up to God's work as he is? I suspect he has a higher happiness than you or I know anything about. And you, who are bearing the sting of remorse, are the punished one, after all."

"That is true," said Eleanor, "But, Una, I tell you that even remorse, heavy though it is sometimes, can not shut me out from the thought that I have my husband, and that he is to me what, in my selfishness and fierceness, I did not suppose he could ever be. Why should such happiness have been given to me?"

"It is the seal of the royal way in which the King forgives," Una answered, her face shining with joy. "When you come to speak of one's deserts, Eleanor, you get on very low ground. You make me think of what I have been, and what the forgiving God has given me?"

"Yes," Eleanor said, thoughtfully. "It is all of grace. But, Una, there is a very solemn side to it. Even God can not take away the results that follow from our sins—can not *always* do it, I mean. The scars remain. I shall always have to think of a scarred life that I have made."

"And yet, my dear sister, you are bound also to remember that his Leader is bound in honor to make even the scars into good for Him."

"Thank you," Eleanor said.

And, though there were tears in her eyes, she smiled. There were thoughts in her heart that she left unsaid. She could not bring herself to say to this almost bride that there lay at times a heavy fear upon her that she had lost her husband's love. He was tenderness itself, and yet could he forget or forgive or absolutely trust her? And Una, looking at the tearful yet shining eyes, felt sad for her—felt almost certain that the new life had opened too late for her to hold her husband's love. And yet felt that not for the world would she have hinted such a thing to the struggling, repentant woman.

So even yet these people did not by any means understand each other, and looked at their lives from their different standpoints, and thought their thoughts and believed that every side was plain to them, and that only the others were in mist. How well it was for them each that their lives lay in hands that understood and saw with clear vision to the end, or to the eternities, for to *lives* there *is* no end. Sometimes the All-seeing Eye and the ever-tender Heart puts it into human hearts to speak the right words at the right time.

It was the morning of the wedding. Indeed, the wedding had been; the solemn words spoken so many times had sounded again, and Una Taylor, who had told her Journal so solemnly long before that certain joys were not for her, had departed with a face in which shone the fulness of human joy and rest. Those left behind were beginning to feel that reaction which is sure to follow an excitement of any sort, and perhaps specially the excitement of a wedding.

Eleanor Harrison went about the little parlor at the Taylors', leaving little touches here and there, that lessened the confusion and the dreariness; doing those things that the nearest friend stops to do when a daughter of the house has gone out from it. There was a sort of half sad, half wistful expression on her face, when her eye sought her husband's, which moved him strangely, and which led him by an impulse, the source of which he did not understand, to bend toward her a moment when they were alone at the farther end of the room, and say:

"Do you want me to quote a sentence that I wrote in my Diary last evening?"

"Yes," she said, smiling. "That is if it was a good sentence, one that will help right the bewilderment of things."

"I don't know as to that, but I wrote this sentence from a full heart: 'I thank God that Eleanor Haddington is my wife.'"

He had a flash, then, from Eleanor Harrison's eyes such as he had never seen before.

"It helps," she said, simply, but the tone and the look that accompanied them made his heart beat, and each of these two foolish ones felt that their true bridal had just commenced.

Well, lives do not stop being lived, unless death comes in and snaps the thread. And these lives are being lived, all of them, to-day. All this happened not long ago, and yet many things have happened since that might be told. But stories have to stop; they can not wind up, for there are the lives going on, something being said and done every day, every hour, that one would like to chronicle. And yet one musn't. Who would read a story that went on, and on, just like a life? It is as much as people can do to *live* their lives. So as there is no place in which to round and smooth this story into finishing, it must just stop.

THE END.

POPULAR BOOKS.

BY "PANSY."

ESTER REID,	$1.50
JULIA REID,	1.50
THREE PEOPLE,	1.50
THE KING'S DAUGHTER,	1.50
WISE AND OTHERWISE,	1.50
HOUSEHOLD PUZZLES,	1.50
THE RANDOLPHS,	1.50
FOUR GIRLS AT CHAUTAUQUA,	1.50
CUNNING WORKMEN,	1.25
GRANDPA'S DARLINGS,	1.25
JESSIE WELLS,	.75
DOCIA'S JOURNAL,	.75
BERNIE'S WHITE CHICKEN; to which is added, THE DIAMOND BRACELET,	.75
HELEN LESTER; to which is added, NANNIE'S EXPERIMENT.	.75
A CHRISMAS TIME,	.15

BY "PANSY" & "FAYE HUNTINGTON."

MODERN PROPHETS,	$1.50
DR. DEANE'S WAY,	1.25

BY "FAYE HUNTINGTON."

THOSE BOYS,	$1.50
MRS. DEANE'S WAY,	1.25

D. LOTHROP & CO., Publishers.

HISTORIC HYMNS.

Collected by REV. W. F. CRAFTS.

Music arranged under the supervision of Dr. E. Tourjée.

A COLLECTION OF

a hundred popular STANDARD HYMNS, of which incidents are given in "*Trophies of Song.*" A pamphlet of thirty-two pages, in stout covers, which affords

A CHEAP HYMN BOOK

for Sunday Schools, Congregational Singing, Praise Meetings, Concerts, Camp Meetings and Special Services. It has doubled the volume of congregational singing in churches, where it has been used, by furnishing the words, at a slight expense, to every person in the congregation. Besides the hymns, "Bible Readings," Responsive Readings, Introductory Responsive Services, &c., &c., are also included. Commended by I. D. SANKEY, P. P. BLISS, and other prominent singers·

Price, in Stout Paper Cover, per 100, - - $7.00.
" " Cloth, per 100, - - - - - 10.00.

Send ten cents for specimen copy.

TROPHIES OF SONG.

BY REV. W. F. CRAFTS.

WITH AN INTRODUCTION BY DR. E. TOURJEE.

A COMPILATION OF

200 STRIKING INCIDENTS,

connected with the origin and history of our most popular hymns, both of the Church and Sunday School, together with articles by prominent writers on "Praise Meetings," "Congregational Singing," "Sunday School Singing," and all the various uses of sacred music. Its suggestions and incidents make it valuable to pastors, superintendents and choristers, and its numerous and thrilling incidents give it interest for the general reader and even for children. Price $1.25.

D. LOTHROP & CO., Publishers,

THE NAME ABOVE EVERY NAME. In sending forth a new and revised edition of this work the Publishers append a few of the many favorable notices which, from various sources, testify to its catholicity, and its adaptation to the wants of the disciples of our Lord by whatever denominational name they may be called.

The Name above Every Name. *or, Devotional Meditations.* WITH A TEXT FOR EVERY DAY IN THE YEAR. By the *Rev. Samuel Cutler.*

This little volume, which is a gem of typography, is just what it claims to be—"devotional and practical." The pure gold of the gospel is here without the base alloy of man's wisdom. It accords with the teachings of the divine Spirit, and tends to exalt in the souls of men the Christ of God.

The texts are fitly chosen, and the exquisite fragments of sacred poetry seem like jewels from a mine of inspiration. None can read this book devoutly without being benefited; and all who read it in the spirit in which it appears to have been written, will lay down the volume with higher views of Christ's nature, and of His work, and reverently acknowledge that if His name be above every name in dignity and glory, it is also, as declared in the inspired canticle, "as ointment poured forth" in its heavenly fragrance. —*Parish Visitor.*

From the Congregationist.

The Name above Every Name. It has a chapter for every week in the year, each chapter preceded with appropriate passages from Scripture and closing with a choice selection from devotional poetry. The whole book is eminently evangelical, and fitted to foster the growth of true and genuine piety in the soul.

The Name above Every Name. By the *Rev. Samuel Cutler.* This has been carefully prepared by its author. The texts are for every day in the year, and have reference to the Scriptural titles of our Lord. The devotional and practical meditations are for every week in the year. The appendix contains five hundred and twenty five titles of our Lord, with the Scriptual reference; also a topical and alphabetical list of the titles, and of first lines of poetry with the author's name.

The work is exceedingly valuable, not only for its meditations, but for the great amount of information which it contains. It is a book which the Christian would do well always to have at hand. *Evagelical Knowledge Society.*

The volume is a precious *vade mecum,* for all who love the "Name that is above every name"—*Protestant Churchman.*

Plain Edition $1.00   Full Gilt $1.50   Red line Edition $2.00

D. Lothrop & Co., Publishers, Boston.

BOOKS FOR YOUNG HEROES AND BRAVE WORKERS.

VIRGINIA. By *W. H. G. Kingston.* 16 mo. Illustrated $1 25
  A stirring story of adventure upon sea and land.

AFRICAN ADVENTURE AND ADVENTURERS. By *Rev. G. T. Day, D. D.* 16 mo. Illustrated 1 50
  The stories of Speke, Grant, Baker, Livingstone and Stanley are put into simple shape for the entertainment of young readers.

NOBLE WORKERS. Edited by *S. F. Smith, D. D.* 16mo. 1 50

STORIES OF SUCCESS. Edited by *S. F. Smith, D. D.* 16mo 1 50
  Inspiring biographies and records which leave a most wholesome and enduring effect upon the reader.

MYTHS AND HEROES. 16 mo. Illustrated. Edited by *S. F. Smith, D. D.* . 1 50

KNIGHTS AND SEA KINGS. Edited by *S. F. Smith, D. D.* 12mo. Illustrated . 1 50
  Two entertaining books, which will fasten forever the historical and geographical lessons of the school-room firmly in the student's mind.

CHAPLIN'S LIFE OF BENJAMIN FRANKLIN. 16mo. Illustrated 1 50

LIFE OF AMOS LAWRENCE. 12mo. Ill. 1 50
  Two biographies of perennial value. No worthier books were ever offered as holiday presents for our American young men.

WALTER NEAL'S EXAMPLE. By *Rev. Theron Brown.* 16 mo. Illustrated . . 1 25
  Walter Neal's Example is by Rev. Theron Brown, the editor of that very successful paper, *The Youth's Companion.* The story is a touching one, and is in parts so vivid as to seem drawn from the life. — *N. Y. Independent.*

TWO FORTUNE-SEEKERS. Stories by *Rossiter Johnson, Louise Chandler Moulton, E. Stuart Phelps, Ella Farman, etc.* Fully illustrated 1 50

SUGAR PLUMS. Poems by ELLA FARMAN. Pictures by Miss C. A. Northam. Price, $1 00. D. Lothrop & Co., Boston.

This collection of sweets, which the critics say is the best verse-book published since "Lilliput Levee," will probably prove to be one of the most popular Christmas-Tree books of the season. The poems are written from a child's own point-of-view, and some of them, like "Learning to Count," "Baby's Frights," "Pinkie-Winkie-Posie-Bell," will be perennial favorites in the nursery. While the book is sure to captivate the baby-memory, we will whisper to the mothers that there is not an idle "jingle" in the volume, but that every verse will subtly give a refining and shaping touch to the little child-soul. The book is attractively bound, handsomely illustrated, and ought to be found in every Christmas Stocking in the land.

Ask your Bookseller for it.

POEMS IN COMPANY WITH CHILDREN. — By MRS. S. M. B. PIATT. Illustrated. Price, $1 50. D. Lothrop & Co., Boston.

A mother's book — one of those dainty, treasured volumes of poetry which naturally find a resting-place in the mother's work-basket, always at hand, to be taken up in a tender moment. It also contains many poems to be read aloud in the twilight hour when the children gather around mother's knee. Of its literary excellence it is needless to speak as Mrs. Piatt stands at the head of American women poets.

THE CHAUTAUQUA GIRLS AT HOME.— By *Pansy*. Author of "Four Girls at Chautauqua,," &c. Boston: D. LOTHROP & Co. Price, $1.50.

The four brilliant young ladies, three from the highest social ranks, and one a teacher with infidel tendencies, who, having abandoned Newport and Saratoga for Chautauqua Lake and its Sunday-school Assembly, were there converted, and, having returned to their city homes, with their simple faith and joyous experience, they enter the First Church, seeking Christian help and a field for usefulness. Hesitatingly they enter the Sunday-school. Their presence there is almost resented by pastor and superintendent, who knew of their former lives of social vaporing, but did not know of their conversion. The rebuff does not wholly dishearten the young ladies. They go to the social meetings, where their persistent attendance brings about an explanation. They confess Christ, are received into the Church, enter into its work with zeal, and by their efforts and influence remodel the Sunday-school, stir up the social meetings, and help to bring about a great revival.

These young ladies in their developing lives represent four classes of Christians, with which every pastor has to deal, and from studying these models pastors can learn helpful lessons, for they are here depicted with a masterly skill. The *First Church* is a representative *dead* Church. The decayed members and the cause of death are pointed out. The question of social amusements for Christians is discussed and answered from the Bible. The Sunday-school is dull and inefficiently managed. How to improve it and make it a success is indicated in a practical way. In short, the whole case of spiritually dead Churches is diagnosticated with the wisdom of a practical physician, and the revivifying remedies prescribed. Pastors, superintendents, teachers, Christians, young and old, should read this book. It contains help for all. "Pansy" has written nothing better — *N. Y. Christian Advocate.*

WIDE AWAKE NOTICES.

WIDE AWAKE. It is, as usual, handsomely illustrated. A charming magazine for the young. One of the best Boston notions we know of.—*The Christian Advocate.*

Every number commends it more and more to public patronage; indeed, it is very emphatically the children's book of the period.—*The Farmer's Cabinet.*

That charming new magazine for girls and boys, the WIDE AWAKE for January is full of facinating pictures and reading matter. Among the articles are, "Piano Fortes," "The Cooking Club of Tu-Whit Hollow," "My Lady's Christmas," "Grim Grendel," "The True Cinderella," "Little Wooden Two Shoes," and a host of other good things. Talk about the youth-giving springs to which Ponce de Leon devoted his life in finding! If he had lived in these days, he would have found them in the boys' and girls' magazines like the WIDE AWAKE.—*The Green Bay Advocate.*

WIDE AWAKE is well-named, for it is certainly all attention to the needs of its readers. There is a brilliant list of contributors, and an equally brilliant line of engravings. Is very bewitching in its manifold appeals to eye and sentiment. Messrs. Lothrop & Co., Boston, the publishers, have hit the young taste exactly in their judicious arrangements for issuing this serial.—*The Commonwealth.*

The WIDE AWAKE, the new illustrated magazine for young people, published by D. Lothrop & Co., Boston, is the very best publication in our country, as well as the cheapest.

WIDE AWAKE NOTICES.

During the next year the readers are promised an entertainment of wit, and wisdom, and song, and poem, and picture, and story, illustrated by the best artists. The contributors to the WIDE AWAKE are some of the most popular writers of the day. We know of no way parents could expend two dollars more profitably than by subscribing for this first-class magazine; and we think that they will be surprised at the amount of reading received for their money.—*The Evangelist.*

The WIDE AWAKE has entered on its second year with ever-brightening prospects. Its success has proved our theory correct, that children like better to read of something like real life—of boys and girls like themselves—than about fairies and prodigies such as never had an existence on this earth. The list of contributors to the WIDE AWAKE numbers many names among authors best loved by children, and the contents of each number evidence in editor and writers a just estimate of the wants of young readers, and remarkable skill in catering to them.—*The Literary World.*

WIDE AWAKE was a good name for it, and the children love it. All the other publications for children are too old. Now while WIDE AWAKE is pleasing in the highest degree to the four-year-old, it is read with just as much interest by the eight-year-old, and grandma insists that no other book was ever made like it, and grandma knows what she is saying.—*The Journal.*

www.ingramcontent.com/pod-product-compliance
Lightning Source LLC
Chambersburg PA
CBHW030344230426
43664CB00007BB/529